D0705756

Militants and Migrants

Rural Sicilians Become American Workers

Donna Gabaccia, 1947-

Rutgers University Press

New Brunswick and London

Samford University Library

Library of Congress Cataloging-in-Publication Data

Gabaccia, Donna R., 1949–

    Militants and migrants : rural Sicilians become American
workers / Donna Gabaccia.

       p.   cm. — (Class and culture)

    Bibliography: p.

    Includes index.

    ISBN 0-8135-1318-9   ISBN 0-8135-1356-1 (pbk.)

    1. Sicily—Emigration and immigration—History.   2. United
States—Emigration and immigration—History.   3. Alien
labor, Italian—United States—History.   4. Labor and laboring
classes—Italy—Sicily—Political activity—History.
5. Sicily—Rural conditions.   I. Title.   II. Series.

JV8139.S5G33   1988

325.45′8—dc19   87-37673

                                                       CIP

British Cataloging-in-Publication information available

Copyright © 1988 by Rutgers, The State University

All Rights Reserved

Manufactured in the United States of America

Militants and Migrants

Released from
Samford University Library

Class and Culture

A series edited by Milton Cantor and Bruce Laurie

JV
8139
.S5
G33
1988

For Thomas

Contents

List of Maps, Figures, and Tables

Maps

Figures

Tables

Acknowledgments

Although I had begun my study of Sicilian red towns and migrants from those towns before I accepted a position at Mercy College, I came to see the project in new and unexpected ways once there. A typical Mercy College class seats Spanish-speaking Figueroa next to native-born Cacioppo; an El Salvadoran shares books with the American, O'Reilly; Budnarski, the native, competes with Wu, the foreigner. What struck me initially about my classrooms was that the homelands of my immigrant students read like a list of the current political hot spots of the world. Many came from areas of Asia and Central America characterized not only by emigration, but by economic change, social unrest, violent political conflict, and often revolutionary ferment. Slowly, I came to appreciate that the same had often been true of the immigrants of the past, represented in my classes by their children and grandchildren, the O'Reillys, Cacioppos, and Budnarskis.

Few ethnic Americans today think of their forebears as rural rebels. Yet in the nineteenth as in the twentieth century, many of the rebellious spots of the world were in the countryside. We know that millions of old and new immigrants left rural homelands to seek jobs and new lives in the United States. Still, rural revolt rarely appears as an important element in historians' descriptions of immigrant workers' backgrounds. If, in a small way, this book corrects the historical record and thus allows us to interpret more carefully the transformation of rural Europeans into American workers, then credit lies in part with my students, ranged in their considerable diversity through scores of Mercy College classrooms.

I happily acquired many debts while pursuing my research on Sicilians in Europe and the United States. As usual, I can thank Jane and Peter Schneider for sound advice, stimulating conversation, and some very fine food on both sides of the Atlantic. In Sicily, Alfonso di Giovanna provided key help in identifying the long-dead militants of the past, and in opening the archive doors that I might learn more about them.

Because of the help of many colleagues and friends, writing this book proved less stressful than major projects sometimes are. Participants in a number of professional meetings contributed commentary and criticism of my written work: for this, I especially thank Lucia Birnbaum, Alan Kraut, members of the Columbia University Seminar on Modern Italian Studies, and colleagues and students at the Universities of Bremen and Bochum, and at the Free University of Berlin. Jane and Peter Schneider saved me from a number of errors. George Pozzetta carefully read many early papers, and, before it was published, generously shared his and Gary Mormino's research on Tampa's Sicilians. Sam Baily and Bruce Laurie both gave the manuscript thoughtful readings, which much improved the final version. Dirk Hoerder and Christiane Harzig not only read and responded with enthusiasm to an early essay, they both contributed to the book with timely critiques of the first draft. With their support, a year spent as a Fulbright Lecturer in Germany (at the University of Bremen) provided both the extra time needed for writing and a supportive setting for doing it.

For help with preparation of the manuscript, I thank Eileen Callan and Rosemarie Farella. Thomas Kozak proofread many pages, and helped me struggle with a balky printer. And here I would like to thank my parents, too, who long ago insisted that learning to type would serve me well in my future, whatever it might be: sometimes I resented that advice—but they were right.

Many people offered aid of a more personal nature; it was equally essential to the completion of this book. I especially thank the many people who allowed my son Tamino to remain happy and curious while his distracted parents typed chapters, cooked meals, earned wages, and mailed Legos back and forth across the Atlantic Ocean. To families, babysitters, friends, and to Tamino's outstanding teachers in White Plains and Bremen, I express my gratitude.

This book is dedicated to Thomas Kozak, my unfailing partner. It was he who first suggested, long ago, that I leave the United States and my English-language parochialism behind. Since then, he has enthusiastically accommodated the travels of an academic labor migrant. My research and writing continue to profit from the transatlantic connections—and home fires—of our shared life. Without our mutual pleasure in both, this book could not have been written.

White Plains, N.Y.
September 1987

Militants and Migrants

Introduction

For historians and for many outside the academy, the word movement has two distinct meanings. On the one hand, movement means mobility or migration, as in the phrase "population movement." On the other, movement describes the desire for change and the organizations and alliances of people working for that change.[1] It may be that our use of the same word for two such different phenomena is purely accidental. Nevertheless, it is an intriguing accident. Population movements and movements for social and economic change both loom quite large in accounts of nineteenth- and twentieth-century European and American history. But while we know a great deal about each movement separately, we know considerably less about their historical interconnections. These interconnections are the topic of this book.

Migration and labor studies have developed in parallel streams, but—in the United States at least—represent separate historical fields of inquiry and sometimes separate disciplines. Demographers and historians of American immigrant and ethnic groups analyze migration, while labor historians focus on labor movements and protests, and anthropologists tackle the subject of peasant revolts.[2] The result is that linkages between the histories of population and labor movements, especially in the countryside, remain poorly understood.

True, we already have some important ideas about the influence of mobility on class consciousness and on workers' and peasants' movements. Working independently in the 1960s, historian Stephan Thernstrom and sociologist J. S. MacDonald both concluded that migration and workers' political organization varied inversely, and hence conflicted in some way. This thought had long been expressed in the Turnerian notion of migration as an individualistic safety valve; migration deflected the social discontent that might otherwise lead to class consciousness, labor organizing, or workers' revolution. When Thernstrom documented the migratory habits of Newburyport's workers, he wondered if he had not discovered an answer to Sombart's eternally repeated question: "Why is there no socialism in America?" Had mobility frustrated political organization by disrupting social relations among the mobile? Most labor historians now reject this possibility. More widely accepted is MacDonald's convincing argument that migration and labor militancy became alternative responses to similar crises. (MacDonald described Italian agriculturalists who chose either to fight or to flee.)[3]

With this broad understanding of militancy and migration, immigration historians argue that the Europeans who moved to the United States represented poor candidates for an American labor movement, and even poorer candidates for a radical one. The problem was not, as Thernstrom suggested, that mobility complicated the otherwise natural task of organization, either politically or in the workplace. Rather, the predominantly peasant immigrants who chose to migrate and not to fight at home re-created familiar personal and community social networks that often made a labor movement irrelevant in confronting the problems of working-class life in the United States.[4]

MacDonald's and Thernstrom's seminal thoughts became the starting point for my research. To explore their rather broad formulations, it seemed important to shift to a new, more detailed level of analysis, and to pay particular attention to change over time. Thus, the heart of this book is a case study. It tells the story of labor militancy and migration in a town that—in the words of a local historian—became a "little Moscow" in the Sicilian countryside.[5] Sambuca was not completely typical of the Italian South—no town is—but neither was it a total anomaly. There were other red towns in the European countryside, although in Sicily they were never more than a sizable minority.

Why another case study? Students of migration have recently expressed reservations about the proliferation of narrow studies focusing on one group. Case studies do complicate historians' efforts to identify general patterns in migration to the United States and the emergence of ethnic group life there. But questions about the United States were not the starting place for this book. Thus I found convincing Samuel Baily's recent call for "village-outward" studies that focus comparatively on specific hypotheses.[6] The village-outward case study offers other useful perspectives, particularly the opportunity to transcend the boundaries of the nation-state, which normally define labor studies. It does not reduce the European experiences of migrants to deep background, and it does not ignore the ongoing interaction that migration fostered between the European countryside and the cities of the United States.[7] Equally important, it is a way of studying migration that replicates migrants' experiences and perceptions: they lived in both worlds.

A village-outward approach requires primary research on several continents and in multiple locations. It is a demanding and expensive—yet rewarding—research strategy. As a result, *Militants and Migrants* does not easily fit the molds of most monographs in either immigration or labor history. Unlike most studies by immigration historians, more than half of the book focuses on Europeans in their homelands before and after mass migration to the United States. Unlike much labor history, the book cannot offer a detailed portrait "from the bottom up" of any one of the several geographically based communities in which Sambucesi lived along with other Sicilians. The emphasis throughout is on the connections between European and immigrant settlements, and on the fact that for many Sicilians both places were significant and familiar.

Three related sets of questions shaped this book. Of primary concern was the impact of massive out-migration on peasants' and workers' movements in the nineteenth-century countryside. Were rebellious towns or rebellious Sicilians less mobile than their more quiescent neighbors—as MacDonald suggested? Some Sicilians did choose to flee rather than fight. But this was only one possible linkage of population and labor movements. Labor militancy also could and did develop during the era of mass migration in many Sicilian towns. How did activists organize? In Sambuca, militants built on a surprising foundation—the family and informal social networks, which are usually assumed to function as alternatives to workers' organizations. Structurally, Sicilian labor organizations closely resembled, and sometimes grew out of, migration chains.

Second, it seemed important to ask whether migration facilitated or undermined the transplantation of rural protest traditions to the United States. Did European traditions influence Sicilians' behavior as immigrant workers? Were immigrants a distinctive subgroup, self-selected as they rejected and severed ties to homeland militants? And what was the impact of the American environment on transplantation?

Answers to questions like these proved quite complex, and mainly negative. European militants had extensive contact with some New World settlements, and almost no contact with others. This was largely the consequence of distinctive migration choices by artisans and peasants. Organizationally, too, Sicilian settlements in the United States varied enormously. The jobs of immigrant workers varied, and could complicate the transplantation of European traditions. So did the coming of World War I and the dawning of ethnic nationalism just as Mussolini rose to power. A flourishing immigrant labor movement was only one possible outcome—and not the most common one. In the United States, one finds many good examples of how mobility could undermine labor militancy.

In other cases, however, the impact of migration on Sicilian labor activism was a supportive one. Questions about returned migrants' confrontation with the labor movements developing in their hometowns are the third main component of *Militants and Migrants*. Many scholars assume that returning migrants became conservative lower-middle-class supporters of fascism.[8] But in Sambuca and some other Sicilian towns, returners often found their way instead into a clandestine but ardent Communist movement of resistance. The political traditions of Sambuca's lower middle classes help explain this surprising outcome.

The organization of the book follows these three sets of questions about militancy and migration closely. The first chapter offers an overview of how social scientists and theorists have thought about rural economic change, peasant rebellion, international migration, and immigrant workers as labor activists. The second chapter examines rural protest and internal migration in Sicily as the island's trade with rapidly developing nations changed from the fifteenth to the nineteenth centuries. In chapter 3, events in Sambuca illustrate the early genesis of one red town. The focus is on the slowly evolving relations of artisans to both the local elite and to the poorer peasant majority of the town. Chapter 4 describes the violent peasant rebellions that shook Sicily and the Italian nation in the early 1890s, and explores the patterns of emigration developing in towns with contrasting political histories. Chapter 5 continues the story of Sambuca, analyzing chain migration from the town and the importance of occupation in shaping settlements of Sambucesi in the United States. Chapters 6 and 7 contrast the social and economic development and diverse organizational histories of Sicilian settlements in Louisiana, Illinois, New York, and Tampa. Chapter 8 returns the reader to Sicily to consider the aftermath of mass migration, and the role played by returned migrants in transforming their hometown into a "little Moscow." Finally, the conclusion makes explicit some broad connections between economic change in American industrial cities and in the European countryside. Overall, it suggests that immigrants' complex experiences, indeed the entire process of what is sometimes called class formation, might productively be viewed from an international perspective, rather than from the viewpoint of the individual nation-state.

Chapter 1
Of Militants and Migrants

That migration and labor movements of the past should be studied together seems obvious when we think of nations of immigrants like the United States. But immigrant workers were not unique to the United States: Canada, Australia, and the South American countries had multi-ethnic workforces; each major European nation received smaller numbers of foreign workers; and even Europe's "native" workers—recruited from the countryside—could sometimes be as culturally unlike their industrial-city compatriots as foreigners.[1] Today, of course, foreign workers make up a sizable minority in the working classes of all western nations.[2]

There are two schools of thought about migrant workers in labor movements, whether in the United States or Europe. A few observers see immigrant laborers as potential activists, even radicals; most, however, view them as severe, if innocent, hindrances to labor solidarity. European and American analyses of foreign workers also differ in important ways, especially about migrant workers' rural backgrounds, their cultural "baggage" of protest and organizational traditions, and the use to which they can put their traditions once they arrive in the industrial city.

The Political Baggage of Immigrant Workers

At one time, both Canadian and U.S. observers viewed immigrants as potentially dangerous radicals. Nativists in the United States saw foreign-born extremists behind the growth of trade unionism and labor agitation in the 1870s and 1880s.[3] The Haymarket affair and massive strikes by immigrant workers before World War I led nativists to picture the immigrant as a bearded bomb thrower and saboteur. Restrictive immigration legislation, enacted in part to end foreign subversion in the United States,[4] created curious bedfellows: antiradicals found themselves in alliance with the American Federation of Labor, and even some Socialist trade unionists, who also supported restrictions of some kind.[5]

American trade unionists sometimes feared immigrant radicalism, but they worried more about employers' use of immigrant workers to restructure industrial workplaces. Immigrants became cheap laborers who broke strikes, and, in the long run, replaced skilled trade unionists as unskilled tenders of new machines. Labor leaders publicized data that purported to show how rarely immigrants organized or joined American unions, suggesting that they were unAmericanized, and thus unorganizable and undesirable.

To Samuel Gompers and his peers, foreign workers weakened organized labor in its struggles with capital.[6] This theme re-emerged in scholarly form in both European and American studies in the past twenty years. Europeans in particular have viewed labor migrations of rural ("southern") Europeans to the cities and factories of northern Europe as part of a carefully timed attack by capital on the labor movements of the industrialized nations. They noted that, at the same time, migration also threatened to perpetuate the underdevelopment of the southern homelands of the immigrants.[7]

In general, European scholars emphasized how difficult it was for immigrants to participate in the politicized labor movements of the north. Tenuous work contracts and prohibitive naturalization procedures inevitably transformed immigrant workers into exploitable competitors. Without the vote, immigrant workers showed little interest in workers' political parties, and the parties remained uninterested in them. The animosity of native-born workers, fueled by cultural differences, was an almost inevitable result.[8] Unlike the earlier American labor movement, however, European observers in the 1960s and 1970s typically appealed to the labor movement and to native-born workers to welcome the foreign-born. They emphasized that all shared a common enemy in capital.[9] By contrast, they had little to say about the desires and intentions of the foreign workers; they seemed to assume that, if welcomed, immigrant workers would participate fully and enthusiastically in existing labor institutions.[10]

American analyses of labor migration focus more on the immigrants themselves than on structures of capital and labor. Perhaps this is because labor migration to the United States began during a distinctive period of relatively free migration, when employers' search for labor played a hidden role, unlike the employer- and state-initiated immigration programs of postwar Europe.[11] A general turn to cultural analysis in American labor history and an enthusiasm for "history from the bottom up" also encouraged American scholars to concentrate on how the traditions and goals of immigrants shaped their behavior as workers and as participants in the American labor movement.

Having discarded the old stereotype of the radical immigrant, American scholars for a time paralleled Gompers in seeing rural European migrants as experientially ill-prepared for and uninterested in building a labor movement in their new homes. Politically, migrants have been characterized as premodern.[12] Some were fatalistically inured to exploitative conditions in the workplace; many intended to return to their homelands; others wanted only security, symbolized by the purchase of a house or a steady job. Still others turned to family, kin, friends, or communal and ethnic self-help to ease the adjustment to urban and industrial life. Communal orientation and a desire for family security was inimical to voluntary association, class-consciousness, workers' organizations, or labor politics.[13]

The genius of Herbert Gutman's work was to reveal the more creative and militant implications of immigrant workers' premodern cultures. According to

Gutman, rural immigrants carried with them older communal traditions of protest which helped them respond to new and difficult working conditions in the United States.[14] Polish and Italian communities, for example, could support fierce and lengthy strikes. Taking this approach in a somewhat different direction, David Brody has shown that immigrant workers could overcome cultural fragmentation to wage fierce workplace struggles, but they rarely organized politically as workers or attempted to link economic struggles to class-based political actions.[15] Perhaps this was so because they so often lived in separate wards and assembly districts, isolated by what Ira Katznelson called "city trenches." Among immigrants, only the most skilled and urban immigrant group—the Jews from eastern Europe— moved temporarily beyond workplace activism to vote Socialist.[16]

In his recent synthesis of many of the new American social histories of im- migrant workers, John Bodnar sensibly urged caution in analyzing the impact of European traditions on immigrant workers or the American labor movement.[17] Bodnar conceded that many rural craftsmen, not just Jews, carried a knowledge of European radical thought in their baggage.[18] Bodnar stopped far short of reviving the old image of immigrant as radical, but he did suggest that a reassessment might be in order. That reassessment must begin in the countryside, where the majority of immigrant workers of the past originated.

That countryside still holds some surprises for historians. The hinterlands of Europe were not inhabited by "potatoes in a sack"—Marx's contemptuous view of peasants incapable of organization or revolt.[19] Instead, the history of nine- teenth-century Europe is littered with abortive rural revolts, which accompanied fundamental political, economic, and social change in the countryside. Barrington Moore recognized this when he discovered the important influence of rural change on the evolution of democracy and dictatorship. According to Moore, the process of modernization begins in the past, "with peasant revolutions that fail. It culmi- nates during the twentieth century with peasant revolutions that succeed."[20]

The success of "proletarian" revolutions in rural lands like Russia, China, or Vietnam first led scholars to recognize that peasants, rural change, and rural discontent had often sparked economic and political change.[21] Since most earlier peasant revolts failed, they have not shaped prevailing interpretations of Europe in the nineteenth century. They have been easy to ignore. The discontents of urban and industrial workers, not peasants, fill the pages of European labor histories.

This view is more unbalanced than wrong. Even European countries undergo- ing industrialization housed sizable peasant and rural populations throughout the nineteenth century. In addition, large parts of southern and eastern Europe re- mained overwhelmingly agricultural for much longer. Rural Europeans, too, had their problems and complaints during the industrial revolution. Country people expressed their displeasure by migrating and by revolting or organizing for fundamental change. The rural rebels of France are probably best known, since France actually experienced revolution.[22] Elsewhere, failed revolts predominated:

after 1700, Ireland, Italy, Poland, Rumania, Bulgaria, Russia, Spain, and most other parts of eastern and southern Europe experienced periods of intense rural conflict.[23] This took a variety of forms, from bread riots to tax revolts.[24] Significantly, Europe's rural rebels shared a number of characteristics with their twentieth-century counterparts: they lived in areas increasingly tied to distant industrial centers through trade, and their homelands often were parts of declining empires.

The rebellions of the nineteenth century should have special significance for scholars seeking to understand the backgrounds and cultural heritage of Europeans migrating to the United States. Instead, many of these revolts have practically disappeared from historical accounts. Before one can understand immigrant workers, one must know the countryside they abandoned, and to which they often returned. Both rural revolts and migration characterized a distinctive period in European history as more and more rural Europeans encountered new markets and centralizing nation-states.

Markets, Capital, and Migration

Scholars of rural migration and of rural unrest seek explanations and causes in rural economic change.[25] Rural areas did not remain stagnant backwaters as the industrial revolution proceeded. J. S. MacDonald, for example, traced the origin of both labor militancy and emigration from rural Italy to what Moore has called "the challenge of commercial agriculture."[26] MacDonald believed that new capitalist forms of agriculture and household production for new markets encouraged peasant cultivators to experiment with either migration or labor militancy in the nineteenth century. He argued further that labor militancy accompanied economic development, while migration and economic stagnation went hand in hand.[27]

Historians' views of immigrant backgrounds have gradually changed to reflect new research on economic change in Europe's hinterlands. Gone are the days when rural Europe was described as a land forgotten by time, or as a last bastion of feudalism and subsistence production. Most recent studies in immigration history acknowledge that migrants left a countryside in economic ferment.

The exact nature of rural economic change, however, is still a source of confusion. Some scholars believe migration accompanied expansion of market relations in Europe's hinterlands. Others, most notably John Bodnar in his important work *The Transplanted*, find the origin of migration in the growth of rural capitalism. According to Bodnar, "most of the immigrants transplanted to America . . . were in reality the children of capitalism. They were products of an economic system and, indeed, a way of life which penetrated their disparate homelands in particular parts of the world at various stages throughout the nineteenth century."[28] Bodnar sees commercial agriculture as the key to explaining emigration, but he assumes that commercial agriculture was also capitalist agriculture. Unfortunately, that was not usually the case.

Historians' confusion about capitalism in the countryside originates in part with the influential work of the world-system analysts, principally in the writings of Immanuel Wallerstein.[29] Our understanding of world-wide migration patterns has been significantly advanced beyond older push-pull models by scholars working within this paradigm.[30] Nevertheless, world-system analyses repeatedly equate commerce with capitalism, and this lessens their usefulness for historians interested in rural unrest or immigrant workers.

The goal of the world-system analysts is to describe the formation of a capitalist world system and the market relations forming it. The nature of capitalism, they argue, is to expand, creating unequal development in its wake. The essential inequality is that between the "core" industrialized nations and the rural areas of the "periphery." As core economies developed in northern and western Europe in the fifteenth and sixteenth centuries, they created peripheries in surrounding rural areas, in most of southern and eastern Europe, and in colonies in North and South America. Changing trade exchanges linked core and periphery. Initially, the periphery exported raw materials and food to the cores; later, it became a market for industrial products and a source of cheap labor. Today's periphery is increasingly the site of world industrial production.[31] In the world-systems model, as in Bodnar's view, rural areas became capitalist once trade linked them into the capitalist world economy.

Critics of world-systems analysis point out that trade with capital scarcely makes a rural economy itself capitalist in organization. Critics define capitalism more strictly as a mode of production, accompanied by unique social and class relations. Only under this definition can capitalism be considered "a way of life." Many scholars argue that few peripheries were capitalist until very recently.[32]

Is this just a debate about useless ideal types? Not for those interested in rural rebellions or immigrant workers. Migrants coming from regions "with capitalism" would almost certainly have developed different political traditions and understanding of class relations than those coming from regions with commercialized but noncapitalist economies. For this reason it is helpful to review the history of markets and capitalist enterprise in the European countryside.

Trade, of course, predated capitalism. As capitalist development created new and ever-wider markets, commercial agriculture developed in parts of eastern and southern Europe. Wheat-raising in the peripheries became increasingly oriented toward export to the core economies.[33] This commercial agriculture was not capitalist in organization: serfs, coerced laborers, and sharecroppers raised much of the grain; family farmers raising their own food marketed small amounts of grain, too. All types of peasants owned their own houses, tools, and animals: they worked in commercial agriculture, but they were not a rural proletariat. Most had relatively limited contact with the market, since lords, landowners, and middlemen organized the grain trade. Grain merchants concerned themselves as much with rents, feudal privileges, and mercantilist regulations as with profits.[34] Once understood as feudal or semifeudal, this type of agricultural economy was recently renamed "tributary" by Eric Wolf.[35]

Capitalism did not need to penetrate rural areas like these; in Europe, at least, capitalism was already present—primarily in rural manufacturing. Capitalist textile production originated in the countryside; mining, salt extraction, lumbering, and other production for profit on a larger scale employed wage earners in all European hinterlands from a fairly early date.[36] Later, of course, the countryside became the site of early capitalist experiments with large-scale manufacturing, in cottages instead of factories.[37] At the same time, local demand for cheap goods continued to support both artisanal and small-scale capitalist producers in rural villages and towns. Small capitalist producers even enjoyed expanding markets for a time, as cottage industry seems to have facilitated rapid population growth.

Wage-earning did eventually become common in commercial agriculture, especially in wheat production. Even then, however, peasants rarely depended entirely on wages for self-support. Why wage labor developed where agriculture was only marginally capitalist in organization is not well understood. But one result was that semiproletarianized laborers on the land probably outnumbered the industrial workforces of many European nations until well into the nineteenth century.[38]

By the nineteenth century, rural Europeans found the use of cash and recourse to the marketplace increasingly necessary. Since small amounts of cash had always circulated in the countryside, goods manufactured in the core eventually arrived to chase it. This is what some scholars have termed capital's "penetration" of the countryside.[39] The term is misleading. Rural people increased their contact with the market; they did not experience new or more extensive contacts with capitalist workplaces or with capitalism as a way of life. Instead, capitalist production in the countryside (in both its small workshop and cottage forms) declined when faced with competition from the core. At roughly the same time, political changes—the end of feudalism and the rise of the nation-state—pushed people toward the marketplace.[40] The end of common rights to land usage and the imposition of taxes on peasant households both encouraged rural families to look for new sources of cash income.

The spread of market relations had a curious effect on commercial agriculture: both wage earning and household production for the market increased as land became private property. Subsistence production rarely disappeared, even in areas with large estates. Thus, although the economies of many peripheral areas in the nineteenth century defy sensible classification, one can say that capitalist production in agriculture developed only in exceptional areas. Usually, no one mode of agricultural production could be called typical. Writing of one region in Calabria,

Pino Arlacchi called it an area of permanent transition—a transition never completed—to capitalist production.[41]

It is obvious how changes like these encouraged rural Europeans to migrate cityward and beyond. Wherever local artisanal or capitalist industry collapsed in the face of imported goods, out-migration inevitably followed.[42] In addition, a general search for cash continued to fuel out-migration, especially when bad harvests or American crops upset the export markets of Europe's centuries-old commercial agriculture, its part-time wage earners, and its family farmers.[43] According to some observers, migrant laborers of the nineteenth century simply followed capital to the areas of greatest capitalist expansion, whether in the city, in northern Europe, or in the United States.[44]

Furthermore, migration did not facilitate the development of capitalist enterprise in rural areas exporting migrants. Scholars disagree only about how migration perpetuated economic stagnation, not that it did so. Some believe that capitalists in core economies had no incentive to invest in such regions once they became suppliers of surplus laborers.[45] Others believe instead that labor migrants who returned with savings went back to subsistence production, thus avoiding wage earning for struggling capitalist ventures in their homelands.[46] In either case, rural capitalist production rarely prospered: migration and economic underdevelopment went hand in hand.

Rural emigrants might best, then, be termed "children of commerce." Their experiences in the hinterlands of Europe could have shaped unique political traditions, since the economies of their homelands little resembled those of the core. Still, it can be dangerous to assume that economic experience so directly determined political consciousness and traditions. A look at rural understandings of class, change, and protest is in order.

Class, Politics, and Peasants

For rural Europeans, new opportunities and new discomforts originated with money, markets, commerce, and the rise of nation-states. Their thoughts on conflict, cooperation, and exploitation, as well as their hopes for well-being, revolved around financial independence, commerce, land, and subsistence. Capitalist workplaces or capitalism as a way of life was not the prime mover. Anger with taxes, low prices (for their goods), or high prices (for the goods they sought to purchase) flared periodically in the countryside. At such times, the state and the market square seemed obvious targets, and peasants and housewives figured prominently in attacks on both.[47] Mistrust of the merchant and the middleman, and intense anti-Semitism in regions where Jews figured prominently among petty traders, were common.[48] This section explores how rural class structures, community solidarities, and peasant mentalities may have influenced rural politics.

Students of today's peripheries have emphasized the peculiarities of class structure in such regions. One study defines elites of the periphery as a "lumpenbourgeoisie."[49] Others distinguish between a "dependency elite" (involved in trade with the core) and a "development elite" (with nationalist and petty-capitalist orientations).[50] Historians have found both in Europe's hinterlands; both groups shared a deeply rooted respect for landed wealth, and valued the life of the rentier above all.[51]

Rentiers, merchants, and petty capitalists also faced a changing world as market relations expanded in the nineteenth century. They desired goods manufactured in the core; as prices for grain declined, they often sought to squeeze additional crop surpluses or taxes from peasants. Their domination of local politics and local marketplaces allowed them to do so, but they often provoked intense opposition from the agricultural majority.[52]

Conflict between rural elites and peasant majority had been universal in Europe since the fifteenth century. American historians have sometimes obscured this fact with their attention to immigrants' communal orientation. Clearly, community solidarity existed, emerging from economic practices, legal codes, and conditions of life in tributary societies.[53] But, at best, communities resembled quarrelsome families: a communal orientation structured conflict, it did not eliminate it.[54] Many of the conflicts of rural Europe had little to do with class, however political they may otherwise have been. (One remembers, for example, the ritualized brawls between opposing parishes at yearly festivals).[55] Other conflicts must be termed class struggles; Eric Hobsbawm has told us much about this aspect of rural life—the jacqueries, the murders of the rich or powerful, and the social banditry.[56] All flourished in Europe's peripheries.

Hobsbawm has argued that rural revolts increased and became more modern in the nineteenth century, perhaps as rural communalism declined.[57] Josef Barton, for one, claimed to have found evidence of such a decline in eastern Europe; he wrote of rural communities in disaggregation.[58] If older rules no longer governed local conflicts, both the type and extent of conflict could have grown, allowing for a kind of revolutionary moment in the countryside. But was there really a universal decline in community solidarity? Most historians of immigrant workers do not assume so. Other historians have found the decline of community in many different centuries, and identified so many different causes for its demise, that this question cannot be regarded as settled.[59]

Similarly, the influence of a distinctive and conservative peasant mentality is problematic for understanding nineteenth-century protests in Europe. Anthropologists have been engaged in a debate on this issue (which originates in the writings of Chayanov) for some time.[60] On the one hand, writers like James Scott continue to argue that peasants resist political and economic change for cultural reasons. Their "subsistence mentality"—which defines family or community self-sufficiency as a desired way of life—prevents them from behaving in ways we deem economically or politically rational.[61] Other scholars, however, insist that peasants do behave rationally, and that it is the difficult economic or political context in which they live that encourages their passivity.[62] In this view, peasants resemble people submerged up to their necks in water; it is hard for them to choose to make sacrifices in order to push their heads higher above the water in the future, since any sacrifice threatens them with death by drowning.[63]

Theoretically, rational and subsistence-oriented peasants should have developed different political traditions as markets expanded in the countryside. We would expect subsistence-oriented peasants to become involved in communal protest, and in patron-client ties to the nation-state. Their values would be familist and perhaps influenced by a backward-looking ethos of limited good and a lost paradise. By contrast, rational peasants might see voluntary association and interest groups aimed at structural changes as appropriate economic and political strategies; they would look forward to a future paradise.[64] Undoubtedly, however, these are ideal and false dichotomies. Rural Europeans by the nineteenth century already had moved several steps beyond subsistence. As the market, and its discomforts, expanded, subsistence may have become a completely rational and defensive economic strategy, and communal protest a new way of influencing the nation-state.

Scarcely the secure and unchanging villages they were once described to be, the homelands of rural Europeans in the nineteenth century seemed alive with an almost chaotic mix of new possibilities, new threats, and new schemes for securing one's place in a changing world; migration and movements for political and economic change, even social revolution, became two such schemes. The question to ask is, of course, did different people really choose each?

Case Studies of Emigration and Rural Rebellion

There are sizable but separate literatures that describe the characteristics of regions with high rates of emigration and the characteristics of regions with peasant rebellions. Smaller numbers of studies turn to the individual level to show which individuals migrated and which rebelled. But the results of regional and individual studies cannot be interchanged: this is the so-called ecological fallacy. The characteristics of regions with high emigration (or rural protest) cannot simply be attributed to the emigrants or the rebels themselves.

If Thernstrom and MacDonald are correct, regions of revolt and rural rebels should differ in significant ways from regions of out-migration and rural emigrants. In fact, as this section demonstrates, it is the similarities between militants and migrants that are most striking on both levels.

Rural European migration rates varied considerably from town to town and from region to region.[65] Between 1830–1930 those areas involved in extensive trade and market relations, often with the United States, were also areas of mass migration to the United States.[66] Historians employing a geographical model note further that towns bound together by regional trade shared similar migration patterns; undoubtedly word of migration opportunities spread through markets.[67] Areas of subsistence production or large-scale capitalist agriculture lost fewer residents; districts with small-scale commercial or "household" agriculture had the greatest number of migrants.[68] Other studies demonstrate that declines in rural industry encouraged high rates of out-migration.[69] Case studies show that widely distributed land encouraged emigration, suggesting that the more prosperous rather than the poorest may have migrated most easily.[70] It seems also that where peasants divided land and property among all their children temporary labor migrations occurred, while in areas of impartible inheritance the migration of noninheriting children was permanent.[71]

Areas of recurring, violent, or successful peasant rebellions shared many of these characteristics. Studies of rural rebellions are harder to summarize, as scholars have consistently disagreed among themselves about several issues.[72] One important debate concerns the origins of peasant discontent. Most scholars now see class conflict and political change—especially the formation of the nation-state—as the key event.[73] (State formation is a factor rarely mentioned in case studies of emigration.) Others emphasize economic causes. Some believe that relative deprivation angered peasants, while absolute deprivation rendered them apathetic, not rebellious. Scholars as diverse as Crane Brinton and James Davies have found the origin of successful revolutions in a sudden and unexpected frustration of rising economic expectations (the "J-curve" theory.)[74]

These differences aside, almost all scholars see peasant unrest as a necessary, but not sufficient, basis for successful revolution. Factors external to rural life heavily influence the outcome of peasant rebellions. Of these, the pressures of war, administrative failure or incompetence in the central government, and disenchantment on the part of the intelligentsia add fuel to peasant initiatives.[75] Most scholars agree further that a truly self-sufficient peasantry, uninvolved in the market or the earning of wages, can revolt repeatedly without ever precipitating political change.

Most studies show that the likelihood of peasant revolt becoming revolutionary war increases as peasants become more involved in commercial agriculture.[76] Rebellious areas have more cash circulating, more imported goods, and more commerce in general than less rebellious areas.[77] In this respect, of course, rebellious areas demonstrate precisely the qualities attributed to regions of mass emigration.

The role of capitalist production in sparking peasant discontent is quite controversial, however. On the one hand, Eric Wolf describes peasant rebellions occurring in regions which much resembled those of massive emigration: oriented toward the market, with the usual complex mix of family farmers, sharecroppers, subsistence peasants, and wage earners, but without extensive capitalist agriculture.[78] MacDonald's findings contrast sharply with Wolf's, for MacDonald found labor militancy in areas of capitalist agriculture utilizing gangs of rural proletarians.[79] (A problem in assessing this disagreement is that Wolf analyzed peasant armed conflict, while MacDonald defined rural labor militancy as electoral support for Italy's Socialist Party.) Armed rebellion in regions of semicapitalist or capitalist agriculture is not completely unknown, either.[80] In a recent review of the literature, Theda Skocpol concluded that almost any peasantry could be considered potentially rebellious. Her point was that the national and international context, the nature of the ruling classes, and the ideologies of leaders—not just the peasants themselves—determined the outcome of rural rebellions.[81]

The conclusion is obvious: regions with high rates of emigration often resembled those characterized by peasant unrest. This tells us little about the character of individual migrants or militants, however. Unfortunately, this point is too often forgotten. Aware that regions with considerable household production for the market produced many migrants, immigration historians have described the migrants themselves as market-oriented family farmers.[82] And they have ignored the evidence that similar regions were ones of considerable rebellion, instead describing household agriculturalists as apathetic or as familists. The individual level must be analyzed separately—but even doing so we will find some striking similarities between militants and migrants.

Most studies of peasant rebellions agree that "middle peasants" participated in the greatest numbers in rural revolts.[83] Middle peasants were neither the wealthiest nor the poorest of their villages; they might own a bit of land, but they could rarely support themselves on it; they worked as lessees, sharecroppers, and wage earners, but they did not depend on wages entirely; they were not peasant proletarians. Middle peasants enjoyed some autonomy and some privacy; they could both feed themselves and purchase weapons for a prolonged struggle. (By contrast, rural proletarians risked starvation when they rebelled.) The spread of the market suspended such middle peasants somewhere between older habits of subsistence and the newer challenges of wage earning and the market. Eric Wolf, who emphasized the role of the middle peasants, seemed to relish reporting that such peasants—typically viewed as conservative and backward-looking—manned the successful revolutions of the twentieth century. Even Jeffery Paige, who found rebellions in South American areas with semicapitalist agriculture, describes peasant revolutionaries as sharecroppers, not wage earners.[84]

Middle peasants rarely had the skills needed to become spokesmen of their own revolts: alienated intellectuals and discontented artisans or industrial wage earners assumed this role. All these groups had special complaints as commerce and new governments changed the countryside in the nineteenth and twentieth centuries. Typically, it was the alliance of middle peasants, industrial workers, and alienated intellectuals that resulted in successful revolts.[85]

Although the evidence is still sketchy, it seems clear that middle peasants and artisans also migrated in disproportionately large numbers in the nineteenth century. At one time, immigration historians merely noted that the majority of migrants in statistical summaries were laborers; currently, historians believe those statistics describe unmarried or journeymen children of struggling middle-peasant parents and artisans.[86] Given the haphazard way in which such occupational data were collected, their meaning will remain difficult to assess. Case studies using better sources demonstrate more convincingly that artisans, fishermen, miners, and petty traders may count for as much as a third of all emigrants to the United States.[87] Middle peasants, if identifiable in the sources, would easily raise this proportion to almost half in many European regions. This suggests that many potential or former rural rebels could have become immigrant workers in the United States.

Conclusion

When both regional and individual levels of analysis are considered together, it appears quite unlikely that distinctive groups of Europeans became migrants or militants in the nineteenth century. The preconditions for migration and labor militancy were often the same. The part that capitalist workplaces played in encouraging militancy and discouraging migration still needs clarification, however.

Furthermore, both migration and labor movements seem to have been characteristic of a particular type of mixed agricultural organization in rural areas entering world markets. One cannot with any certainty sort rural populations into two separate categories, one labelled migrants and the other militants. Nonagriculturalists and middle peasants could be found in large numbers in both groups. It would be surprising, then, if there were no historical connections either between the developments of the two movements or between the individual militants and migrants themselves.

The implications for our understanding of immigrant workers should also be obvious. Migrants left homelands in economic ferment, and part of that ferment was the rural revolts of the nineteenth century. Whatever their behavior as immigrant workers, rural Europeans were neither apathetic nor unfamiliar with the principles of collective action in their homelands. As such, they cannot automatically be regarded, as they often have been, as poor candidates for participation in the labor movements of their new homelands.

Chapter 2
A Mobile and Unruly Countryside

In the nineteenth century, visitors from northern Europe hesitated to call Sicily part of Europe, as if they knew when they had crossed the border separating core from periphery. In part, it was Social Darwinism that encouraged tourists and even scholars to see Palermo as an Arab city, or to remark on the Asian, Oriental, or African vestiges they claimed to have uncovered in the Sicilian countryside. But other considerations influenced visitors, too. Northerners often simply found conditions of life in southern Italy as unfamiliar and uncomfortable as those outside Europe.[1]

The economic chasm that separated Sicily from northern Europe would with time be used to explain mafia violence, recurring peasant unrest, high rates of crime against property, and the mass migrations that followed Italian unification—to explain anything, in fact, that made Sicily seem different from northern Europe. The economic gap was real enough. But whether it could explain so much is less certain. Northern Europe's standard of living had surpassed that of southern and eastern Europe well before the nineteenth century. But peasant discontent, migration, and mafia did not assume new dimensions and character until, roughly, the century between 1830 and 1930.

While not ignoring the economic chasm or economic change, this chapter examines some of the other factors which shaped migration and rural unrest in Sicily before 1890. In particular, it focuses on the expansion of market relations, on the peculiarities of class relations (especially the sensitive place of middle peasants), and on the formation of the nation-state—factors which, according to Sicilian scholars, influence militancy and migration. Although agricultural production had been integrated into world-wide trade since the fifteenth century, Sicily's residents began to use money frequently only in the nineteenth century. The slow spread of market ties and the formation of the Italian nation-state in turn influenced population movements, and helped forge the context in which Sicilians devised new forms of rural organization and protest.

Two Steps from Africa: Sicily and the World

Scholars, like tourists, have seen Sicily as different, treating the island's history apart from the general flow of European history. South of Rome, European history seems to turn around. When feudalism was ending in northern Europe, it was beginning again, albeit in a new form, in Sicily and some other southern regions. While Britain, Spain, and France sent colonists overseas, Sicily became a colony. While large-scale textile production took off in Holland and England, it collapsed in Messina and Palermo. While the proportion of the active population employed in agriculture declined throughout northern Europe, it actually increased in much of southern Italy. Finally, Italy joined the ranks of modern European nation-states quite late; even as a nation, after 1860, Italy united such a diverse collection of regions that governance sometimes seemed an impossible challenge.

Economically, Sicily and much of the Italian south is still described as a kind of way-station, stuck or moving (depending on one's optimism and political perspective) along the continuum between the developed or core countries and the underdeveloped or peripheral countries of Asia, Africa, and central or South America. In the hopeful years after World War II, economists pointed to Italy as a potential model for economic development, "a school for developing nations."[2] Italy's economic success, however, was unequally shared by northern and southern Italians. By the 1960s, younger scholars turned to dependency theory with hopes that what had been written about the Third World might shed light on the persistent inequality that divided the nation into two halves.[3] Even today, parts of southern Italy have not completed the transition to capitalism.

Many scholars have found fascinating parallels in the histories of Sicily and Latin American countries. The two areas once shared a common fate, when both became Spanish colonies in the fifteenth century. Spain sought different products from each—Sicily exported wheat and wool—and Spanish conquest was imposed and maintained (haphazardly in the case of Sicily) under very different conditions in the two regions. Still, some similarities are striking. In both regions, new elites seized and colonized lands to meet Spain's colonial and mercantilist requirements. In both areas, Spanish conquest created, extended, or consolidated large agricultural estates (the *latifondo* in Sicily; the *hacienda* in Latin America). With time, complex layers of middlemen brokers emerged to mediate commercial and political linkages between Spain and its numerous colonies.[4] Population transfers accompanied Spanish colonizations after 1492, most obviously in the repopulation of parts of Spanish America. In Sicily, too, the new Catalan barons built towns in uncultivated mountain regions and induced coastal dwellers, Albanians, and mainland Italians to settle there. The barons imported some African slaves as well. Northern Italians (who organized Sicily's wheat trade, as they did commerce in many other parts of the Spanish empire) flocked to Palermo and other port cities.[5] Sicily in the fifteenth century was a land of immigration, not emigration.

Spain never consolidated its political hold on Sicily; perhaps it never needed to, for the wheat and wool trade it sought continued successfully through centuries of political strife. By the late eighteenth century, however, a Bourbon French dynasty had unified Sicily and Naples into the Kingdom of the Two Sicilies, and from that time until the Napoleonic Wars, commerce linked Sicily to Naples and France, not Spain.[6] When it became part of the Kingdom of the Two Sicilies, Sicily's remaining luxury industry (silk production in Palermo and Messina) collapsed; local barons preferred imported French goods. There is evidence, however, of a humble linen and cotton industry that utilized both small factories and cottage production to satisfy the needs of more modest consumers and strictly local markets.[7]

The Napoleonic Wars again reoriented Sicily, this time toward England. The years before 1815 represent a turning point in Sicilian economic history. First, high prices for wheat during the war years allowed thousands of provincial Sicilian wheat speculators to reap immense profits, creating a new elite in Sicily's rural towns. The *civili* (as they called themselves) pressed both for political independence and for the end of feudal privileges, especially entailment and common rights to the land. Second, this new elite cooperated and sometimes competed with English investors in extending oil, citrus, and wine production, while they simultaneously expropriated communal lands and consolidated their control of the wheat trade. In a few areas, the new elite also acquired sulfur mines. While the civili functioned as a kind of development elite, they also strove to imitate the social lives and consumption habits of the older aristocracy. Few lived as rentiers at first, but most aspired to the idle life of the rentier.[8]

The unification of Italy in the 1860s continued economic trends already obvious in Sicily by the 1830s. Wheat remained the most important export; peasants raised the grain both on the older large estates and on the newer smaller holdings of the civili. At the same time, Sicily's economy continued to diversify as sulfur, wine, and citrus crops successfully found foreign markets. Sicily enjoyed a near monopoly on world sulfur production until the early twentieth century. The United States, England, and France purchased Sicilian oranges and lemons. France and England purchased wine in large quantities until late in the century.[9] Although Sicilian peasants did not benefit from land reforms instituted by the new Italian state, they did at least enjoy expanding employment options in some areas, since many of the new crops required more labor yearly than wheat did.

By the turn of the century, exporters of all these products reported crises. Losses caused by poor wheat harvests in the 1880s and early 1890s were aggravated when American grain arrived on world markets, depressing prices seriously.[10] Even earlier, small-scale artisanal and small-scale capitalist producers —left unprotected from 1860 to 1887 under the liberal policies of the new Italian state—lost local markets to outside producers of cloth and some other goods.[11] Sicilian vines fell to a phylloxera epidemic just as France's wine industry recovered from an earlier infestation and just as France responded to Italy's protective tariffs by shutting its doors to Italian wines.[12] Around 1900, Florida oranges began to compete successfully with Sicilian citrus fruits on the American market.[13] Finally, a new technique allowed United States producers to produce sulfur from native sources, reducing American dependency on Sicilian mines in the first decade of the century.[14] Ordinary Sicilians bore the impact of all these reverses.

Scholars usually trace peasant unrest and mass emigration to these economic crises of the late nineteenth and early twentieth centuries. This explanation is too simple. For one thing, recent research reports that the crises of the 1880s and 1890s were neither as intense nor as long-lasting as once believed.[15] Furthermore, peasant unrest in western Sicily—while not unaffected by these economic blows—had a history that both preceded and extended well beyond the crises of these two decades. Peasants responded not just to economic change but to the political unification which made Sicily part of the new Italian nation. While one might speak of a long-term crisis for Sicilians, as market relations disrupted older habits of production and exchange, the crises of the 1880s and 1890s formed only one set of episodes in the much longer and intertwined histories of peasant revolt and migration in the area.

A Cash Crisis? Sicilian Towns, 1860–1900

A major difficulty in outlining the long-term crisis introduced by the market was the stubbornly diverse nature of the Sicilian countryside. Western Sicily by the late nineteenth century was a region of marked contrasts, not least of which were visual. Mediterranean gardens surrounded the teeming city of Palermo, while not far away loomed the treeless, sun-bleached stony mountains of the interior. In a few Sicilian towns, residents still spoke their Albanian dialects (called "Greek" by Sicilians) and worshiped in eastern-rite churches. Nowhere outside of Palermo was Italian regularly spoken, not even by local notables. House forms, town plans, local costumes, marriage customs, diets, favored saints, and local amenities like roads, cemeteries, or piped water all varied from town to town and from region to region.[16]

To find patterns in Sicilian emigration and protest, and to test how changing markets may have affected the development of either, one cannot despair in the face of this diversity. But what categories make sense? The Italian state imposed one kind of bureaucratic and administrative system, copying the model of France.[17] After Italian unification, three provinces made up western Sicily: Trapani, Palermo, and Agrigento (see Map 2.1). Each province took its name from its administrative city, and each was divided into smaller units (*circondari*), again named after the local administrative city. Trapani, Marsala, and Alcamo made up the province of Trapani; Palermo, Termini Immerese, Cefalù, and Corleone together formed the Province of Palermo; Bivona, Sciacca, and Agrigento made up the province of Agrigento (or Girgenti, as it was then called). For the purposes of record keeping, the Italian state recognized 137 independent communes in these three provinces. Of these, the main city of Palermo stood out

Map 2.1
Western Sicily, circa 1890

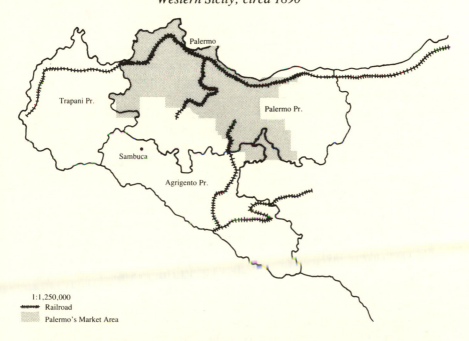

1:1,250,000
Railroad
Palermo's Market Area

as unique in many respects; the largest city by far in the region, Palermo was the traditional home of the island's aristocracy as well as the main commercial center for the western half of the island. Overall, of course, the bureaucratic units devised by the Italian state rarely corresponded to Sicilian market areas; nor did they unite towns of generally similar agricultural or industrial character. This fact has complicated most studies of Sicilian change which focus on provincial or regional analysis.

Analysis of economic and political change in western Sicily is more sensibly pursued at the communal level. Contrary to what one might expect, the sources for the study of western Sicily's 136 rural communes in the late nineteenth century are quite good. (Because of its distinctive qualities, Palermo cannot be considered part of rural Sicily, and it is omitted from the analysis of local economics and migration in the paragraphs and chapters that follow. Nevertheless, it—like many capital cities—played a central role in regional politics, so Palermo could not be, and was not, omitted from the history of rural unrest.) Industrial and agricultural surveys undertaken by the Italian government provide detailed information about the economies and class structures of Sicilian towns.[18] They also reveal much about market relations in the Sicilian countryside. Data on communal migration and militancy patterns are also readily available. Demographers have reported intercensal population balances adjusted for mortality and fertility for all Sicilian towns after 1861; national emigration reports supply annual statistics on applications for *nulla osta* (permission to leave) or passports for each commune after 1882.[19] A flourishing tradition of local history has produced a massive literature on local and communal politics and on rural protest. This literature supplements less-than-systematic national and provincial reports on friendly societies and workers' organizations, strikes, union membership, and electoral politics at the communal level.[20] (Sicilian local history is particularly well covered for the years 1860–1914; the early nineteenth century and the years between the outbreak of World War I and Mussolini's ascendancy await greater attention from scholars.)

Many studies of Sicilian agriculture, peasant uprisings, and emigration distinguish between a modernizing coastal zone of intensive agriculture (where grapes and citrus crops grew) and a backward and isolated wheat-raising region in the inland mountains.[21] To oversimplify, coastal Sicilians are believed to have migrated while mountain dwellers revolted. This distinction between mountain and coastal people is not a pointless one; it does, however, falsely characterize Sicilian wheat production, and it obscures variations in market relations, forms of agricultural and industrial organization, and class relations. Most provincial and regional units in Sicily encompassed coast, hill, and interior mountains. As in most Mediterranean lands, transhumance and population movements in Sicily had also long linked coastal and mountainous regions. Topography never strictly defined market areas, nor did class relations correspond neatly to geographic location. For this reason, it makes more sense to group towns according to similarities in economy, class relations, and markets than to use topographical or administrative units for an analysis of migration and rural revolt.

The extent of local, regional, and international market relations in western Sicily can be measured in a variety of ways in the nineteenth century: by the coming of a railroad line; through exports and imports; or by local sales of staple goods like bread, pasta, agricultural implements, matches, wine casks, or cloth. In the 1890s, railroad lines reached one Sicilian town in three: most so linked were towns along the north coast, but one small line connected Palermo to interior wheat towns, and another ran from Porto Empedocle on the south coast to important sulfur towns in Agrigento and Caltanisetta provinces.

Not surprisingly, given Sicily's long history of commercial agriculture, only 20 percent of Sicilian towns reported no significant agricultural exports during the 1880s. In most towns, subsistence production of food coexisted with cultivation of a market crop. Two-thirds of west Sicilian towns exported some wheat; 40 percent exported some grapes and/or citrus fruits.[22]

Similarly, products from the outside reached even small Sicilian mountain towns by the 1880s. The most common item was cloth, imported from Naples, England, or northern Italy. Trade in food also linked some Sicilian towns into small regional markets. Goods produced in Palermo typically found their way to all the towns within fifty kilometers of the city, creating a rather sizable market area centered on Palermo on the north coast. (See Map 2.1.) With Palermo's artisans so close by, many of the smaller towns around Termini Immerese, Cefalù, and Palermo housed few artisans and no workshops of a semicapitalist nature or bigger size.[23] Beyond the reach of Palermo, however, greater local self-sufficiency in industrial production prevailed. A fairly large population of artisans, some in good-sized workshops, still manufactured necessary items for local markets around Corleone, Alcamo, Trapani, Mazzara del Vallo, Sciacca, and Agrigento.[24]

To assess the extent of market relations in the Sicilian countryside around 1880 it is helpful to remember the ways in which Sicilian men and women entered the marketplace—as consumers, as marketers of crops or goods, and as wage earners. In other words, it seems important to focus not merely on the extent of market relations in the countryside, but also on the kinds of market relations that existed in different regions within western Sicily.

First, the frequency or enthusiasm with which Sicilians used cash should not be exaggerated. Sicilian proverbs consistently warned against the dangers of the marketplace, urging caution and craftiness to those who would succeed there.[25] The accounts of folklorists clearly document that wives and mothers "husbanded" the family's supply of cash, and bought goods that the family required. Women normally made major purchases (cloth, furnishings, and household goods) in preparation for children's weddings.[26] Fewer women expended cash for everyday food purchases; only half of Sicilian towns could claim even one person who made bread or pasta for sale.[27] Some of a family's cash went each year to taxes, but other outlays were less common. In wheat-raising areas, few peasants paid land rents; relatively few Sicilians outside the largest cities paid house rents.[28] Finally, although many peasant men produced wheat for distant markets, they rarely sold their share of the product; they and their families ate it.[29] Artisans and grape or citrus cultivators, on the other hand, did market their own goods, and they also sometimes paid cash to rent lands.[30] Because more cash passed through the hands of such peasants and artisans, towns exporting grapes and citrus and towns with considerable local industry imported more food and supported more bread and pasta makers than average in the 1880s.

Such towns were the exceptions, however. It is clear from the regional evidence that purchases strained and sometimes exceeded cash sources in many Sicilian towns, even before the agricultural crisis of the 1890s. Many Sicilians might easily have experienced the spread of market relations as a cash crisis. Most Sicilian towns, for example, already imported considerable amounts of cloth by the 1880s; at that time, town clerks in all three provinces reported declines in domestic production of cloth for home use. The number of western Sicilian towns importing cloth (82) or cloth and food (44) far exceeded the number of towns where peasants could earn a cash income by marketing grapes or citrus fruits (54).[31]

Nor could wage earning necessarily correct this imbalance. Unfortunately, published sources do not reveal precisely what wage-earning options existed in western Sicily's 136 communes. Even regional evidence is flawed: census categories used in 1881 and 1901 varied considerably and were quite confusing. The Italian census does suggest that independent artisans outnumbered industrial wage earners in 1901, and that between one-third and two-thirds of western Sicilian agriculturalists (depending on region) worked at least part of the year for wages.[32] These figures, however, are too rough to shed much light on the existence of a cash crisis in particular towns.

At best, one can identify Sicilian towns with some capitalist or semicapitalist production in agriculture or industry, and thus some local wage-earning opportunities. Overall, wage-earning possibilities seem to have been quite limited. Only one Sicilian town in twelve claimed a considerable number of workshops employing wage earners from outside the family. Salt extraction, fish salting, boat manufacture, wheat and olive grinding, wine production, cask making, tanning, and rope making all employed wage earners in towns beyond the reach of Palermo's exports.[33] In fourteen towns, sulfur mining employed some wage earners and many more pieceworkers (paid by weight mined). Wage earning in agriculture also existed, as census figures suggested. Sicily's large wheat estates, while only minimally capitalist in organization, nevertheless did employ wage earners in large numbers at harvest time; these large estates and their harvests dominated agriculture in one-quarter of west Sicilian towns.[34] A fair conclusion might be that in slightly less than half of all west Sicilian towns, most men and some women worked at least occasionally for wages in large-scale or profit-oriented enterprises. Few Sicilians outside of Palermo, Marsala, Trapani, or the sulfur towns supported themselves entirely with wages. Payment in kind remained common everywhere.

When opportunities to earn cash by marketing or wage earning are reconciled with records on local imports, it is possible to distinguish between towns where a cash crisis almost certainly existed in the 1880s, towns where a crisis could easily result if any one source of cash income declined, and towns where residents had several options for earning cash to pay for imports. In thirty-one towns, residents had no obvious wage-earning options and no marketable crops; yet they had to pay taxes, and they purchased cloth (and sometimes small amounts of food as well). In such towns, a cash crisis could have been particularly pressing. In sixty-four Sicilian towns, cash-generating possibilities and imports seemed in rough balance, although a contraction of wages or a decline in agricultural prices—as occurred in the late 1880s and 1890s—could easily have precipitated a crisis. In the remaining forty-one towns, men and women enjoyed more flexibility because they could find work on large wheat estates, in small-scale industry or mining, or as cultivators of market crops. Thus residents of these towns had several ways to earn the cash they needed for taxes, cloth, and food.

Sicilian class relations did not vary directly with the cash crisis, but could potentially influence how Sicilians perceived that crisis. Land was widely distributed in sixty-two west Sicilian towns and concentrated in another fifty-nine. Discrete and clearly demarcated classes characterized the second group of towns. In twenty-three towns a small group of absentee owners of large estates faced a majority of partially proletarianized and landless peasants. In twenty-six, a sizable group of civili rented or contracted their medium-sized holdings to landless sharecroppers. (Sicily's fourteen sulfur towns also belonged to this group of towns with discrete classes.) Few middle peasants lived in such towns, but outside of Palermo's regional market, towns like these usually housed a middle stratum of petty merchants, artisans, small entrepreneurs, and journeyman wage earners.[35] Somewhat more typical of Sicily in the late nineteenth century were towns with intricate, complex, and fluid class hierarchies. Eighty-seven fell into this category. In these towns, one or two aristocratic owners of large estates appeared occasionally in town, while a small local gentry lived there permanently. Beneath them existed a marginal group of estate managers, pharmacists, other professionals, and substantial merchants. Small numbers of independent artisans or fishermen mingled socially with substantial peasant landowners (middle peasants), who distinguished themselves in turn from smaller groups of peasant lessees, sharecroppers, and wage-earning day laborers. In such towns, marriage, a small inheritance, or a year of good or bad luck in field or workshop could move families one or two steps up or down in local estimations.[36]

In general, widely distributed lands, agriculture organized by peasant households, fluid classes, and the cultivation of grapes and trees were most pronounced in coastal areas, while concentrated landholding, large-scale agriculture, discrete classes, sulfur mining, and wheat raising characterized more mountainous areas. Market relations and capitalist enterprise, however, did not prevail more obviously in highland or lowland; and thus neither did a cash crisis. Table 2-1 summarizes the data about western Sicily's 136 rural communes. Ties to world markets, local class relations, and the experiences of wage earning or of raising and consuming one's own food varied immensely in Sicily in the 1880s. All these factors prove useful in explaining peasant unrest and—to a somewhat lesser extent—migration from the island during the late nineteenth century.

Population Dynamics before 1880

The market influenced population movements in Sicily in obvious ways. While the colonization of Sicily by Spain in the fifteenth century had encouraged the expansion of baronial towns in the mountains, Sicily's reorientation toward northern Europe in the eighteenth century resulted first in population stagnation and then in reversed population flows. By the late eighteenth century, Sicilians moved about frequently, but primarily locally: from smaller to larger towns, from the mountains

Table 2.1

Market and Class Relations in Western Sicilian Towns, circa 1880s

	Discrete classes	Fluid classes
Severe cash crises (31)*	14	12
Cash crises threatening (64)	22	34
No cash crisis (41)	13	27

*Includes towns for which complete information on class structure was not available.

toward the hills and coasts and, most dramatically, toward the three coastal commercial centers of Palermo, Catania, and Messina. Sicilians were increasingly likely to move in these directions during the years of relatively slow population growth under Bourbon rule. Between 1798 and the first Italian census of 1861, the population of Sicily climbed from 1,660,267 to 2,408,521. The search for work probably motivated many moves, since towns planting citrus or grapes during this time attracted impressive numbers of in-migrants. Citrus towns on the coast near Palermo, for example, increased their populations three to six times over in sixty years.[37]

Sicilians did not settle down noticeably after Italian unification. Only after 1880 did they begin to venture abroad, however. And only after 1900 did emigration rates from the region as a whole surpass rates of out-migration from many towns in the 1860s, 1870s, and 1880s. Decades of regional migration preceded international migration.[38]

Population movements from 1861 to 1880 generally followed the patterns of the past. Small towns in the mountains lost residents while larger towns in hill and plain attracted the migrants. Palermo absorbed a substantial part of Sicily's population growth during these years. There were exceptions, of course. Despite their mountainous locations, Sicily's fourteen sulfur towns attracted in-migrants at a rate of 4 per 1,000 each year between 1861 and 1870. (Towns with no industry lost about the same proportions.) Grape and citrus towns continued to attract migrants during the 1870s (5 per 1,000 yearly), while wheat-raising towns lost population during the same decade (4 per 1,000 yearly). Annual out-migration rates of 4 or 5 per 1,000 were well below typical rates of emigration after 1900 (when towns lost an average of 10 to 15 residents per 1,000 yearly), but they do contradict any picture of stagnant rural villages in the Sicilian countryside. A sulfur town like Lercara Friddi with 9,154 residents in 1871 attracted 2,200 new residents in ten years. During the same ten years 650 persons deserted the nearby wheat-raising town of Valledolmo (population 7,000).[39] No rural Sicilian could fail to note the comings and goings among the neighbors. The Sicilians who organized and protested in the nineteenth century were people who knew about other alternatives, including the possibility of moving away in search of better conditions.

Overall, western Sicilian towns which developed severe cash crises after 1880 had already begun to lose population before 1880, while towns with mines, industry, or marketable crops (and no crises) attracted new residents. Movement from village to town, from mountain to plain, or from provincial workshop to Palermo seems not to have undermined the development of rural protest in Sicily by the late nineteenth century. By no standard was western Sicily politically and socially peaceful for any lengthy period during the century. In one sense, peasant unrest had been a constant feature of rural Sicilian life at least since the development of commercial agriculture. More striking and interesting is the marked transformation—some would call it modernization—of rural protest over the course of the nineteenth century. While the market's impact on population movements seems direct even before international migration began, the linkage between cash crises and labor movement or political modernization is less straightforward, and more difficult to isolate from other influences. If migration and labor movement actually became conflicting strategies for social change by century's end, then differences in their origins and patterns of development must be sought in the preceding decades.

Jacquerie in Evolution

The traditional form of peasant protest in Sicily was jacquerie—violent peasant riot—as it was almost everywhere else in rural Europe. We cannot know for sure when Sicilian peasants first revolted; perhaps there had always been recurring revolts in the countryside. Evidence suggests that the formation of a capitalist world market and the development of commercial agriculture in the sixteenth century produced a period of particularly intense unrest in Europe's periphery. Fernand Braudel writes of social war, brigandage, and glimmers of class consciousness in the Mediterranean of that century. These revolts remained unfinished revolutions, however.[40] Thereafter, Sicilian peasants continued to revolt periodically—in 1772, 1799, 1820–1821, 1848, 1860, 1866, 1892–1894, 1901–1904, 1917–1921, and 1945–1950.[41] Each and every one of these periods of unrest has been termed traditional peasant jacquerie by at least some authors.

This terminology tells us too little, however. It leaves the false impression that peasant revolts have no history, that they have been fixed, almost natural features of rural life—unpredictable, irrational, and beyond control, yet timeless. This is precisely how outside observers often saw peasant revolts, not just in Sicily, but everywhere in the European countryside. Literate men found peasant behavior—and not just in this matter—inexplicable, pointless, and violent. Scholars have been kinder to rioters and mobs, exploring the moral economy and community sentiments that motivated peasants and workers in revolt. As the world view and motives of peasants changed over the centuries, so too did their protests and revolts.[42]

Peasant revolts in Sicily much resembled those in other parts of Europe, at least in their outward forms.[43] Without much warning, a mob of men, women, and children descended on some enemy, his immediate family, and his kinsmen. The rioters humiliated or killed them, and usually looted and destroyed their property. Then, as quickly as they had appeared, the rioters were gone. No leaders could ever be identified, nor witnesses found. Denis Mack Smith notes with some irony that Sicilian peasant rioters could easily have learned such behavior from their aristocratic neighbors, who, under Spanish rule, had for centuries engaged in bloody factional battling among themselves.[44]

While observers all over Europe claimed not to understand what motivated peasants to revolt, in most cases the motives were quite clear. They could be summed up in one word—revenge. Scholars have seen jacquerie as the peasants' efforts to punish wealthy or powerful men who violated communal notions of fairness, decency, or traditions in some way. Thus, to borrow Charles Tilly's term for them, most peasant revolts were reactive.[45] Resentment of French rule had resulted in an early exception to this pattern—the famous Sicilian Vespers of 1282 were clearly aimed at political change.[46] Before the turn of the nineteenth century, however, most rural rioters seem to have been motivated by the desire for revenge on a local strong man or baron who had usurped communal lands or mistreated peasants in some way.

Economic exploitation probably cannot satisfactorily explain all peasant revolts, at least from the late eighteenth century onward, for revolts tended to cluster chronologically in telling ways. In Sicily, peasant uprisings usually followed hard on outbreaks of urban unrest, which usually originated in political struggles and aspirations. In 1820–1821, for example, some of Palermo's aristocrats and republican merchants tried with artisans' help to instigate a revolution against the unpopular Bourbon rule recently restored in Naples. Their goal was independence for Sicily. Not long after the suppression of street fighting in Messina, Catania, and Palermo, peasants in the countryside also rioted. (At least one author suggests that they followed the call of local artisans in doing so.) Peasants vented their ire both at the local well-to-do, including the newly prosperous civile elite, and at the symbols or supporters of Bourbon power in the countryside.[47] It seems hard to deny that Sicilian peasants had their own recurring hopes for independence during these years—independence from both outside rule and from a newly arrogant provincial elite.

A similar wave of unrest followed attempted urban revolutions in 1848, and erupted again in the wake of Garibaldi's march through Sicily in 1860.[48] In both years, Palermo's artisans, capitalists, and liberal aristocrats led the way, and in both these years only some rural artisans and peasants followed their example. In general, rural towns with market-oriented peasants or artisan producers as well as towns with some capitalist small-scale manufacturing numbered among the most rebellious. Peasants in Palermo's immediate hinterland revolted quite frequently, as did the marketers of new crops like citrus fruits and grapes. Finally, towns with mines and/or considerable local industry experienced jacquerie more frequently than did either predominantly agricultural or wheat-raising towns. These were not towns that would develop early or particularly severe cash crises, and most had remarkably fluid class hierarchies. Notably absent from the list of rebellious towns of 1820, 1848, and 1860 were those towns dominated by the large wheat-raising estates. Similarly, where subsistence production prevailed, towns remained remarkably quiet, unmoved by urban unrest.

Peasant knowledge of and reaction to events in Palermo might easily explain the repeated jacqueries in nearby towns: all the rebellious towns of 1848 and 1860 had close ties to Palermo. Traveling vendors carried not only urban goods but urban news into Palermo's hinterland. Similarly, citrus cultivators enjoyed ties to Palermo's port, since they marketed their oranges there. (Wheat and grapes, by contrast, found their way to southern and western ports.) Distant towns with considerable industry probably followed revolts in Palermo through newspaper reports as well as word of mouth, for most Sicilian artisans, and even many miners, could read.[49]

By 1866—a year when Sicilians protested the draft and new tax policies of the unified Italian state—and even more clearly by 1892–1893, the Sicilian countryside began protesting on its own initiative. No urban unrest preceded the rural revolts of the 1890s. Furthermore, smaller towns and a broader range of towns experienced unrest during these years. One can see an important shift in the ecology of rural rebellion between 1860 and the 1890s; the once quiet wheat-raising towns with large estates figured prominently among the towns with the most violent and repeated revolts in 1892–1893.[50]

Not only did rural unrest become less reactive to urban events over the course of the nineteenth century, the focus of jacquerie violence also evolved. Before 1821, peasants attacked mainly rich men and their wealth; after that time they attacked rich men in positions of political authority, and they attacked the symbols of state authority at the local level. Attacks on Italian state authority and on local officeholders quickly replaced attacks on Bourbon tax collectors and municipal offices after national unification. Draft offices, municipal records, town halls, and local officials all found themselves under attack in 1848 and throughout the 1860s.[51] In 1866, leaders of the new Italian nation even worried that Sicilian tax and draft protests might develop into a wider insurrection.[52]

It is not surprising that peasant anger during this period of rapid political change focused on the state. The protests make particular sense if we assume that the tax man—with his demand for cash—personified a growing cash crisis for struggling rural people. Once again, there seems ample evidence that peasants had clear reasons for taking their complaints to municipal and government offices. The neatness of this interpretation collapses, however, in the face of the Sicilian data. Peasant unrest was most common in areas where relatively more cash circulated; the cash crisis was a threat mainly to quiet towns. We know that reactive tax revolts characterized the formation of nation-states throughout Europe.[53] In Sicily, at least, it was the least economically vulnerable towns that voiced the most objections to the process of state making and to the political changes that accompanied unification. This suggests that it was those with resources who revolted, while those struggling to find adequate cash resources were more likely to move around than to struggle.

After the tumultuous decade of national unification, rural Sicilians abandoned their riotous protests. Of course, there had been many other periods of calm in the Sicilian countryside; these always ended—after twenty years or so—in a period of peasant jacquerie. The 1870s and 1880s heralded instead the decline of jacquerie as the peasants' preferred form of protest. By the 1890s, jacquerie would figure as only one type of protest, employed mostly by women. The decline of rural jacquerie reflected important changes at the local level, changes primarily affecting male artisans and peasants. These changes can best be summarized as a growing interest in mutual aid—*mutuo soccorso*. In Sicily, as in many other parts of Europe, a burst of male sociability accompanied the formation of the nation-state, inspiring men to form interest groups and experiment with voluntary associations of many kinds. The growth of mutual aid in Sicily changed the patterns of protest associated with peasant jacquerie in the countryside.

Mutuo Soccorso

Unfortunately, it is still necessary to emphasize that voluntary association was indeed widely practiced by South Italian men by the late nineteenth century. Despite the fact that social scientists have largely discarded Edward Banfield's interpretation of South Italians as amoral familists, incapable of voluntary association, historians continue to argue that nuclear family interests prevented cooperation among Italian peasants. Humbert Nelli's recent essay on Italians in the *Harvard Encyclopedia of American Ethnic Groups* documents the tenacity of Banfield's ideas.[54]

The Sicilian evidence suggests that familism—to the extent it actually existed—waned quickly after Italian unification. The Sicilian proverbs collected by folklorist Giuseppe Pitrè in the 1880s do not reveal thinking like that of Banfieldian amoral familists, who "pursue short run family interests."[55] While many proverbs did glorify nuclear-family solidarity, they also reveal Sicilians' strong desire for cooperation with neighbors, kinsmen, and friends. The proverbs recommend cooperation at least as often as they warn against it. Without cooperation, in fact, a Sicilian family could expect little respect from the community. Social status literally grew out of a generous network of cooperative and reciprocal (thus moral) social relations. Both men and women worked to surround their families with such networks.

Familism, as Banfield used the term, was not the Sicilian ideal. Cooperation, however, did not always mean voluntary association. Friendship, kinship, and neighborliness, or patron-client links, could and often had to suffice.[56] And poor Sicilians often experienced considerable difficulty even in maintaining satisfactory informal networks based on such ties. Voluntary association after 1860 never completely replaced informal networks as a cooperative social strategy among Sicilians. Women continued to rely on informal neighborhood networks and on kinship for cooperation, while peasant men in particular may have simultaneously extended their informal networks and their participation in voluntary association.

Voluntary association had a long history in Sicily. Craft guilds and religious confraternities had existed since the sixteenth century.[57] Artisans dominated both associations. When the revocation of traditional rights to monopoly abolished artisans' guilds in 1812, local craftsmen quickly reorganized as religious confraternities, groups independent of the church but assuming responsibility for organizing religious processions for a favored patron saint.[58] Obviously, Sicilian artisans had never been familists. Their identification with their trade was strong; the social respect that master artisans enjoyed—so evident in Pitrè's collection of proverbs—grew in part from the close and ritualized cooperation that these men enjoyed among themselves.[59]

After the formation of the Italian nation-state, artisans and petty-capitalist entrepreneurs, along with some industrial wage earners, began organizing new kinds of associations, sometimes in cooperation with marginal and ideologically dissident members of local elites. Until 1880, in fact, mutual benefit societies and other types of workers' clubs and voluntary associations developed almost exclusively in towns with either industry or sulfur mines. Many of these early associations mixed political and economic aspirations, although economic self-help became the dominant theme as time passed.

Perhaps because large numbers of Sicilians had just begun experimenting with new forms of voluntary association, there are few clear patterns to be found in men's organizations in the 1860s and 1870s.[60] (Few, for example, at first called themselves mutual benefit societies.) Groups organized in the 1860s tended to name themselves "the honest workers"; in some cases, it is obvious that these were societies formed by journeymen wage earners or employees in capitalist workplaces rather than by independent master artisans. In the early years of the decade, police often noted radical or "ultra" republican influence in such workers' clubs —usually a local republican student, a teacher, or a doctor was identified as the troublemaker. A few such groups declared their continued allegiance to the republic Garibaldi had proclaimed while marching through Sicily in 1860.

By the late 1860s, and especially in the early 1870s, police became even more

concerned about Socialist influence in workers' societies. Police identified Socialists and formal sections of the First International in thirty-four Sicilian towns,
mainly in the southern and western regions of Agrigento province where local
industry still flourished. Dissident Freemasons also worried those responsible for
maintaining public order. Police surveillance seems to have worked effectively for
a time; formal public associations of Socialists and masons usually disappeared
quickly.[61] Mutual aid societies replaced them. These seem to have been regarded
more favorably by the police, but not a few of them were founded by men suspected of Socialist sympathies.

After twenty years of uncertain experimentation, Sicilian men embraced mutual
aid in respectable numbers after 1880. In the first five years of the decade, workers
and peasants organized 108 mutual benefit societies; 144 more appeared by 1890.
Only in very small towns with no industry and in towns of subsistence peasants
were there no mutual aid societies. Thus, by the early 1890s, four of five Sicilian
towns claimed at least one such society, and most had more than one. Fairly
typical was Petralia Soprana, a town of just over 7,000 in 1881. There, an early
workers' society founded in 1873 disbanded during the early 1880s, after its
members were accused of contact with Socialists in Turlin. Shortly thereafter, in
1883, sixty workers organized again, this time as the Society for the Mutual
Benefit of Workers. A year later, fifty other men formed a Catholic society
for mutual aid; they named their association after Saint Joseph, the patron of
friendship.

Three-quarters of the Sicilian societies for mutual aid formed in 1880–1885
limited membership either to artisans/workers or to agriculturalists. Although few
sources speak directly to the point, all seem also to have limited membership to
men. Unlike the jacquerie, with its commune-wide base, voluntary association
revealed interest groups and cleavages based on gender and occupation in many
Sicilian towns.

The Sicilian evidence strongly suggests that voluntary association of peasants
occurred for the first time after 1880, when they joined together to practice mutual
aid. By 1892, when well over half of western Sicily's 136 rural towns had a
workers' mutual benefit society, only about a third boasted a society open to
peasants. The real proportions may have been somewhat higher than this, since
society names did not always indicate the nature of their membership, especially
after 1885.

If voluntary association became popular quite suddenly in the early 1880s, it is
worth trying to understand why this was so. The regional data provide some clues.
The sudden proliferation of mutual aid among artisans in the early 1880s probably
reflected a change in Italian electoral law, which granted some artisans the right to
vote in 1882.[62] And since not all peasants showed equal enthusiasm for mutual
aid, this variation provides hints for understanding what motivated peasants to
organize for the first time. Peasants who organized voluntary associations may

have done so under artisan leadership or example, since towns with peasant associations but no local industry were rare. Wage-earning peasants in wheat-raising towns with large estates also organized earlier and in far greater numbers than did peasant marketers of grapes and citrus fruits. Peasants who subsisted on the food they raised and who had no additional ties to the market did not organize for mutual aid at all. As a result, the spread of mutual aid among peasants did not clearly follow the patterns of peasant jacquerie in the 1860s. Towns with severe cash crises had proportionately fewer mutual aid societies, but in economically less vulnerable towns, mutual aid might be weak (where peasants earned cash by selling grapes and oranges) or strong (where local industry persisted or where peasants earned wages on the large wheat estates). Problems in the workplace, and especially problems related to wage earning seemed to have sparked peasant interest in mutual aid, while it was political change that spurred artisans to organizational action.

Among scholars who have noted the spread of mutual aid in southern Italy, there is disagreement about the meaning and function of the many societies formed after 1880. Some authors see them as family-oriented yet community-based circles of assistance with humble but essential insurance functions like burial of the dead.[63] Others suggest that mutual aid societies gave visible organizational form to existing informal networks—the clienteles of local strongmen or the rival parish enthusiasts of one patron saint or another might become mutual benefit societies.[64] Furthermore, while some scholars believe that mutual benefit societies developed directly into class-conscious trade unions and workers' political parties in the 1890s, others see the mutual benefit society as a training ground for small-scale, market-oriented artisans and peasants aspiring individually to upward mobility. In this last case, the function of the society was to provide education, credit, and cultural programs to artisans and to middle peasants.[65]

Sicily's mutual benefit societies provide at least some evidence for all these interpretations. If we allow societies' names to indicate their goals, we find considerable diversity, even in the early 1880s. Many of the earliest mutual aid societies aimed at economic self-help, largely burial benefits; some provided a meeting room to facilitate sociability, much as had clubs formed in the 1850s and 1860s by civile men. Other early societies had clear political ambitions, and this helps explain, perhaps, why mutual aid remained a male form of organization.[66] By 1890, at least one Sicilian town in seven had a political society. Some took the name of their political boss or patron, but others called themselves democratic, independent, or "supporters of Garibaldi" (republicans). To these politically oriented associations, one might add the small but growing numbers of Catholic societies, in one town in ten. (The Catholic Church at that time still adamantly demanded its communicants reject secular politics and the Italian nation-state, a political position in itself.) *Rerum novarum* was still some years in the future, but small numbers of Catholic priests already worked with humble Sicilians at the local level for mutual aid. Catholic mutual aid societies abjured not only secular politics but occupational divisions as well; by the 1890s, they would announce their rejection of class struggle, too. Significantly, some Catholic societies appeared in small towns with no industry, where mutual aid was otherwise uncommon. They also had more appeal to grape and citrus marketers than to agricultural wage earners or industrial producers of any kind.[67]

After 1885, Sicilian mutual aid societies began to take more grandiose and abstract names, presumably of the virtues they sought to cultivate among their members. In a move that may have reflected the contemporaneous onset of emigration, a few took the name of the discoverer Christopher Columbus; others proclaimed their nationalism by calling themselves after Sicilian or Roman heroes or—more patriotically—after members of the Italian royal family. Obviously, self-improvement was one important reason for joining together in mutual benefit societies. It would, however, probably be a mistake to see in this trend toward abstract names the transformation of occupational pragmatism, political ambitions, or desire for familial security into a vague bourgeois idealism. While many societies did name the ideals supposedly most valued by middle-class Europeans and Americans (progress, self-improvement, education, or "civility"), others named the virtues that had ornamented protest banners since the French Revolution (harmony, brotherhood, strength, unity, and cooperation). Only equality was strikingly missing from this list of ideals Sicilians associated with mutuo soccorso.

In short, mutual aid societies probably had all the goals that scholars have imagined, and more. The fact that their goals strike us as a contradictory hodgepodge may not matter. The importance of the mutual aid society did not lie simply in the goal it pursued, but rather in the new model for organization that it represented. Sicilian men by the 1880s and 1890s had learned that voluntary association could further many interests, not just those of patron saints or local artisans. Increasingly in the 1880s, wage-earning peasants, too, came to appreciate the mechanisms of voluntary association and of mutual aid, and to explore their possibilities.

However much ordinary Sicilians disapproved of the actions of their nation-state—as earlier protests clearly indicate they did—national unification seems also to have encouraged men to identify their interests and pursue them in new ways. Why this was so is not completely clear in the regional evidence, however. While cash crises might have seemed a problem to be solved through interest-group pressure on the state, it was not in towns with severe crises that voluntary association flourished. Nor is it obvious why political change, in the form of national unification, would have encouraged wage earners—particularly disenfranchised peasants—to think about their workplaces or everyday lives in new ways, or to see in them problems to be solved through organization and self-help.

One important possibility has been ignored up to this point, and that is that crime represented another and more individualistic alternative to peasant jacquerie and mutual aid during this period. Banditry, for example, has long been understood as a prepolitical form of protest. We know that theft did increase in Sicily with the end of feudalism, primarily because those who attempted to exercise older common rights to plants and animals suddenly found themselves accused of crimes against newly private property. Furthermore, Anton Blok has argued that latent and open class conflict—whether in the form of theft, protest, or organization—also encouraged the development of mafia in the late nineteenth century, at roughly the time when mutual aid became popular. Protesters, "thieves," and organized peasants threatened the status quo in many wheat-raising towns with large estates; mafiosi came forward to offer landowners a service, by coercing and controlling potential activists, thieves, and other troublemaking peasants with threats of physical violence. Blok found mafia strongholds in the same towns where Sicilian peasants first organized mutual benefit societies during the 1880s. His history of mafia in western Sicily also suggests that periods of mafia violence generally coincided with years of peasant activism and protest.[68] What Blok's analysis ignores is the strength of mafia in the citrus-exporting towns around Palermo, where mutual aid never attained the popularity it did in wheat-raising towns, and where peasants remained surprisingly quiescent in the 1870s and 1880s. There, mafiosi extorted money from small and large cultivators alike, by threatening to destroy crops or property or by seizing control of the fruit trade.[69] Crime and mutual aid might seem logical alternatives, but they did not always conflict with each other; mafia, furthermore, could develop independently of either.

Conclusion

In many respects the histories of population movements and rural protest in Sicily before 1890 confirm the findings of scholars who have written about rural unrest and migration in the contemporary world. The slow decline of subsistence production, the process of state formation, the spread of market relations, and the activism of middle groups all had important consequences in the Sicilian countryside of the past century. As is true today, subsistence producers in Sicily in the past did not often revolt, organize, or migrate. The Sicilian evidence suggests further that food-raising but market-oriented middle peasants like the ones described by Wolf figured far more prominently in peasant jacquerie than in the later development of mutual aid. Other middle groups—especially independent artisans and the more proletarianized industrial wage earners—moved easily from protest as rural jacqueristes to initiatives in mutual benefit societies and other voluntary associations. By contrast, the peasants working for wages on the large wheat estates rarely revolted in the early years of the century, while they migrated in large numbers. After 1880, however, as emigration from Sicily began, they frequently organized for mutual aid. Perhaps their behavior had changed as wage earning began to surpass subsistence wheat production in importance—that is, as more and more wage-earning peasants found themselves purchasing the grain they needed to eat. Perhaps this, too, is a key to the onset of transatlantic migrations.

It is fair to say that the history of Sicily's militant (and later "red") towns began not so much with the old rural tradition of jacquerie as with its gradual and incomplete transformation by men's voluntary associations. Towns with no voluntary associations for peasants, artisans, or miners before 1890 rarely developed into leftist strongholds, whatever their past history of violent and recurring peasant revolt. Thus, the timing of mutual aid's sudden popularity in the countryside seems especially important.

Was it mere historical accident that mutual aid became popular during the same decade when significant numbers of Sicilians first began emigrating to the New World? The links between population movement and an emerging labor movement were not completely obvious in the regional and communal patterns discussed in this chapter. They become more obvious at the local level. The next chapter introduces Sambuca di Sicilia, and a study of the town's activists and emigrants.

Chapter 3
The Genesis of a Red Town

From a distance, Sambuca di Sicilia looks much like the other towns of its region. It seems large for its setting at the foot of completely desolate mountains. Can the irrigated valleys and vineyards to the south actually support not only this small city of 8,000 but also the citizens of the other three towns visible in the distance? (See Map 2.1.)

The typical sights and sounds of provincial Sicilian life are much in evidence in today's Sambuca: the loud voices behind curtained windows, the public garden, the dust, the vegetable trucks with their raucous calls to buy, the men's clubs, and the improbably grand (if rundown) palaces stretched along the wide straight main street.[1] But there are differences, too. Few tourists travel to see Sambuca's humble public squares; they are not particularly noteworthy. They are, however, clean: no refuse collects there, and no skinny dogs search for scraps. Street cleaners and a three-wheeled garbage truck appear regularly, at dawn, announcing their arrival with an unforgettable alarm. Even more impressive, the rubble left by an earthquake in 1968 has been entirely cleared away. There are no abandoned districts of earthquake-damaged buildings such as one finds in some nearby towns.[2]

Sambuca is a red town—"still" a red town, its political activists might add, for they are concerned about declining support among the young. The decline has been slow but regular since the 1950s, a time when three-quarters or more of town residents gave their vote to parties of the left, chiefly the Communists. Town government remains firmly in the hands of Communists and Socialists, as it has since the end of World War II. Their hegemony is obvious everywhere in the town: at the Antonio Gramsci elementary school, in the mock labor festivals of children (replete with five-year-olds' renditions of militant songs), and in the high visibility of *l'Unità*, the Communist Party newspaper, at the local newstand. And —one must add—in the regular appearance of street cleaners. This is municipal communism, Sicilian-style. The piazzas are clean; the mayor finds new local sources of water during drought years; corruption, while not unknown, is not a major theme in village gossip.[3]

Sambuca's leftism makes it somewhat exceptional in the Italian South. As a region, Italy's South gives most of its votes to the Christian Democratic Party; the strongholds of Socialist and Communist parties are elsewhere in Italy—in the north and center. Still, more than a quarter of western Sicilian towns give considerable support to the parties of the left, and there are other local centers of leftist enthusiasm in Italy's other southern provinces. The Communist Party in particular worked hard to attract rural and peasant membership in the South in the years after World War II.[4] If Sambuca's history is at all typical, their success was built on earlier roots, especially the rebellions of the turn of the century.

Residents of Sambuca readily offer an explanation for the success of the left in their hometown. Retired schoolteacher, enthusiastic poet, and son of a Socialist shoemaker, Baldassare G. spoke for many of his fellow townsmen: "Why this town and not Santa Margherita Belice [a nearby neighbor]? Because Sambuca's elite was more arrogant! They showed off, especially during Mussolini's time. They drove around in cars, and lorded it over starving peasants!"[5] For G., an analysis of his town's peculiar political history begins with an understanding of relations between rich and poor, relations he believed differed from those of other towns in the region, especially in the twentieth century. While archival research revealed a more complex picture than this, Baldassare G.'s explanation is essentially correct.

This chapter summarizes the first episodes of Sambuca's turn to the left, a tale completed in chapter 7. Sambuca's history is unique, but not at all atypical of an important group of Sicilian towns that developed politically in similar ways in the twentieth century. Early events in Sambuca demonstrate that rural unrest and emigration sometimes had common origins, and that both could develop simultaneously. It documents further how that growth occurred, as disgruntled artisans looking for allies in local political struggles eventually (although in Sambuca quite belatedly) turned to the peasant majority of wheat cultivators. Unrest in areas of considerable and early emigration and the important if problematical connection between artisans and peasants are themes that will appear and reappear in subsequent chapters.

Much of this chapter (as well as chapters 5, 6, 7, and 8) is based on a systematic comparison of the backgrounds and lives of Sambuca's political activists and the emigrants from the town. The evidence comes from Sambuca's local archives, especially population registers and series of vital records. Local sources identified over 3,500 Sambucesi migrating to the United States at least temporarily before 1934.[6] (For further information, see Appendix. While emigration historians have not often used such sources, a number of scholars of internal European migration have exploited them systematically and imaginatively.[7]) Because of their pride in their red town, Sambuca's political leaders have lionized the town's earliest militants, making it easy to identify and gather information about the early leaders of the Socialist and Communist parties.[8] Reconstitution of the families of Sambuca's militants and migrants revealed much about the backgrounds of both groups; it outlined as well the occupational, kinship, and neighborhood ties that organized political association and chain migration from the town.

Sambuca Becomes Italian

Like every Sicilian town, Sambuca has a long and unique history.[9] Originally centered around an Arab castle (hence its original name: Sambuca Zabut), the town by Norman times claimed about 1,000 residents. Most Sambucesi found housing in seven crooked passageways, which today are called the Saracen alley-ways. Sambuca was one of a cluster of small settlements (*casali*), its lands divided into two separate manors: one was a church holding, another a baronial estate. As the Catalans arrived and refeudalized Sicily, three nearby villages disap-peared—their inhabitants having fled to live in the better fortified Sambuca. By 1500, Sambuca thus claimed 5,000 inhabitants, even though a sizable Jewish population had been recently expelled.

Sambuca's street plan reflects its sudden expansion: as new residents built down the ridge away from the Saracen alleys, they constructed a lower town with long straight streets in a gently modified grid. This grid in more vigorous form charac-terized most of the new baronial towns founded by Spanish lords. The number of religious orders and churches also increased suddenly around this time, perhaps reflecting Sambuca's new size and the Church's considerable land holdings there. By 1629, the town had orders of Carmelites, Augustinians, Franciscans, Capu-chins, and Benedictines; it claimed ten churches (a number that would grow in the centuries ahead) and a religious confraternity.

Despite its rapid growth, Sambuca soon saw its neighbors Menfi and Santa Margherita surpass it in political importance, probably because Sambuca had been inherited by lords both farther away and politically more marginal by the seven-teenth century. After the plagues of 1575–1620 (when local residents discarded their old patron Saint George for Maria dell'Udienza), the town grew again, from 5,800 to 8,000 residents by 1750. Population then stagnated under Neapolitan rule, and at the time of Garibaldi's Sicilian campaign, Sambuca had about 8,900 inhabitants.[10]

Sambuca in the nineteenth century was a typical wheat-raising town, its popula-tion polarized between a landowning elite (the civili) and a population of landless peasants. Like many of the towns of southern and western Sicily, it still housed a sizable group of artisans as well. As we will see, Sambuca shared these character-istics with towns which by the 1890s numbered among Sicily's most militant.

The isolation and provincialism of this unremarkable Sicilian town should not be exaggerated. In the nineteenth century, the rise of a new elite and political unification worked in complex and sometimes contradictory ways to alter the eco-nomic and political options of residents of this and other small provincial towns.[11] Both emigration and new forms of rural rebellion can be seen as new strategies, developing in overlapping rather than conflicting fashion.

As early as the fifteenth century, Sambuca's carters carried wheat to the southern port of Sciacca for export.[12] While observers noted occasional other exports (of capers, pistachios, oil, and cheese), these rarely assumed much importance.[13] Grape and citrus cultivation, while expanding in other parts of the island, did not find much success in Sambuca until after World War II.

Sambuca's estate managers and wheat speculators formed a new local elite during the speculative and inflationary Napoleonic Wars. Sambuca's civili usurped communal lands; they purchased large wheat estates from the impoverished aristocracy in the 1830s; and they acquired parcels of church lands as they became available during the 1850s and 1860s. Perhaps because so many religious orders had owned land in Sambuca, the town's gentry population grew larger than in other towns. By 1880, elite families were about 10 percent of Sambuca's households.[14] In addition, the average civile family in Sambuca seems to have owned more land than was common in other Sicilian towns. Agricultural surveys usually contrasted large land holdings (the wheat estates) with newer medium-sized plots held by local elites. Medium-sized in Sambuca meant about fifty hectares; elsewhere, medium-sized holdings ranged from five to ten hectares.[15] Obviously, the material possibilities for elite arrogance existed in Sambuca well before the twentieth century.

Sambuca's peasant majority (65 to 75 percent of the population) raised wheat on land owned mainly by the town's elite. Local records suggest that land tenure and conditions of labor divided cultivators into three rough and overlapping categories. Middle peasants (*burgisi*) owned (or leased long term) plots of one, two, or three hectares; they also possessed substantial houses and work animals. But they formed the smallest group of Sambuca's peasants, only about 10 percent of the peasant population.[16] Local records identified a second type of middle peasant, the *agricoltore,* who seemed to have been a peasant lessee with three-to-six-year contracts on small and medium-sized plots belonging to civili and local artisans.[17] These middle peasants, too, owned houses and animals. They, too, constituted a small group, perhaps 10 to 15 percent of the peasant population. Middle peasants ate the wheat they raised and marketed small amounts of grain and other produce locally.

The vast majority of peasant men appeared in Sambuca's records as poor peasants—*contadini;* they worked as sharecroppers for one year at a time on rotating plots on the large wheat estates, and at harvest time they earned wages there. In Sambuca, about two-thirds of the families of poor peasants lived in houses they owned. Most owned simple agricultural tools, like hoes, but few could keep work animals, having lost access to pasture lands with the end of feudalism.[18] Still, the term *bracciante* or *giornaliere di campagna* (agricultural day laborer) rarely appeared in Sambuca's records before the twentieth century. This hints at the still secondary importance of wage earning in local agriculture. Wage earning was limited to harvest and plowing seasons on local wheat estates in

Sambuca and adjoining communities. Most of Sambuca's peasants were semi-proletarianized sharecroppers and wage earners; they ate the wheat they raised, marketed nothing, and earned little.

Sambuca was distant enough from Palermo's market to need a sizable artisan population, roughly 15 to 25 percent of local household heads. Most artisans owned small plots of land, four- to ten-room houses, and the tools of their trade.[19] The list of trades represented in Sambuca seems excessive for a town of 8,000 to 10,000 inhabitants: weapon makers, decorative painters, barbers, plasterers, shoemakers, seamstresses, carters, locksmiths, rope makers, potters, confectioners, cabinetmakers, carpenters, blacksmiths and ironworkers, tinkers, tile makers, photographers, midwives, butchers, tanners, marble carvers, masons, tailors and tailoresses, watchmakers, pasta makers and bread bakers, wigmakers, basket makers, and stonecutters. Of these, shoemakers, carpenters, masons, and seamstresses formed the largest groups. Many artisans or their wives also operated small shops, selling coffee, dry goods, and small amounts of food. In the 1890s, Sambuca claimed in addition two cloth merchants, a leather merchant, a pharmacy, and six small shops selling liquor and wine.[20] An industrial survey in the early 1890s noted a local specialization in the production of agricultural implements. Six foundries had abandoned small-scale artisanal production for "more modern" techniques; together, they employed twenty-eight ironworkers. Cabinetmakers and bakers, too, had organized larger workshops employing journeyman labor.[21]

Finally, until the early 1880s, local clerks regularly included most female residents of Sambuca among the noncultivators of the town, calling them *industriose*.[22] (Women's work in the fields was highly seasonal; they traveled only once during the year to the large estates, and they harvested the small local grape crop.) Sambuca's women spun and wove, mainly (although not exclusively) for domestic use.[23] They also wove straw mats and made brooms for middlemen capitalists from Sciacca.[24] Few women besides midwives and tailoresses reported specific trades to local clerks before the mid-1880s.

Several sources hint at the meaning of economic and political change for Sambuca's elite, artisans, and peasants in the nineteenth century. While northern Europeans typically called Sicily's rural elite backward and lacking in entrepreneurial skills, impoverished, and slavishly imitative of the older aristocracy, a somewhat different picture emerges at the local level.[25] From the years of the Napoleonic Wars until the grain crises of the late 1880s, Sambuca's civili seem to have enjoyed a period of rising social and political fortunes. As they monopolized land released from church and feudal controls, they reshaped their hometown, building thirty-room mansions, refurbishing a local theatre, constructing a public garden, and paving streets so that their new carriages could carry them about in visible splendor.[26] Local men in the 1850s formed their own social club, the *circolo civile*, with furnished rooms on the main street; its main purpose was recreational, although it also helped institutionalize boundaries between the elite and the upwardly mobile.[27] Finally, Sambuca's elite bore increasingly large families in the nineteenth century. Eight or ten legitimate children and uncounted illegitimate ones was not an unusually large group of progeny for a civile man by century's end. Jane and Peter Schneider's research suggests that large families symbolized the growing confidence of the elite in its new local prominence.[28] Crude and ignorant the civili may have been; they were also clever, ruthless, and, in their own way, ambitious. Unlike Sambuca's former baronial rulers, who for two centuries had lived elsewhere and rarely visited the town, the new rulers seemed determined to leave their mark locally, and Italian unification provided them with new opportunities to do so.

Many civili welcomed unification, at least initially, as an escape from the outside interference of the Neapolitan dynasty.[29] When a troop of Garibaldi's followers (the Orsini column) camped just outside Sambuca, local civili sent a message immediately, welcoming them and offering hospitality. The band collected mules, horses, and wagons before heading for the nearby town of Giuliana. Sambuca's wealthy Ciaccio family sent a special gift of 59 *onze* and a horse for Orsini, while a group of civile men collected and donated an additional 450 onze to show their support for Garibaldi.[30]

Sambuca's gentry reaped the rewards of unification in the form of church lands, the vote, control of municipal government (and with it the right to tax), and municipal spoils.[31] Although divided into two hostile nonideological factions (termed the "ups"—from the upper town, and the "downs"—from the lower town), the elite nevertheless held local government firmly in its own hands. They forced their poorer and unenfranchised fellow citizens to bear the costs of local administration and improvements through taxes on animals, hearths, and food purchases, while practically eliminating taxes on land, which they as landholders would have had to pay. They also voted loyally for representatives of Italy's "historic left" nationally. Not a few thought of themselves as republicans and liberals.[32]

For Sambuca's artisanal producers, the nineteenth century brought mixed blessings at best. On the one hand, the rise of a new elite and its willingness to spend, if not to invest, created many local jobs for masons, tailors, and cabinetmakers. A period of rising expectations seems to have ensued. Like gentry families, artisans' families grew larger after the 1860s.[33] Some of Sambuca's wealthier artisans even intermarried with the marginal elite of the town in the 1860s and 1870s.

In other ways, however, artisans' experiences differed significantly from those of the civili. The vast majority of artisans did not own enough property to vote; they had no access to either local prestige or local spoils, except through servile relations to individual patrons. Furthermore, as we have already seen, the liberal trade policies of the new Italian state allowed outside producers to challenge artisans' monopoly on local markets. It seems, however, that only Sambuca's female spinners and weavers suffered initially from such competition. Production of cloth for local sale and home use declined rapidly during the 1880s. Both local records and those of the Italian state reveal this change: women were no longer listed as *industriose* around 1880;[34] Women in artisanal families were subsequently listed as seamstresses. By 1896, a government survey reported only forty domestic looms still in use in Sambuca.[35]

For Sambuca's wheat cultivators the changes of the nineteenth century seem most elusive. Excluded from political life during the previous centuries, they remained firmly excluded after national unification. Neither feudalism's end nor national unification transferred land to ordinary peasants in Sambuca. With little change in local agriculture, few peasants became marketers of grapes or citrus fruits. Peasant families rarely achieved the size of artisan or elite families unless they owned some land; among the poorest, low fertility and high mortality—the result of poor diet and unsanitary living conditions—limited peasant family size until the end of the century.[36] Nor was there evidence of rapid proletarianization among Sambuca's peasantry. Only the smallest amounts of cash passed through peasant hands; they used it mainly to pay taxes and to provide daughters with dowries of cloth and household goods.

The major change for Sambuca's peasant families during the nineteenth century was the decline of domestic spinning and weaving. Women who had been weavers at first sought work as seasonal agricultural laborers. (Sambuca's clerks did not begin to list such women as peasants until the early 1880s, when they already comprised about 40 percent of the agricultural laborers in the region.[37])

Falling wheat prices, poor wheat harvests, and limited options for female employment took their toll during the 1880s. Peasant men, for example, completely replaced women as agricultural laborers between the two Italian censuses of 1881 and 1901. This may have been a result of a stagnating or declining demand for labor during a period of expanding population: whether employers or public opinion deemed men preferable employees is not clear. Under- and unemployed peasant women probably appeared in the second census as housewives. Sambuca's clerks also began using the term *casalinga*—housewife—during the early 1890s, and it was no accident that the poorest of peasant women, not their wealthier peers, were most likely to receive the label.

By 1901, then, the average Sicilian peasant family had one fewer worker than the average family of twenty years earlier.[38] Yet taxes still had to be paid and daughters dowered. In years when bad harvests or rapacious estate managers cut into the family wheat supply, available cash went for food, not to the tax man or the savings jar. A cash crisis had arrived in Sambuca's peasant households, as local records showed: a common charitable act for church or rich man in the 1890s was to provide a cash sum to dower the daughters of five or six poor families.[39] Many families fell behind on their taxes, as well, and found themselves in debt to the employers who also taxed them.

Scholars agree that the new civile elite were hated long before the agricultural crises of the late nineteenth century.[40] (In Sicilian proverbs we find no monarch or aristocrat glorified for protecting the powerless peasant.) Class hatreds were said to be especially extreme in the towns dominated by the large wheat estates—the wheat raisers, like Marx, divided the world into two antagonistic groups, the rich and the poor.[41] For Sambuca's peasants, the newly rich were everywhere visible—as the older aristocracy had not been. Even if peasants envied civile wealth (and proverbs like "the poverty of the rich is worth more than the wealth of the poor" suggest this was so), they also hated the landowners' pretensions—their "arrogance," to use Baldassare G.'s word. Only on elite land could peasants raise their food or earn their wages; this was a source of considerable resentment, especially when nouveau riche men attempted to force peasants to observe disadvantageous feudal customs. And the national government was not viewed as more sympathetic—it was just one more in a long list of foreign invaders.[42]

Local social structure and the contrasting experiences of Sambuca's elite, artisans, and peasants shed some light on the more general patterns that the previous chapter summarized as cash crisis, jacquerie in evolution, and the growth of mutual aid. In 1848, Sambuca experienced a peasant jacquerie, when local population registers were burned and the tax man was attacked. This was the last such riot in Sambuca. For fifty years thereafter, rural protest gradually assumed new forms; by the twentieth century, agricultural strikes, land occupation, and voting Socialist expressed peasants' discontent. This transformation of rural protest in Sambuca occurred against a background of considerable and growing population movements. Sambuca's genesis as a red town dates to the period of emigration to the United States.

Mobile Artisans and Their Organizations

The years between 1870 and 1900 stand out in the political and migratory histories of Sambucesi. Like Sicilians in other towns, Sambucesi experimented with new forms of voluntary association during this period. They also showed a persistent interest in life beyond their communal boundaries. Mobile artisans figured prominently in the early histories of both emigration and labor militancy in the town. Without their early initiatives, Sambuca might never have become a red town, nor might the town have sent so many of its citizens to live in the United States.

Numbers of Sicilian artisans moved about well before Italian unification, and usually the search for work and better local markets for their goods motivated them. When Sicily's barons abandoned the countryside to live in Palermo in the seventeenth and eighteenth centuries, artisanal workers followed them to build their houses, to clothe them, and to provide them with other goods and services.[43] Similarly, the growth of a sizable rural elite in towns like Sambuca encouraged artisans to move there in search of clients. While Sambuca slowly lost population overall during the 1860s, the town also attracted some in-migrants during that decade and even more during the next. Local records show that about half of those seeking new homes in Sambuca were families of young artisans: shoemakers, plasterers, barbers, masons, pasta makers, and confectioners.[44] In-migrants came from nearby towns and from as far away as Palermo. Simultaneously, other artisans left Sambuca to ply their trades elsewhere. Almost half of the young artisans marrying in Sambuca in the 1850s, 1860s, and 1870s never bore children in their hometown—a possible clue that many left before starting families.[45] Artisans more often found their spouses in other towns, a further spur to their migration. Both ironworkers and cabinetmakers from Sambuca regularly apprenticed in Palermo, while shoemakers, tailors, and others traveled occasionally to Palermo or to Sciacca (the nearest port city) to purchase supplies.[46]

Because of their training, literacy, and mobility, artisans knew of and reacted to events in the cities of Sicily and the world beyond. This explains in part why they played a crucial role in the urban revolts and jacqueries of the early nineteenth century and in the voluntary associations of the later nineteenth century. Sambuca's artisans became the town's first activists. They also became the town's first emigrants, and for much the same reasons: their knowledge and social contacts reached well beyond the boundaries of their hometown, and their resources allowed them to undertake new ventures when they felt discontented with the status quo.

Organizational experimentation in Sambuca began among elite men, but artisans soon joined and then surpassed them. Because of their long opposition to Bourbon rule, a small number of the Sicilian elite found attractive not only republican but also socialist and internationalist thought. Though "ups" and "downs" factions were nonideological, a few elite men in Sambuca can be considered ideologues. During the late 1860s and throughout the 1870s, police kept Sambuca's local intellectual Navarro della Miraglia under surveillance; they believed him to have been in Paris during the Commune, and to have supported the Sicilian rebellions of the 1860s.[47] It is important to emphasize the utter social respectability of this man. His father was a much-honored notary and lawyer—a small piazza in Sambuca bears his name. Navarro's family included the head of Garibaldi's republican support committee in Sambuca and a former teacher of Francesco Crispi, who would become Italy's first Sicilian prime minister. Navarro himself wrote short stories and novels, which prefigured but never achieved the popularity of Giovanni Verga's naturalistic tales. Many of Navarro's stories drew on his life in Sambuca.[48]

Apparently, Emmanuele Navarro established contacts with a small but active group of International Socialists working in Agrigento province during the 1870s. Police reported a section of the First International in Sambuca in 1873.[49] By 1876, with the help of men from nearby Menfi, Sambuca also claimed a small lending library for workers.[50] Since the town's peasants remained overwhelmingly illiterate (as "x"s in town marriage records confirm), literate artisans must have formed the bulk of Navarro's associates among Sambuca's ordinary citizens. Certainly, the alliance of artisans with dissident intellectuals was typical of other Sicilian towns.

Shortly after they received the vote in 1882, Sambuca's literate and most prosperous artisan men organized for mutual aid. There were two mutual aid societies, but no records of them survived on the local level. One group seems to have had political ambitions, since it called itself the Unione Elettorale; it may be that this group functioned as an artisans' machine for the "downs"—the civile faction that already included a few substantial peasant landowners in the lower town (where an important cluster of artisans' workshops was also located).[51] Sambuca's second mutual aid society called itself the Franklin Society, taking its name from Benjamin Franklin, whose homilies for humble workers became popular in many Sicilian towns in the 1880s. This organization probably emphasized self-improvement.[52] (It is easy to imagine, but impossible to document, that a reader at the workers' library of the 1870s suggested Franklin as an appropriate model for the new organization formed several years later.) Since no records survive, we can only guess that poorer or illiterate artisans—still nonvoters at this time—formed this group.

Mutual aid in Sambuca reflected artisans' attempts to differentiate themselves somewhat from the local elite; politics seemed to encourage at least some to action. That Sambuca's artisans might be interested in entering and influencing local politics is not surprising, since some of them had just received the right to vote. Enfranchised artisans could not, however, simply assume leadership of their hometown by going to the polls conscientiously. The elite outnumbered the literate and enfranchised artisanry. A tax list from 1896 reports that for every eligible artisan voter, two civili already had the vote.[53] If artisans were to influence local politics they either had to cooperate with elite bosses or they had to bring new voters—the illiterate among them—into the polity. In Sambuca, artisans attempted to do both. The Unione Elettorale probably accepted elite leadership, and sought benefits within the existing spoils system. The second strategy—of self-improvement, modeled on Ben Franklin—aimed at increasing the electorate. If every artisan man in Sambuca gained the vote, artisans could hope to control local government. This emphasis on democracy in local politics constituted an important step to the left.

No evidence suggests that artisans at this time saw peasants as potential allies. Sambuca had no peasant mutual benefit society, as did some other Sicilian towns. It is essential to emphasize the point that such an alliance was not necessarily logical in local eyes; peasants and artisans did not, in any meaningful sense, form a working class. Cases of artisan men combining industrial with agricultural work were quite rare in local records before the 1880s. Artisans shared with the elite a contempt for agricultural labor; they regarded themselves as townsmen, not rustics.[54] While an artisan might own land, he rarely worked it himself: instead, it was leased to a middle peasant. And since artisans and peasants infrequently intermarried, relatively few artisans had close kinship ties to the peasant majority.[55]

Sambuca's artisans remained the main proponents of change in Sambuca during the tumultuous 1890s. Available sources paint somewhat conflicting pictures, but one thing is clear: Sambuca did not number among the most rebellious towns in 1892–1893. The majority of its population—the peasants—remained quiet, as they had since 1848. Unrest in Sambuca began in late 1893 when artisans, who now began to see themselves acting in the interests of all humble taxpayers in the town, organized a *fascio* of workers around the tax issue. By that time, many nearby towns had not only organized similar groups but had begun to experience strikes and protests of various kinds.[56] Sambuca's fascio maintained contact with a Sicilian central committee. It also moved to join the newly constituted Italian Socialist Party.[57] But, unlike the others, Sambuca's fascio appears to have worked only behind the scenes; it organized no public protests.

Perhaps this is why local tradition traces the origins of socialism in Sambuca to Michele B., a shoemaker and a fascio activist. In 1894 Michele B. was sent to jail, where he met Nicola Barbato, one of western Sicily's best-known early rural socialist activists. Many of Sambuca's early Socialist Party members reported that Michele B. "brought socialism" with him when he returned to his hometown.[58]

Prison conversions are not unusual events in the history of radical movements, but this local version leaves an important question unanswered. Why, after all, was Michele B., along with two other men from the town, jailed? Two clues point again to local politics and to a heated debate about local taxes as the source of the conflict. In early 1894, Sambuca's elite-dominated council suddenly lowered taxes. It probably did so under pressure, but we can only guess at the nature of this pressure. Elite faction fighting reached a peak in Sambuca in the early 1890s; losers regularly challenged winners in court, and artisans bounced onto and off of tax lists as their literacy tests were challenged, accepted, and (sometimes) stolen or destroyed. At about the time that workers in the town organized their fascio, an opposition faction emerged and offered candidates for office. (Its challenge proved strong enough that it assumed municipal leadership briefly at the turn of the century.)[59] One of the artisans jailed in 1894 seems to have belonged to this group; whether or not he was a Socialist before his imprisonment is not clear. It may have been the case that Sambuca's fascio adhered to the Socialist Party before its members became socialists in any ideological sense. Local Sicilian history provides countless examples of nonideological factions indiscriminately seeking outside alliances. Sambuca's "ups" also followed local precedents when, in late

1893, they bowed to pressure and lowered taxes, while simultaneously arranging with higher authorities for the imprisonment of their challengers. Threats and efforts at cooptation had long characterized boss politics at the communal level.[60]

By the time the Italian government lifted restrictions on workers' organizations in 1901, Sambuca had a functioning Socialist circle. The jailed shoemaker Michele B., who also worked as custodian at the town's school for boys, led the group. Elderly Socialists in the 1970s recalled that B. had talked to them about socialism during the school break. B.'s methods of recruitment largely determined which boys came under his influence—few peasant boys attended school at all. It also meant that most of the early activists became Socialists at a surprisingly young age—at about ten or eleven. (After that age, even artisan boys stopped their formal schooling to begin work and apprenticeships in shops.)

Once repression of workers' organizations ended, the artisan Socialists promptly rented rooms above a shoemaker's shop in the lower town. Local legend has it that they got the rooms cheap because a woman had recently died there of tuberculosis, and no one else dared take the space. A sympathetic midwife—herself the wife of a shoemaker—gave the Socialists disinfectant to clean the rooms. This was the only obvious role women would play in Sambuca's left for many years. Since Socialist initiatives, like mutual aid, developed in response to political change, women's absence was predictable.

Sambuca's Socialists hung a red flag on the wall, and they quickly opened an evening school to teach workers how to read and write. Their strategy facilitated the spread of Socialist ideals, of course; more important, perhaps, it also helped qualify the illiterate to vote in the years before 1913. Significantly, Sambuca's Socialists demanded the end of spoils politics and corrupt patronage at the municipal level. They continued to claim democratic principles for themselves, and they thus claimed to speak for ordinary Sambucesi of all backgrounds.[61]

Socialism in Sambuca remained largely an artisans' movement for many years. Local records tell us about the origins of ten of the early Socialist activists. Most were young men born in the 1880s and early 1890s. Four worked as shoemakers, three as tailors, and two as petty merchants (a seller of wine, the manager of a tobacco shop). With the exception of Michele B., most came from less prosperous artisanal families, and most lived in the lower town. Only one early Socialist activist was a peasant, and he owned some land; one of the Socialist shoemakers had a peasant father, while a second had a father who apparently mixed work as a peasant lessee and as a carter. Brothers became Socialists together: two sets of brothers supplied, in fact, half of the early activists. Blood and affinal ties linked several others. Local sources show quite clearly that the Socialist circle was the product of an existing social network: many of the parents of the first Socialists had chosen each other as marriage witnesses fifteen to thirty years earlier.[62]

Typical of Sambuca's Socialist founding fathers was Biagio R., born in 1886 in the lower town to a father listed alternately as a shopkeeper and operator of a wine shop and a mother listed as a shopkeeper. Biagio R. worked at several trades: he was trained as a cabinetmaker, but sometimes worked as a salesman, and operated a little tobacco store. Biagio was the youngest son in a family of four sisters (two of whom married in Sambuca) and four artisan brothers (most of whom eventually migrated to the United States). Three of the sons of the R. family became Socialists. Biagio later joined the Communist Party several years after his marriage to Antonina R., a seamstress and the daughter of a carter and his wife, a cafe operator. Biagio R. remained in Sambuca most of his life; he had two children, one of whom trained as a doctor and later moved to Ribera and several other Sicilian cities in search of work.

At first, Sambuca's artisan activists did not seem to have much appeal for the peasant majority, and there is, in fact, little evidence that they hoped to. One elderly peasant man, who later joined the Socialist and then the Communist parties, reported that peasants initially associated the Socialists' red flag with the devil. They crossed themselves defensively whenever they had to pass Socialist headquarters.[63]

The limits of early Socialist organizing in Sambuca are reflected in a local list of the men most influenced by the artisans' school. Upwardly mobile sons of artisans outnumbered all others: a lawyer son of a rope-maker father, a teacher born to a shoemaker, two artists (sons of a carter and a shoemaker), and a doctor born to a carter father. A very few upwardly mobile sons of peasants also appeared on the list: the oculist son of a peasant lessee and a tailor from a family of middle peasants. Compared to a handful of masons, shoemakers, and tailors trained in the school, only a single poor peasant appears on the list.

Many citizens of Sambuca today proudly see the Socialist-trained autodidacts of their town as the origin of a lively, democratic, and popular culture in Sambuca.[64] Until the second decade of the twentieth century, however, left-wing self-improvement, municipal power struggles, and popular culture remained largely in artisan hands. Peasants stayed apart. Perhaps peasants did not see lowered taxes or self-improvement as appropriate responses to their problems, or perhaps—as the peasant informant suggests—religious fears held them back.

Whatever the reasons for their caution, peasants in Sambuca did ultimately turn to the Socialists and the Socialists to them. The timing of this transformation, explored in chapter 8, is surprising. Only during the years of massive emigration and return migration to their hometown did Sambuca's peasants join the ranks of Socialist activists and transform Sambuca into a visibly red town.

Migration as Context

Sambuca's political transformation occurred against a backdrop of increasing mobility. Emigration from Sambuca to the United States began just as the town's artisans formed their first autonomous voluntary associations in the early 1880s. Figure 3.1 plots applications for *nulla osta* (permission to emigrate) and for passports by Sambucesi in the years between 1884 and 1915. Local records show a roughly similar pattern in the migration of young draft-age men. While only one percent of young men called for the draft in the 1880s had already emigrated, a quarter of those called in the 1890s had left their hometown. After 1900 the percentage of emigrated draft-eligible men rose to over one-third, reaching a peak in the years just before World War I, when 50 to 75 percent of the men called to service were already living in the United States. Even after World War I, 10 percent of the young men called for the draft had left their homeland.[65]

Figure 3.1 and the local sources both hint at historical linkages between migration and rural unrest in Sambuca. During the 1880s, when artisans organized self-help and local political initiatives, they also began migrating in considerable numbers. All the men listed in draft lists as migrants during the 1880s were artisans. My file of Sambuca's 3500 migrants also revealed disproportionate migrations of artisans during the 1880s and 1890s. (These data are analyzed in greater detail in chapter 5.) During the general rural unrest of 1892–1894, neither Sambuca's activist artisans nor the more passive wheat cultivators of the town migrated in great numbers. Migration from Sambuca dropped sharply after 1891, even though Sambuca experienced less unrest than many other Sicilian towns.

Figure 3.1

Applications for Nulla Osta *and Passports from Sambuca, 1884–1915*

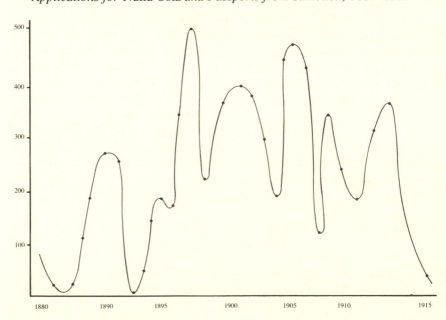

Table 3.1

Emigration from Militant and Nonmilitant Italian Regions

	Annual Applications for *Nulla Osta* or Passport, per 1,000					
	1882–1885	1886–1889	1890–1893	1896–1900	1901–1905	1906–1910
Sambuca *Militant*	3.4	9.8	16.2	34.8	35.2	32.5
Apulia *Nonmilitant*	0.5	1.3	1.3	2.7	8.1	14.0
Basilicata	13.9	23.4	16.5	18.0	29.7	28.8
Abruzzi-Molise	4.2	11.3	8.4	12.9	34.4	30.7

This decline, common in most Sicilian towns, reflected American economic crises during these years.[66] Finally, rising mobility does not seem to have undermined unrest in the town. Half of Sambuca's early Socialist artisans migrated to the United States at some point in the early twentieth century without weakening the spread of socialist ideals among local artisans. At worst, migration may have hindered artisans' efforts to organize among the mobile peasants of the town. But even this seems questionable: first, because artisans (who did join the Socialist Party in growing numbers) were more mobile than poor peasants, and, second, because the first Socialists elected to local government with peasant help assumed office during the years of highest emigration from the town.[67]

The migration patterns of this red town present quite a contrast to regions of Italy with comparable political histories. J. S. MacDonald, for example, compared the militant but immobile southern region of Apulia to the politically apathetic but highly mobile deep south provinces of Abruzzi-Molise and Basilicata.[68] Table 3.1 compares Sambuca's emigration rates to these regions. Only before 1890 did migration from Sambuca fall well below the migration rates of provinces like Basilicata or Abruzzi-Molise. Thereafter, migration from the town equaled or surpassed migration rates from both these provinces. Furthermore, Sambuca sent proportionately many more of its residents abroad than did the militant province of Apulia. Sambuca provides some tantalizing, if limited, evidence on the complex relationship of migration and labor militancy as rural strategies for social change.

Some Hypotheses

Because each town is unique, the results of this case study must be interpreted with caution, and—in the next chapter—compared with those for Sambuca's nearest neighbors. The case study of Sambuca does, however, provide more than a series of good anecdotes; it also suggests some hypotheses for comparative study. For one, Sambuca's history reveals the central role that artisanal producers played in the development of both migration and militancy. We need to know if Sambuca was unique in this respect.

Scores of studies in recent years have pointed to the varied but always critically important activities of artisans and skilled labor aristocracies in the labor movements of most industrializing nations.[69] Our understanding of the artisans of the declining or economically stagnating peripheries of the world is much less complete.[70] In this context, Sambuca's artisans must be viewed as lower-middle-class. They owned land; many also worked as petty merchants; a few organized small capitalist manufactories of iron tools, pasta, and furniture. While the masters and journeymen of Sambuca's most capitalist workshops were strikingly absent from the list of Sambuca's early activists and autodidacts, the small-scale trades were well represented. Similarly, Sambuca's few agricultural activists came from landowning peasant families, not from the landless families of the poor. In Sambuca, the men most oriented toward the market became the first activists. These were not, however, the local men most severely affected by the cash crisis that accompanied market relations. It seems logical to consider why lower-middle-class peasants or artisanal producers would espouse an ideology appealing generally to the interests of people quite unlike themselves—wage laborers in an industrial economy dominated by the interests of capitalists.[71]

Artisans' discontents provide part of an answer to this puzzle. These were both political and economic, and in both cases the civili appeared as the cause. Before the emergence of the civile elite, artisans had formed the small pinnacle of rural society, at least during the many months of the years when feudal lords lived in Palermo. Over the course of the nineteenth century, artisans saw upwardly mobile civili far surpass them in wealth and in local power. Even if, for several decades, artisans enjoyed growing local clienteles as a result, they could and did resent the arrogance of the new elite. Resentment sharpened when the new Italian state—forgetting that artisans, like civili, had supported anti-Bourbon initiatives—granted the franchise only to substantial landowners. The experience of status decline allowed artisans to identify civili as their own local ruling class, without ever having experienced exploitation in capitalist workplaces or at the hands of elite employers.

Sicilians distinguished only two classes; thus, the political division of newly and obviously rich civile voters from unenfranchised artisans made the latter, although relatively well off by local standards, seem poor. The similarities between Sicilian folk categories and the Marxist vocabulary of class enabled Sambuca's artisans to find in Marx's thought a logical description of their everyday experience of elite arrogance.

It seems important to emphasize that this arrogance was primarily political. The economic fate of artisans in the late nineteenth century was not the single most important factor motivating their turn leftward. Despite threats from outside producers, there was no obvious or sudden crash in local industry in Sambuca, except in the domestic production of cloth. Large cohorts of artisan sons born in the 1860s and 1870s did experience difficulties setting up shops after 1880, since their numbers so far exceeded those of their fathers, and these difficulties might explain the early migration of artisans or the clear generational pattern among Socialist activists. Still, the history of the male trades in Sambuca reveals that as large numbers of artisan sons abandoned their workshops, new individuals and sometimes even families arrived in Sambuca to replace them.[72] The number of artisans at work in Sambuca declined very little between 1880 and 1920, despite substantial emigration from the town.

Artisans could have aimed some economic resentments directly at civili as well. Once the artisans' best customers, Sambuca's elite came to prefer imported goods in the 1870s and 1880s, threatening old ties of patronage to local tradesmen. Local novelist Navarro condescendingly described young civile men returning from trips "to the continent" with Parisian finery.[73] Civile homes, Jane and Peter Schneider report, often included imported furniture or a piano as well as imported cloth and clothing.[74]

But how exactly did artisanal discontents like these translate into support for Italy's new Socialist Party? First, artisans had to have the opportunity to learn the tenets of socialism. Here, intellectual elite dissidents like Navarro della Miraglia and scores of internationalist and freethinking schoolteachers, law students, and druggists played an important role. So did the mobile lives of Sicily's artisans: all manner of news spread rapidly with carters and journeymen tramping through the Sicilian countryside. Peter Schneider has also argued that artisans' emphasis on self-improvement—surely reinforced and extended by the spread of mutual aid in the 1880s—encouraged many to grapple seriously, and collectively, with new ideas from the outside.[75]

Finally, it is worth emphasizing that throughout the early 1890s, many European Socialists, especially those most influenced by the French Socialist Party, debated how best to undertake organization of a wide variety of peasants in the countryside. The possibility that Socialists might support land reform—an early example of a more general strategy that would later divide Socialists—was much discussed, although not always at Party congresses. While not themselves peasants, Sicilian artisans may at least have felt that Socialists viewed their agricultural world as an important and a central one.[76] Still, the Italian Party never adopted an agrarian program during these years—land reform proved too controversial for Socialists hoping for a revolution. It seems most likely, then, that artisans saw in the Socialist Party mainly an important oppositional political force, one that could bring their fundamentally political complaints to some form of successful conclusion, primarily at the local level.

Conclusion

Sambuca's artisans provide yet another example of the importance of middle groups in rural unrest and migration. Politically frustrated and economically disappointed after a period of rising expectations, artisans had the necessary resources to respond, and they saw the new Socialist Party as an appropriate vehicle for voicing their political grievances. Structurally, Sambuca's artisans can be seen as the equivalents of the activist middle peasants discussed in chapter 1. Not surprisingly, Sambuca's artisans also found their few agricultural allies among the middle peasants of the town.

By contrast, the poorest in Sambuca, those most obviously affected by a cash crisis in the last decades of the century, seemed unable to risk rebellion—or migration. Ordinary peasants had experienced no obvious period of rising expectations; while their tradition of jacquerie and their hatreds of the civili reflected a native sense of injustice, peasants may have despaired in the 1860s and 1870s, seeing even traditional protest forms as unproductive under new circumstances. Peasants had few resources of their own. Wage earning, often as migrant workers, would change that fact; only then would peasants re-emerge as vigorous protesters and participants in Sambuca's labor movement.

Without its population of artisans, Sambuca would not have become a red town. Still, in the nineteenth century, the town's Socialists had not reached the peasants—a problem that troubled relatively few socialist parties, or socialist theorists, after the 1890s.[77] Sambuca was a "late bloomer" among Sicilian red towns, in part because the town's artisan activists had not established working ties to the peasantry before they became Socialists. But this was not true of all Sicilian towns. In many towns in western Sicily, artisans and peasants had begun building tentative alliances during the 1880s. These alliances help explain both the fervor and the complexities of the revolts of the 1890s.

Chapter 4
From Fasci to Emigration

The Sicilian countryside exploded in 1892–1894, this time without the spur of revolt in Palermo. The unrest began inauspiciously, but eventually far exceeded the modest actions of Sambuca's artisans. Beginning in the fall of 1892, *fasci* first appeared in Palermo, then in larger Sicilian towns, and finally in the smaller provincial towns. These peasants' and workers' organizations took their name from the Roman word meaning "bundles of sticks." The name conjured images of unity and strength. Within a year, two-thirds of western Sicily's 136 rural towns had a fascio.[1]

A new period of peasant jacquerie seemed imminent by early 1893. Newspapers noted peasant demonstrations in several towns. In only a few cases did the local fascio organize the earliest protests. Soon thereafter, however, fasci led astonishing new protests throughout the countryside. In January, peasants in Caltavaturo occupied former demesnial lands, demanding their distribution to poor peasants. Thirteen deaths resulted. That summer peasants in many inland towns staged lengthy and coordinated strikes at harvest time. They demanded higher wages, new sharecropping contracts that would deliver more grain to the peasant, and an end to common contractual abuses and usury. The pace of all types of protest picked up after the harvest strikes. While Sambuca's artisans worked quietly and behind the scenes, fasci elsewhere organized giant protests against taxes. Spontaneous attacks on town offices occurred in some towns. In Piana dei Greci, a crowd of women destroyed municipal offices. Sulfur miners struck and, at the start of the new agricultural year (circa September 1), sharecroppers refused to enter new agricultural contracts on the old terms. Throughout the summer and fall of 1893, the fasci of many Sicilian towns joined Italy's new Socialist Party. Several strikes of agricultural laborers ended successfully, but still peace did not return to the countryside. Public protests continued, as did the incidence of violence, occasional deaths, and arrests.

The Italian government, led by the liberal Giolitti, failed to restore order; after a ministerial crisis, Sicilian Francesco Crispi assumed office. While protests demanding the reduction or abolition of local taxes continued, Crispi in late December telegraphed Sicily's prefects, urging them to intervene at the local level and demand additional tax reductions from municipal councils. (Some councils —like Sambuca's—had already succumbed to local pressure.) But even this request failed to pacify the rebellious countryside. Police officers killed twenty-eight protesters during the first days of January, 1894. Crispi then responded by announcing a state of siege on January 3. With 1,600 persons placed under arrest, the revolts ceased. (Some Sicilian activists remained in jail until 1896.) The fasci were abolished, and all workers' organizations suppressed. In Sicily, and in the nation as a whole, repression of peasants' and workers' societies continued until the liberal Giolitti reassumed office in 1901.[2]

Writers in the 1890s, and scholars since, have viewed the Sicilian events of 1892–1894 from many conflicting perspectives, finding in them the recurrence of traditional peasant jacquerie, the first steps toward the creation of a moderate, modern, and reform-oriented Sicilian trade-union movement, and a failed Socialist revolution.[3] The debate about the Sicilian uprisings of 1892–1894 foreshadowed in many ways the questions raised in the 1960s, 1970s, and 1980s about peasant participation in successful revolutions and in Marxist movements in the underdeveloped countries of Africa and Asia. Had Sicilian peasants truly become Socialists? Or had their pursuit of simple economic justice, their century-old desire for revenge against local elites, or their petty-capitalist hunger for property led them into a misalliance with Socialist outside agitators? While the evidence from Sicily does not allow definitive answers to all these questions, it does provide some clues to the origins of the revolts and the motivations of angry Sicilian men and women in 1892–1894. It also allows us to see how these events influenced—and were in turn shaped by—the migrations of Sicilians that began in the 1880s and grew rapidly after 1900. This chapter shows that Sambuca's residents were by no means unique in experimenting simultaneously with migration and labor militancy in response to local economic and political difficulties.

Regional Evidence of the Rebellions

The story of the fasci and the revolts of the 1890s has been told many times.[4] Rather than offer yet another narrative account of the events of 1892–1893,[5] this section focuses on the diversity of protest patterns during those years. Rural rebels' repertoire of protest forms had changed by the 1890s. By examining where protest occurred and in which forms, the origins of the uprisings of 1892–1893 can be traced to Sicilians' diverse experiences as peasants and workers at the local level. Such an analysis is possible mainly because historians of the Sicilian revolts have already written accounts which focus on many of the western rural towns.

Not all peasants in Sicily rebelled in the 1890s. Thirty-one west Sicilian towns remained absolutely quiet during these years, their residents apparently oblivious to or uninterested in the revolts and initiatives of their neighbors. Communication barriers or isolation may have left some Sicilians largely unaware of developments in other towns; this might explain why three of western Sicily's four offshore settlements experienced no unrest. But other factors were at work, too. About half of the towns in the district around Termini Immerese also stood apart from the general revolt. The apathetic lived mainly in towns with no agricultural exports and local industry. In western Sicily as a whole, towns where peasants marketed grapes and citrus fruits also numbered disproportionately among the nonrebellious.

There is some evidence that the peaceful towns actually did house the old-style, submissive peasants glorified by conservative folklorists like Salomone Marino, who deplored the revolts of the 1890s.[6] Peasants who raised their own food—whether as their sole endeavor or in combination with a market crop—did not revolt in the 1890s. As a later section shows, some of these apathetic peasants may have found themselves too busy planning their moves to America to care about improving their lives at home. In many, but not all, apathetic towns, peasants also entered the marketplace almost exclusively as consumers; they had few sources of income, and sought cash mainly through migration. Otherwise, however, the severity of local cash crises did not neatly predict levels of activism in the 1890s.

Quiet towns of mobile or submissive cash-hungry peasants remained the exceptions. In most Sicilian towns, peasants revolted in jacquerie; tax protesters demonstrated in city squares; peasants and workers organized new societies with new goals; police noted scores of "incidents" and "agitations"; Sicilian wage earners struck for better wages and improved working conditions.[7] In a few towns, peasants revolted spontaneously, but in most, a local fascio was at work.

Spontaneous peasant jacquerie had a long history in Sicily, as chapter 2 demonstrated. Yet only a relatively small number of peasant protests in the 1890s could be called spontaneous. And even spontaneous actions often departed from the script of traditional jacquerie to assume a more modern appearance in the 1890s. Harvesters in Licata and Montemaggiore Belsito, angered by low wages, struck spontaneously and briefly in September 1893. Unlike peasant rebels of earlier decades, they did not seek revenge on their estate managers; they made no effort to humiliate or harm them. Instead they sought specific material goals—better wages. In doing so, they undoubtedly followed the example of peasants in nearby towns, where organized strikes had been underway since late summer that year.[8] Tax protests also erupted spontaneously in several towns; these revolts more closely resembled those of the 1840s and 1860s. In a few, however, fasci were organized immediately after the first unorganized demonstration.[9]

In many towns with spontaneous revolts, reporters noted violence, arrests, and agitations, but they could not specify what provoked the protest or what the demonstrators hoped to accomplish. Women figured prominently in such spontaneous actions.[10] Although their participation shocked some observers from outside, women's activism was nothing new; women had always taken to the street during periods of peasant jacquerie. Furthermore, as housewives controlling the family purse, women were responsible for saving enough cash over the year to pay taxes. Many women resented being told—as they were in Piana dei Greci—that they should take jobs as servants if they could not pay their taxes. The local officials who gave them such advice were, of course, the same men who levied the taxes and who hoped to employ them.[11] Female jacquerie, while common enough in the 1890s, rarely resulted in either repeated protests or formal organization. Women, unlike men, had no experience with voluntary association; nor did many men in the 1890s attempt to mobilize female discontent in order to build or dominate female societies.

About twenty Sicilian towns experienced spontaneous revolts or rebellions resembling jacquerie in 1892–1893. These towns varied considerably in economic structure, market relations, and location. They could not easily be distinguished from either their peaceful neighbors or from the more militant and organized towns around them. Perhaps this was because women's experiences varied less than men's in Sicily's rural towns, so that women's protests showed less clear patterns of local variation. In any case, women in subsistence towns, in areas of market cultivation, and in towns with large wheat estates all sometimes revolted. Since women figured so prominently among spontaneous revolters, the existence or absence of benefit societies in a town worked no influence on the incidence of jacquerie in the 1890s. Obviously, older forms of communal protest like the jacquerie did not simply disappear when challenged by mutual aid. The evidence suggests instead that older protest traditions survived among the women excluded from the newer voluntary associations and—like all peasant men previously— from politics itself.

Even when we take women's experiences into account, however, we clearly see the results of twenty years of voluntary association at the local level in the rural uprisings of the 1890s. Most Sicilian towns (eighty-two) had fasci, and in most of these towns (seventy-four), the fascio went on to organize protests of some kind.[12] In twenty-four towns, protesters and their demonstrations focused on high taxes; in seventeen towns, the fascio led strikes and/or land occupations. In twelve towns, peasants and workers organized both tax protests and work stoppages, while in another twenty-one towns, residents undertook local initiatives that cannot easily be characterized, but which nevertheless attracted police attention—arrests or the use of armed force were noted. Sambuca numbered among this last group of towns.

The most rebellious of western Sicily's towns numbered about fifty. These Prime Minister Crispi termed "Palermo's crown of thorns." As Map 4.1 indicates, his metaphor, however appealing, was inaccurate, since organized and militant towns were scattered through most western Sicilian districts. Unlike geography, local economy did clearly influence the form that organized revolt took in the 1890s. Of twenty-nine towns with strikes and/or land occupations, twenty-three were either wheat-raising towns dominated by latifondi or towns with sulfur mines or other forms of local industry. Not surprisingly, the strike and the seizure of property developed as new forms of protest only in areas of large-scale agriculture and industry. By contrast, peasants involved in market-oriented but smaller-scale

Map 4.1
Palermo's "Crown of Thorns," 1892–1893

production were more likely to organize tax protests, if they protested at all: twenty-two of thirty-two towns with tax protests exported oranges, lemons, or wine. The case study of Sambuca reminds us that artisans, too, may have acted largely in response to the tax issue.

Because local discontent varied, the fasci themselves differed in structure and function from town to town. Some men already united in mutual benefit societies transformed their group into a fascio while continuing to practice mutual aid. In towns with many wage earners, the fasci often did function as trade unions or, among wheat-raising peasants, as syndicates aiming to expropriate the large wheat estates. In a few towns, wage earners and their fascio organized agricultural and industrial cooperatives. Peasants' cooperatives had existed before the 1890s, but beginning in 1892 some tried legally to lease large wheat estates for the first time. (This strategy, which became more popular later in the decade, was called peasant latifundism.[13]) Elsewhere, as in Sambuca, fascio members concerned themselves primarily with municipal politics. Fascio and Socialist circle were indistinguishable in many towns. The diversity of both protest and organizational forms understandably produced conflicting interpretations of the significance of the Sicilian revolts, as reported above.

The many functions of local fasci reflected diverse local needs. Wheat cultivators, even if they earned wages only seasonally, most resembled industrial proletarians in facing an exploitative foreman or employer—who took directly from their year's food supply on the threshing floor each harvest—in their workplaces. Their typical form of protest was the strike or land occupation. Their fasci resembled mutual aid societies, trade unions, cooperatives, or syndicates. Unlike the wheat cultivators, artisans and grape or citrus cultivators knew no directly exploitative employer.[14] For them economic woes originated in an impersonal market. Far more personal than the market's invisible hand was that of the tax collector, so artisans and market-oriented peasants blamed local officeholders (the rich) for taxing the homes and food purchases of the poor while exempting their own substantial land holdings from taxation. Their typical form of protest was the antitax demonstration in front of the city hall. Their fasci resembled political factions or, in a few cases, credit unions.

The cash crisis described in previous chapters did not directly shape either protest or organizational forms. Subsistence peasants who imported cloth or food were especially hard-pressed for cash in the 1890s; grape cultivators were less pressed since they had at least some cash income. Yet neither group of peasants protested against taxes unless they also shared their hometowns with at least small populations of artisanal or wage-earning industrial workers. When this was the case both groups protested. (Twenty-two of thirty-two towns with tax protests had at least some local industry.) Where there were no artisans or wage earners, there were few tax protests, except in the form of spontaneous female revolts. This suggests that peasant men still relied heavily for leadership on industrial producers.

In fact, artisans and industrial wage earners actually did organize many of the protests and workers' societies of the 1890s; Sambuca was quite typical in this respect. Not only did artisans, industrial wage earners, and sulfur miners make their hometowns the best organized and most active in the region, artisans and small merchants appeared especially frequently among the leaders of the fasci in agricultural towns. In wheat-raising Contessa Entellina, for example, a carter served as president of a peasants' fascio.[15] In listing over 200 local fasci activists, Francesco Renda found that 27 percent gave petty industry and commerce as their occupations. Another 33 percent were small peasant proprietors, men Eric Wolf might call middle peasants. Six percent of fasci activists can be considered ideologically dissident members of the provincial elite—mainly professionals.[16] This pattern is even more pronounced in Sicily's first generation of nationally prominent labor activists, many of whom began their lives as activists in the 1890s. Of twenty-one west Sicilian men included in a comprehensive biographical dictionary of Italian labor activists before World War II, nine came from artisan families and nine from families of the provincial elite.[17] Typical was Girolamo li Causi, who would become the most prominent Sicilian in Italy's Communist Party. Born in Termini Imerese soon after the suppression of the fasci, li Causi grew up in an artisan's family; his father, a shoemaker, was a long-time emigrant to the United States.

As was true in Sambuca, west Sicilian artisans and industrial wage earners also became the strongest early supporters of socialism. More than forty west Sicilian towns had Socialist fasci or independent Socialist circles by 1893 (only a year after the founding of Italy's Socialist Party.)[18] This means, for example, that almost half of Sicily's fasci established contact with the new party. Enthusiasm for socialism grew quickly in towns with some industry—55 percent had a Socialist circle by 1893—but found little support in towns with no industry, of which only 10 percent had a Socialist group. Unfortunately, the evidence does not always show whether it was the more traditional independent producers (as in Sambuca) or the wage earners who joined Sicily's early Socialist Party sections in the largest numbers. It is clear, however, that wage-earning peasants on the large wheat estates acted in predictable ways, showing considerably more interest in the Socialist Party than did subsistence peasants or peasant marketers.

Because independent artisans, industrial wage earners, and wheat peasants all might support the Socialists, one finds surprising variety among the seven towns that elected Socialists to municipal office in Sicily in 1893. One was a sulfur town; two were wheat towns with large estates; three exported some grapes; four had considerable numbers of small peasant landowners.[19] Socialists in other towns failed to elect representatives but succeeded in smaller ways. For example, towns with Socialist-oriented fasci were more likely to see their municipal councils lower local taxes in December 1893 or January 1894 than were towns with no Socialist presence.[20]

West Sicilians' protest and organizational repertoires had become more varied by the 1890s, reflecting differences in gender, experimentation with voluntary association, and economic challenges. New male initiatives in the form of Socialist politics, cooperativism, trade-unionism, syndicalism, and organized seizures of private land rendered jacquerie an increasingly female protest form. Already in the 1890s, many male leaders proudly rejected the violence and spontaneity of women's protests. Their alternatives to jacquerie were, however, far from fixed and coherent during these years. Newly proclaimed Socialists engaged in a wide range of activities, not all of which closely fit Marxist theory or departed completely from past traditions. Rural rebels had not firmly committed themselves to a program addressing the rather distinctive problems of industrial or agricultural wage earners, or to a program that could satisfy the small-scale market-oriented producers, whether peasants or artisans.

Nowhere is the changing and diverse character of Sicily's early labor movement more obvious than in the new forms of protest adopted in the 1890s. Rural protests in Sicily drew as much on local Sicilian traditions as they did on any theory of revolution. The survival of jacquerie among women documents the continuation of

communal solidarities; communal ties also persisted in the newer workers' societies and in their organized protests. Peasants, for example, sometimes joined a
local fascio en masse, rather than as isolated individuals.[21] Women and children
did join some fasci, although in most of these cases they belonged to separate
sections. In fact, aside from the political initiatives in towns like Sambuca, only
the workplace protests of wage earners completely excluded women and children.
The absence of women from strikes undoubtedly reflected the monopoly poor
Sicilian men had acquired over wage earning by the 1890s.

New forms of rural protest borrowed heavily from the example of Sicilian
industrial workers, who had been striking in small numbers since the 1860s. (Perhaps this helps explain the fact that wage-earning peasants were most likely to
strike if they lived outside Palermo's market area, in towns where they could have
observed or heard of work stoppages among local journeymen workers.) Sicilians
also borrowed from the rituals of earlier voluntary associations in building a
modern labor movement. From the religious confraternities, Sicily's fasci took the
public procession; they then reoriented these public manifestations toward the
piazza, the municipal office, the contested workplace, and the fields. Little wonder
that marchers in the 1890s often carried pictures of their secular and religious
patrons along with their newer revolutionary or reform slogans.[22] From the mutual
benefit societies, fasci borrowed the election of officers, the use of a formal program, and the dedication of a banner representing the group.

Unlike the use of banners or processions, the cultural legacy of jacquerie
violence, while still important, became controversial among workers and peasants
in the 1890s. It is worth emphasizing that organized protests resulted in more
deaths than did peasant jacquerie during these years. Sicilian Socialists usually
insisted this was not so, because fasci members as demonstrators rarely sacked city
halls, looted or destroyed property, or murdered local landlords or public officials.[23] Fasci leaders consciously distanced themselves from earlier peasant revolters, as well as from contemporary female mobs, by insisting that demonstrators
march in orderly fashion with either flags and signs or chants clearly identifying
their society and its demands—such as "Down with the municipal council,"
"Down with taxes," "Land for the peasant," or "Victory to the fascio!" Organized
demonstrators gathered in the main piazza, heard speakers, sent an emissary with a
statement to landowners or town council, and then dispersed until another day.[24]
Nevertheless, most of the ninety-two deaths of 1892–1894 occurred during organized protests. While organized protesters refrained from violence, the enforcers
of public order did not. In fact, protesting peasants probably faced greater risks
participating in an orderly demonstration than they did as revolting jacqueristes. It
was the new, not the old, that seemed to threaten and challenge the police.

Typical were events in Giardinello, where a fascio leader had urged his protesting sisters to disperse upon request. Hearing a shot, he turned to see hastily
called-in troops firing on the departing women. Eleven died. Several days before

this incident, a similar mob of women had sacked the municipal office, killing both the municipal employee responsible for maintaining fair grain scales and his wife.[25] On that day the rioters suffered no casualties. Perhaps troops became more aggressive facing a disciplined demonstration. Perhaps troops could not so easily anticipate where the "mobs" would strike, or perhaps the more traditional crowds could disperse more quickly when threatened.

Very much a region in economic flux, western Sicily had in the 1890s a young labor movement which freely mixed the old with the new, as these examples suggest. For twenty years after the Sicilian revolts, the leaders of Italy's Socialist Party tried to find an agrarian program that would reflect Marx's thinking while still accommodating the needs and interests of their diverse group of rural supporters.[26] As early as 1901, Sicilian observers wrote of a split developing between workplace-oriented rural Socialists in Sicily's wheat-raising towns and the more party- and politics-oriented Socialists of Palermo.[27] In Sicilian cities, and in smaller towns like Sambuca where market-oriented artisans dominated the Party, Socialists also focused their energies on reforming municipal governments. By contrast, rural activists in agricultural towns usually continued other initiatives of the 1890s, vacillating between building peasants' leagues, cooperatives, and unions and leading recurring seizures of the large wheat estates. Eventually these differences would harden into conflicts between syndicalists and reformers.

In 1894, of course, few foresaw the development of these distinctions in Sicily's nascent labor movement. In the early 1890s, small-scale producers, wage earners in agriculture and industry, and some sharecroppers concerned mainly with subsistence seemed part of one momentarily united movement. However illusory or transitory their alliance proved to be, it has seemed significant to scholars viewing it from the perspective of twentieth-century events. Fewer than thirty years after Sicilians organized, struck, and occupied lands, a somewhat similar Russian coalition produced the first of many successful proletarian revolutions in primarily agricultural countries.[28]

The possibility that peasants had become convinced Marxists flabbergasted many Sicilian intellectuals in the 1890s. That possibility would continue to flabbergast observers of peasant life and peasant rebellions in the twentieth century. Theory does not predict that peasants—usually characterized as cautious, land hungry, or familist—could find Marxist thinking attractive. Did they not value property ownership and small-scale family-oriented production above all else? Rather than question their assumptions about peasant familism, caution, or land hunger, many observers in the 1890s suggested that crafty Sicilian peasants saw Socialist slogans merely as clever new means to their inherently conservative end—carving small private-family plots out of giant wheat estates.[29]

Undoubtedly, this explanation is too simple. There is little evidence that Sicilian peasants were either cautious or familist by the 1890s. Furthermore, local traditions rendered Socialist messages comprehensible and even convincing. Eric

Hobsbawm, for example, has noted that Sicilians' millenarian hopes allowed peasants to accept quite easily the revolutionary promises of Sicily's early Socialists.[30] (Undoubtedly, the many anticlericals among them found this aspect of Marxism attractive, too.) Like Sambuca's artisans, peasants of many types could—if for varying reasons—recognize Socialists' descriptions of class struggle as depictions of local reality. Marxist class analysis not only matched Sicilian folk categories of rich and poor, it offered explanations of local municipal politics, high taxes, and peasants' yearly experiences on the threshing-room floor.

Most importantly, Sicilian peasants cannot so easily be dismissed as familist petty capitalists, interested only in tiny privately owned plots of land. Sicilian peasants hungered for land because it fed them; it is less obvious that they expected to own land either privately or in small family plots. Common rights to land usage had a long tradition in Sicily. So did communal ownership of land. If anything, Sicilian peasants might have seen private ownership of land as one source of their problems, for the local elite's power had often originated in their usurpation of these communally held lands. Private ownership of land and elite arrogance should have been historically associated in peasant minds, since the two emerged together. Peasants in Sicily in the 1890s could still easily recall a time, only two generations earlier, when land had been used—some of it collectively—rather than owned. As chapter 2 showed, much of the crime of late-nineteenth-century Sicily represented peasants' efforts to continue to use land communally, as their grandparents had, without respect to ownership. Memories of citizens' rights to water or tracts of pasture land, and to the wild animals or plants that grew uncultivated remained equally fresh. Both memories allowed Sicilian peasants to understand in their own way the Socialist critique of private property and demand for collective ownership. Does this mean that Sicilian peasants were indeed "backward looking" participants in a labor movement? Probably not. They remembered mainly those parts of the past that they deemed to their own advantage: feudal payments and services and servile relations to feudal lords may have been part of local memories, but they were not part of peasants' demands for the future. As one student of Vietnam's peasantry observed much later, they sought "not to restore traditional practices, but to remake them."[31]

To note these aspects of peasant mentality is, of course, no proof that class struggle alone explains the fasci revolts. As this section emphasized, events of the 1890s were too complex for any simple explication. The leaders of the fasci, for example, knew that some workers' organizations of this period represented peasants and workers in name only. In some cases, local elite bosses organized their many political clients into fasci; mafiosi, too, went fishing in the troubled waters of these years. So did Catholic priests, including one nicknamed "the Socialist." But these cases were the exceptions, not the rule.[32] Anger with elite arrogance, whether in the town hall, the workplace, the tax office, or the marketplace fed rural anger throughout western Sicily in the 1890s.

For many students of rural rebellions, the most interesting aspect of the Sicilian unrest of 1892–1894 is its outcome: Sicilian rebels failed to spark a successful revolution. Sicilian landowners and the Italian nation-state trembled but did not collapse. Many of the essential ingredients of twentieth-century revolutions, described in chapter 1, were present in Sicily in the early 1890s—administrative incompetence, alienated intellectuals, angry industrial producers, and a long tradition of violent peasant revolt. But no revolution ensued. It is natural enough to ask why this was so. Is it possible to identify a missing ingredient that somehow explains why this revolt failed to introduce a period of revolutionary change?

In fact, one can identify many missing ingredients. Most obviously, Italy in 1893 was not Russia in 1917; the nation—while new, economically troubled, and administratively fragile—was not at war.[33] Ideologically, too, the alienated intellectuals and local leaders of Sicily scarcely resembled those of the twentieth century. Socialists all over Europe had only just begun to recognize the theoretical problem of rural rebellion as a challenge; the Sicilian revolts helped them do so.[34] Unlike rural activists today, Sicilian activists could not turn to a Russian precedent, or to the writings of Lenin, Mao Tse-tung, or Frantz Fanon on organizing in the countryside. Like the Mexican revolution, this was a revolt without theory.

The identification of additional missing ingredients in the Sicilian countryside perhaps depends on one's theory of revolution. An area in transition, western Sicily claimed a mixed population of middle peasants, small-scale artisans, and both an agricultural and urban proletariat. Should we blame the revolters' failure on the sizable group of small-scale producers? Karl Kautsky might have done so; many Marxists in the early twentieth century continued to argue that middle peasants and artisans, with their tax problems and private property, could scarcely pursue a Marxist revolution. Or was the problem instead the even more sizable population of proletarianized Sicilian peasants who lacked the resources to feed themselves and buy weapons for a prolonged struggle?[35] This possibility has gained considerable support among those studying peasant rebellions in the last fifteen years.

Probably it is best to leave such arguments to those hoping to perfect a historically valid theory of revolution. Rather than try to explain why the revolts of Sicily failed to spark a real revolution, it is perhaps more instructive to view the Sicilian revolts from a different perspective—one suggested by Barrington Moore's work. The events of the 1890s in Sicily constituted a failed revolution. But unlike the earlier failed revolutions of northern Europe, the Sicilian revolts neither introduced a century of successful capitalist economic development, nor did they put Italy on the road to democratic government.[36] The outcome of failed revolution in the nineteenth century, at least in Italy, was unlike the outcome in England. The economic aftermath of the Sicilian revolt was not capitalist development but economic stagnation. Indeed, Sicily's failed revolution scarcely interrupted the island's long history of persistent rural rebellion; it did nothing to prevent the subsequent development of red towns in the Sicilian countryside.

Failed revolution and economic stagnation in Sicily have usually been seen in relation to an important turning point of another kind. By the late nineteenth century Sicily had found a new export—human migrants going to work in the industrializing centers of North America. The next section turns again to the relation of militancy and migration, this time from the vantage point of the communal and regional evidence from western Sicily.

Militancy and Migration

The long-term legacy of the fasci Siciliani and the Sicilian revolts of the 1890s is the subject of a small scholarly debate. According to Eric Hobsbawm and many Italian scholars of the left, the 1890s revolts introduced an era of modern class-based politics in Sicily, as Marxist ideas gradually spread through the twentieth-century countryside.[37] In this view, Sicily's red towns developed quite directly from the militant towns of the 1890s. But others see in the failed 1890s revolts a rather different kind of turning point. With the repression of the fasci in 1894, the numbers of Sicilians emigrating in search of work or new lives increased quickly. This raises the interesting possibility that peasants and workers frustrated in their efforts to change life at home had chosen instead to strike out individually as emigrants.[38]

There is a way to reconcile these interpretations, both of which accurately describe important developments in western Sicily after the revolts of the 1890s. Sicilians did emigrate in striking numbers, especially after 1900. But at the same time some Sicilians, like those in Sambuca, became modern leftists. It could easily have been true that different Sicilians or different towns pursued each strategy. And if we assume that migration need not inevitably hinder militancy, then the two interpretations summarized above need not conflict. As Sambuca's history showed, the same people sometimes could both fight and flee. In fact, high rates of migration accompanied increasing labor militancy in at least some west Sicilian towns. Other towns, however, showed a clear preference for only one strategy.

Compared to other Italians, Sicilians responded rather late to the lure of the United States. Emigration rates in Calabria, Abruzzi-Molise, Basilicata, and the Naples area exceeded those in Sicily three to four times over during the 1880s and 1890s. The numbers of emigrating Sicilians rose steadily but comparatively slowly during these two decades. Among South Italians, only Apulians seemed less interested than Sicilians in finding jobs and homes in the New World before 1900.[39]

An explanation for the delayed departure of Sicilians emerges in a number of recent studies. It was certainly not the case that massive rural protests or efforts to improve life at home had discouraged Sicilians from migrating during the 1880s. (While mutual aid spread, these years numbered among the most peaceful years in the Sicilian countryside.) Instead, Sicilians simply may have had fewer economic reasons than other South Italians to look to the United States for wage-earning opportunities. The Sicilian cash crisis, while important, was far from universal, as chapter 1 showed. Internal migration still satisfied Sicilians looking for work or change. Modest opportunities to earn cash existed in most Sicilian towns; sulfur towns and towns exporting grapes and citrus attracted in-migrants for precisely this reason. Furthermore, markets for Sicilian grapes and citrus fruits did not collapse until the late 1800s, guaranteeing the circulation of cash for a decade after emigration from other South Italian regions had begun in earnest. Even the limited introduction of new crop rotations noted on some Sicilian wheat estates in the 1880s meant modest but positive change, since peasants began eating the beans they planted as fertilizer in such rotations.[40] Thus, while visitors from the north saw only abject poverty and feudal vestiges, it was likely that many Sicilians, not just Sambuca's artisans, experienced the 1870s and even the early 1880s as modestly hopeful years.[41] Perhaps this explains their reluctance to migrate.

Sicilians' hopes fell quickly during a series of very poor wheat harvests in the late 1880s and early 1890s. It seems likely that migration, like revolt, might be traced to a J-curve of rising expectations suddenly frustrated. Emigration dropped temporarily in the early 1890s—perhaps in response to agitations at home, and certainly because of the American depression of those years. After the suppression of the fasci and the return of prosperity in the United States, Sicilians began migrating in proportions equal to or even surpassing those of other Italians. It has been estimated that of every four Italians arriving in the United States before World War I, one hailed from Sicily.

A closer look shows that suppression of the fasci probably was not the most important cause of Sicilians' new-found enthusiasm for emigration. First, and most important, Sicilians did not abruptly stop working for change at home as migration to the Americas began in the 1880s, peaked in the years around World War I, and declined thereafter. Roughly one-third of Sicilian towns had experienced unrest in the 1820s, 1840s, 1860s, and 1870s; unrest peaked in the 1890s, but in both the first two decades of the twentieth century about two Sicilian towns in five again experienced protests of various kinds. True, Sicilians after 1894 did not rebel, protest, and organize in the same numbers as they had in 1892 and 1893. But it would be inaccurate to conclude that they abandoned collective action in order to emigrate. Sicilian peasants again struck and occupied the wheat estates in the years between 1901 and 1905; sulfur miners struck repeatedly until 1906; the numbers of rural peasants and artisans choosing Socialist candidates increased in the years before World War I, and new waves of land occupations occurred after the first world war, and again after the second.[42] The geography and forms of Sicilian protest changed between 1820 and 1950, but the incidence of rural unrest remained surprisingly unchanged over a period of 130 years. Over any twenty-year period, 30 to 40 percent of Sicilian towns experienced some unrest. The 1890s stand out as years of uniquely widespread rebellion, while twentieth-century militancy returned almost to the rates of the past. The long historical perspective shows no marked decline in rural militancy; it is thus unlikely that rejection of social change at home or the suppression of the fasci in 1894 could have caused the Sicilian pattern of belated but substantial migration after 1900.

Just as western Sicilian diversity resulted in conflicting interpretations of the 1890s revolts, so, too, that diversity can clarify scholarly disagreements about militancy and migration after the suppression of the fasci. No one interpretation satisfactorily summarizes all western Sicilians' experiences as labor activists and as migrants. The histories of western Sicily's 136 rural towns reveal at least three distinctive patterns of militancy and migration for the best documented decades between 1860 and 1921.[43] Sixty-five towns either experienced unrest regularly throughout the sixty years or, like Sambuca, they became increasingly militant during and after the 1890s. (I have labeled these as militant towns.) Another thirty-five towns experienced unrest only before and during the 1890s, not thereafter; these towns might be called declining militant. Finally, thirty-six Sicilian towns must be considered nonmilitant. The residents of a few such towns protested or rioted briefly during the 1890s, but in most no peasant unrest of any sort was ever recorded. Comparing militant, declining militant, and nonmilitant towns reveals much about the continuing sources of rural discontent in the twentieth century. More importantly, such a comparison allows assessment of how labor movement shaped emigration patterns in the region.

Not surprisingly, the Sicilians living in militant, declining militant, and nonmilitant towns had quite diverse experiences as workers, producers, and consumers. In towns where wage earners worked in large-scale or semicapitalist agriculture or industry, unrest recurred regularly after 1860: 71 percent of towns with large wheat estates, 86 percent of sulfur towns, 72 percent of towns with considerable local industry, and 62 percent of towns with some local industry became militant towns. In clear contrast, where peasants worked in family groups raising grapes, oranges, and lemons for export, militancy rarely persisted after the 1890s. Towns which imported food or goods from Palermo, as well as very small towns (with fewer than 2,000 residents) often remained totally quiet. Overall, towns with serious cash crises numbered heavily among the nonmilitant and declining militant, while towns with wage-earning options in agriculture and industry became militant towns. The peasants of many declining militant towns had organized tax protests or rioted as traditional jacqueristes in the 1890s before (apparently) lapsing into apathy. It seems likely that militancy declined in towns where women and market-oriented peasants abandoned tax protests in order to seek cash as migrants. The relation of rural unrest and migration was never straightforward or simple, however.

Table 4.1 compares estimated rates of net population change in towns with and without protest in a number of important decades. Once Sicilians began migrating to North and South America, people who lived in quiet towns did migrate in higher proportions than Sicilians living in rebellious towns. This was especially

Table 4.1

Population Movement and Protest, 1861–1930

	Annual Adjusted Net Population Balances per 1,000						
	1861–1870	1871–1880	1881–1890	1901–1910	1911–1920	1921–1930
Towns experiencing protest during decade	−4.3	−4.1	−4.9	−12.7	−2.0	−18.4
Towns experiencing no protest during decade	+0.6	+3.0	−7.1	−26.5	+0.8	−8.5

true in the years just after 1900, when the migration rates of quiet and militant towns showed the clearest difference. In the years just before and after World War I, however, Sicilians in active towns were more likely to emigrate than those from quieter towns. Comparing migration rates from militant, declining militant, and nonmilitant towns reveals similar, but somewhat less distinctive patterns. Overall, nonmilitant Sicilian towns had somewhat higher rates of emigration before 1900; after 1900 differences between militant and nonmilitant towns diminished. And after 1910, residents of militant towns often surpassed those of less militant towns in migratory zeal.

One last set of comparisons is instructive. Both militant and nonmilitant towns varied considerably in character. Among the militant towns, for example, towns with large wheat estates and sulfur towns appeared in disproportionate numbers. Yet the residents of sulfur and wheat towns developed contrasting migration patterns. The migrations from the different subgroups of towns reveal the complex social and economic realities that lay behind individuals' emigration decisions.

Table 4.2 summarizes this comparison. It was not the case, for example, that the residents of towns with recurring unrest always rejected emigration as a popular strategy, even in the important years before 1900. In fact, Sicilians from the militant wheat-estate towns seemed particularly mobile, from the 1880s on. Nor was it true that the suppression of the fasci led immediately to rapid increases in migration from militant towns. The residents of sulfur towns, for example, seemed unaffected by the repression; they migrated in large numbers only much later, in the twentieth century. (By contrast, migration from nonmilitant towns often increased very rapidly after the suppression of the fasci in 1894, a fact that cannot easily be explained.) Sicilians living in wheat-estate towns also seemed to respond to the suppression of the fasci, for their numbers as emigrants doubled after 1895. The fact that large numbers of peasants and workers migrated from the wheat-exporting towns did not undermine the labor movement developing in such towns. And surprisingly, the residents of politically quiet towns did not always show a marked preference for emigration either. The relatively peaceful grape and citrus towns—where peasants' market crops provided them with at least some yearly cash—had lower rates of emigration than the wheat-estate towns for much of the period before World War I. By contrast, towns with no local industry showed the expected pattern of low militancy and high emigration.

Unlike rural militancy, then, migration from Sicily did not vary strictly in any simple way with local market relations, class structure, or cash crises, particularly in the years after 1900. Some students of emigration have speculated instead that geographic locale heavily influenced migration rates, especially in the 1880s and 1890s.[44] This speculation is quite plausible. Map 4.2 shows the spread of migration as a popular rural strategy after 1880. From the migratory populations of a politically and economically diverse group of mountain towns in the regions south of Palermo and Termini Imerese, America fever spread northwest and southeast

Table 4.2

Migration Rates from Selected Types of Sicilian Towns, 1884–1915

	% Militant	Annual Average Applications per 1,000 for *Nulla Osta* or Passport					
		1884–1890	1891–1895	1896–1900	1901–1905	1906–1919	1911–1915
Sulfur	86%	1.0	1.3	2.8	11.2	27.5	25.3
Much industry	72	3.2	5.2	8.7	17.5	28.2	22.5
Large estates	71	6.8	10.6	22.4	32.1	35.2	26.7
No industry	32	6.2	12.5	22.1	38.1	40.3	26.5
Exports grapes or citrus	8	2.3	5.2	12.1	27.2	35.7	22.4

Map 4.2
Geography of Migration from West Sicily

● Early Onset of Migration (Before 1890)
○ Late Onset of Migration (After 1900)

by 1900. The number of emigrants from a widening circle of towns grew as information traveled through markets and through regional networks of contacts with the early emigrants. (This theme is explored in the following chapter.) From a strategy typical only of a small group of towns in the south central mountains, emigration had become popular all over the western half of the island by 1910.

The characteristics of towns with heavy or light emigration tell us little about the backgrounds of emigrants themselves, and thus relatively little about individual decision making, including the decision to rebel or to venture off to the United States. Once again, the individual level must be analyzed separately—and once again, flawed national statistics complicate the task. For example, the occupational categories used in Italian emigration statistics are as confusing as those appearing in the census. They do suggest, however, that artisans—one of the most militant groups in Sicily—generally resembled those from Sambuca in emigrating early and in disproportionate numbers.[45]

A report in the *Statistica della Emigrazione* for 1888 summarized Sicilian clerks' assessment of emigration from their towns: artisans and petty merchants figured prominently in their lists of migrating countrymen. Masons, "workers," shoemakers, barbers, stonecutters, fruit peddlers, carpenters, dry goods salesmen, fishermen, street peddlers of various kinds, and sailors migrated during the 1880s.

Town clerks, including one from Sambuca, gave "lack of commerce and work" as the principal reason for migration.[46]

Furthermore, it seems likely that an early emigration of artisans predated later and larger migrations of peasants from many small agricultural towns just coming into Palermo's regional market in the 1880s. National statistics recorded a small flurry of application for emigration from towns with little local industry in the mid-1880s; for roughly ten years thereafter no one from many of these towns applied to leave Sicily. Migration typically began again in earnest circa 1895, presumably as prices for either citrus fruits or oil dropped, and as phylloxera attacked local vines.

In short, there was no single legacy of the Sicilian revolts of the 1890s. The suppression of the fasci did not always cause rapid increases in migration, even though increasing numbers of Sicilians did begin traveling to the United States. Recurring peasant rebellions did not always offer Sicilians an alternative to emigration; neither did high rates of emigration inevitably undercut the development of a labor movement in Sicilian towns. Both militant and mobile, Sambucesi resembled the residents of other wheat-raising towns with some local industry. The notion that migration could function as an effective safety valve for rural discontent finds only mixed support in the western Sicilian evidence. The wheat-raising towns had higher-than-average rates of militancy despite their higher-than-average rates of emigration. These wheat-raising towns; their activists, migrants, and settlements in the United States; and their subsequent development into red towns will be the focus of the chapters ahead.

Conclusion

This chapter has shown that Sambuca was no anomaly, but easily fit into one of several Sicilian patterns of migration and militancy. While we may never know why the Sicilian rebellions failed, a careful look at the evidence did outline the complex legacy of the fasci revolts of the 1890s. Not the least part of this legacy were several distinctive Sicilian migration patterns which require further attention.

The rest of this book explores the significance of western Sicilian migration patterns for the further development of labor movements among Sicilians at home and abroad. Even when migration did not signal the automatic death of rural protest, it usually did form an undeniable part of the context in which subsequent rebellion or organization would occur. It is important to ask how Sicilians organized under these conditions. Did activists constitute a sedentary core, constantly reestablishing ties to the ever-changing rural population? Did they themselves analyze the ways in which mobility could complicate their work? To answer questions like these requires a focus on the relations of Sicily's artisanal workers—the most obvious group of activists—and wheat-raising peasants. Both the case study of Sambuca and the regional analysis pursued in this chapter showed that the development of leftist political and workplace initiatives resulted from the alliance of these two groups. In particular, it seems obvious to hypothesize that migration changed relations among artisans and peasants remaining in Sicily.

The evidence from both Sambuca and the region as a whole also suggests that artisans' and peasants' migration patterns differed. Massive emigration of artisans in the 1880s and 1890s could easily have left some Sicilian towns without a population of discontented and resourceful activists. Sambuca's history suggests yet another possibility—that emigration itself somehow pushed artisans to open their labor movement to the peasant majority in new ways.

Furthermore, both case study and regional analysis established that artisans emigrated in considerable numbers, often quite early. This means that the Sicilians working as migrants in the United States almost certainly counted among their number men familiar with voluntary association and with the local protests of the 1880s and 1890s. News of rebellion and European political change as well as organizational know-how and ideological commitment to a class-based labor movement certainly could have traveled in artisans' luggage to the immigrant settlements of the New World. In this way, artisans could have transplanted Sicilian traditions of protest and labor organization to the immigrant settlements of the United States.

Furthermore, unless Sicily differed from other European nations experiencing attempted and failed revolutions in the nineteenth century, the failure of each successive period of Sicilian protest undoubtedly encouraged (or even forced) some activists to migrate. The biographies of Sicily's early labor activists, like that of Girolamo li Causi's father, often included periods of time spent in the United States as migrant workers. Immigrant settlements founded during the suppression of the fasci, for example, might have attracted particularly high numbers of activists. Migration, in other words, would shape the context for mobilization in the United States as well as in Sicily.

The role of a few migrating activists need not be overstated in considering the transplantation of Sicilian protest traditions to the United States. Many of the Sicilians who migrated there had directly or indirectly experienced unrest in their hometowns before departure for the United States. This was especially true of those who migrated during the 1890s or after the new wave of unrest that swept the Sicilian countryside in 1901–1905. Over two-thirds of the emigrants leaving western Sicily between 1894 and 1900 left areas with recent periods of violence and conflict. After 1900, the residents of persistently militant towns still accounted for almost half of all Sicilians applying to go abroad. Thus, the western Sicilian case provides little justification for describing immigrant workers as hostile to or unaware of workplace protest, voluntary association, or political action. Not all emigrants could claim familiarity with all forms of rural unrest, of course, but neither were they politically passive, fatalistic, familist, or simple premodern jacqueristes.

The evidence from case study and from regional analysis points in one direction. Just as migration did not always hinder the development of a rural labor movement, it could not automatically transfer to the United States a population of immigrant workers uninterested in and incapable of organizing a movement for social or economic change. Unrest in the countryside had long historical roots; new branches could sprout on the other side of the Atlantic. More than Sicilian traditions would determine the form of that new growth, however. For one thing, relations of peasants and artisans did change in significant ways as large numbers of both groups emigrated to the United States. The work and community experiences of peasants and artisans in the United States also visibly influenced the transplantation of European traditions and practices. The next four chapters address in turn the effect of chain migration and immigrant settlements on Sicilian labor movements on both continents.

Chapter 5
Links in the Migration Chain

The lives of individual migrants provide a somewhat jolting contrast to the structural analyses of emigration offered in the previous chapter. Just as rural protest looks different when viewed through the lens of a case study (see chapter 3), so, too, do important new aspects of migration emerge when we turn to the individual and local level. The term chain migration never appeared in the last chapter, yet it is the chainlike connections among migrants that stand out when studying individual lives.[1] One of the purposes of this chapter is to focus on those connections, and to outline what the social organization of migration reveals about the emerging Sicilian labor movement in Europe and the United States.[2] The chapter begins with the stories of four migrants from Sambuca, and proceeds outward to consider the individual characteristics of all migrants from the town, the social ties linking them into chains, and the significance of their migration as a socially organized movement.

Antonino C. was born in Sambuca in 1889.[3] His father, a cabinetmaker, had first migrated to Brooklyn in 1880. His mother, a seamstress, married his father when he returned to Sambuca in 1884. By the time the family left their home on Sambuca's main street to settle permanently in Brooklyn in 1891, it included a four-year-old daughter as well as two-year-old Antonino. Almost twenty years later, the C. family had grown but still lived in Brooklyn on Hopkins Street. Twenty-one-year-old Antonino C. worked as an upholsterer, perhaps in the same cabinet and furniture factory that employed his father. His older sister made vests at home, while six younger brothers, ranging in age from sixteen-year-old Michael to one-year-old Joseph, went to school or stayed at home with their mother. The C. family lived in a neighborhood of small businesses, small tenements, and middle-sized shoe, metal, garment, and furniture factories. Three of Antonino C.'s aunts and uncles lived nearby. About 300 people from Sambuca lived in the two square miles surrounding the C. family's apartment; most of their immediate neighbors were western Sicilians, but not Sambucesi. Antonino C. remained in Brooklyn—indeed, in the same neighborhood—for much of his adult life. He married, and eventually became a cabinetmaker, following in the footsteps of a grandfather in Sambuca and his own migrant father. In 1933 Antonino C. still lived close to two of his brothers, young men who worked as clerks in local businesses.

Shortly after Antonino C. and his family went to Brooklyn, Baldassare D., an illiterate twenty-four-year-old peasant from Sambuca, sailed with many other agricultural workers to Louisiana, hoping to earn wages as a sugar-cane harvester. In 1896, Baldassare D. married a young woman from Sambuca in New Orleans. The witnesses were three friends, migrants from Sambuca, since neither Baldassare D. nor his bride had close relatives in the New World in 1896. The D. couple and their quickly growing family lived a migratory life for the next thirteen years. In 1898, a daughter was born in Houma, a sugar town in southern Louisiana. During the next years, children were born to the family in three other sugar parishes, as well as in the city of New Orleans. Then, in 1910, Baldassare's family returned to Sambuca, where his siblings had remained. They moved into rented quarters not far from his birthplace. The D.s had two more children before World War I. Baldassare's eldest daughter, as well as two sons, eventually returned to the United States. Another son, a peasant, died in Sambuca just after World War I, while a second daughter remained at home (and unmarried) until after her mother's death in the early 1950s. The two youngest sons of the D. family—born after its return to Sambuca—also lived the rest of their lives in their hometown. Both combined work in a trade with agricultural wage earning. In the 1930s, fascist police placed the youngest, Audenzio D. (a shoemaker), under surveillance as a Communist troublemaker.

A third migrant, Giuseppe I., was a peasant who left Sambuca in 1898 with his wife and three small children. The family moved to Louisiana, where for over five years they lived and worked in Patterson, presumably as full-time employees on a sugar plantation. During these years, three children were born to the L.s. By 1905, the growing family had traveled to Illinois, where two more daughters were born. Five years later, they were living in Rockford, Illinois, a town where the mother of the family had several relatives. Giuseppe L., by then a man of fifty-three, worked as a laborer in an agricultural implements plant. His two oldest sons operated knitting machines in a local hosiery mill. River Street, their home, housed about half a dozen other families from Sambuca in 1910. The L. family never returned to its hometown, although one son eventually left Rockford for Brooklyn. They lived, however, in a city which yearly saw the arrival of Sambucesi from other American cities and from Sicily.

In 1906 Calogero M., a literate shoemaker born to a middle peasant/carter in Sambuca's lower town, migrated to the United States. Several of Calogero's brothers followed him there in the following years. Calogero M. had, as a boy, learned socialism from the school custodian Michele B., and he had joined Sambuca's Socialist circle not many years before his emigration. Once in Brooklyn, the twenty-five-year-old M. worked in a shoe factory and subscribed to the syndicalist newspaper *Il Proletario*. He returned to Sambuca the year before World War I, while his brothers, also shoemakers, remained in Brooklyn. There, they became active participants in a mutual aid society established by Sambucesi.

Although the life history of a migrant is in many respects unique, each one described here shared a number of common experiences with at least some of the others. All can be considered labor migrants; one was a labor militant before migration, and a second had close ties to Sambuca's activist leftists after returning to Sambuca. None of the four migrated as a lone individual; all went to American destinations that attracted many of their fellow villagers. While all migrated as links in migration chains, two also had ties to an organized labor movement, in one case on both continents. Thus, while migration and labor sometimes developed as competing movements, these life histories show that the two sometimes also attracted the same persons.

Most of the evidence on these migrants' lives, and for this chapter, comes from a migrant file describing over 3,500 migrants who left Sambuca in the fifty-five years after 1879. The migrant file, and the sources used to create it, are discussed in the appendix. Both Sicilian and American sources were used to describe the lives of Antonino C., Baldassare D., Giuseppe L., and Calogero M.; their life stories reflect my efforts at transatlantic record linkage.

With close social ties to others, Sambuca's migrants resembled those from most European countrysides at the end of the nineteenth century. Called "chain migration," the phenomenon has attracted much scholarly attention in the last twenty years.[4] Few studies of migration ignore it completely, but chain migration is explored in this chapter for a specific reason. Just as chapter 3 described the social organization of labor militancy in Sambuca between 1880 and 1910, this chapter describes the social organization of migration during roughly the same years. Social ties among emigrants both reflected and rearranged hometown social worlds; at the same time, they built the foundation for immigrant communities in the United States. Thus chain migration shaped the context in which labor activists would work on both sides of the Atlantic.

By focusing on the social organization of migration and labor militancy, the two can be compared as contrasting, overlapping, reinforcing, or competing social movements. This offers yet another perspective on the linked histories of militancy and migration. A comparison of the two shows that the social tie critical to rural protests in the 1890s—that between artisans and poor wheat cultivators— developed first outside Sambuca's labor movement. Migration helped bring artisans and peasants into problematic but long-lasting cooperation in Sambuca. Ironically, perhaps, chain migration also split the two groups into geographically distant and relatively unconnected settlements in the United States. Sicilian labor movements in Old World and New clearly reflected these two opposite aspects of chain migration. The final chapters of this book show how mobility could simultaneously support and undermine militancy on opposite sides of the Atlantic.

Selective Migration

Migration from Sambuca was not random. This section explains which Sambucesi chose to migrate; later sections describe migrants' relations to each other. Just as it was helpful to identify which Sambucesi became labor activists before examining the kind of movement they built, so, too, it is important to establish which Sambucesi chose to migrate before examining the links in the migration chains they created.

Only a small minority of Europeans chose to leave their homelands in the nineteenth century, but scholars have only begun to understand migration as a self-selection process.[5] In Sambuca, the push of poverty was neither as extreme as scholars once believed it to be, nor as much of an obstacle to emigration as more recent studies have suggested.[6] Migration rates from Sambuca varied with economic and occupational status, and with sex. Social, particularly familial, events also influenced individuals contemplating emigration, especially during the peak years of movement out of the town.

Because of the nature of the migrant file, only rough estimates of migration rates from Sambuca could be made. These do suggest, however, that some Sambucesi viewed migration far more positively than others. Not surprisingly, the civile elite of the town did not often migrate: about 11 percent of the elite population of Sambuca in 1881 had migrated by 1935. Among humbler Sambucesi, only shepherds displayed an equal disinterest in leaving their hometown—about 13 percent migrated. Both artisans and the poorest peasants of Sambuca became the most enthusiastic migrants, with migration rates of 37 and 42 percent respectively. Middle peasants seemed more hesitant to move; only 23 percent of the 1881 population of Sambuca's *burgisi* and *agricoltori* left for the United States in the next fifty years.[7] (This finding is surprising, since so many recent studies have stressed the mobility of small landowners' sons.) Overall, middle peasants made up about 12 percent of the migrant file; artisans made up almost a third, and poor peasants about half.

While some Sambucesi of every occupation and class chose to migrate, the majority of every group remained behind. Were migrants different in any visible ways? Clearly, men were more likely to migrate than women.[8] Among Sambuca's elite, those exercising professions (a dentist, a pharmacist) or those with kin ties to artisans seemed more likely to migrate than those with substantial landholdings. It is worth noting, however, that the brother of one Sambuca baron also went to live in New York at the turn of the century. People in Sambuca today report that when substantial landowners emigrated, they did so "for their health"—an intriguing interpretation, when one considers how strongly Sicilians feel about the superiority and health-giving qualities of Mediterranean air.

Among humbler Sambucesi, family status and changes in family life influenced decisions about migration. Sambucesi of illegitimate birth showed an especially strong propensity to migrate. At least three-quarters of the children born to unmarried or unknown mothers in the years after 1871 went to the United States. Undoubtedly, they hoped to leave their embarrassing status behind them. Their distinctive names—Erring Priest, Beautiful Dream, Pretty New Arrival, or Wind from Africa—may have frustrated their hopes, since they followed them to the United States.[9]

Parental decisions about the transmission of property often determined which children migrated. In artisan families, one son usually remained in Sambuca to inherit family lands; other sons first learned a trade and then were encouraged to migrate. Several daughters could receive houses as dowries, allowing them to remain in their hometown.[10] By contrast, Sambuca's peasant landowners divided their small holdings equally among all sons. This practice may have depressed migration rates among this group until well into the twentieth century, since even a handkerchief of land ensured the owner a social status higher than that of the landless peasant majority of Sambuca. Surprisingly, oldest children rarely inherited, but whether this was an old custom or a parental response to the crises of the 1880s is unclear. In general, the oldest children of both sexes were most likely to migrate, while the youngest sons and daughters remained behind to care for the parents in old age and to inherit family properties.[11] Clearly, relations among inheritance, birth order, gender, and migration deserve more attention than they have as yet received.

Another surprise in the migrant file was the number of migrants from Sambuca who had experienced a death in their immediate families just prior to emigration. Groups of siblings migrating together often had just lost their mother, or their father had recently remarried. (Widows rarely remarried, so a father's death influenced migration patterns less noticeably.) Apparently, young Sicilians feared stepmothers, as proverbs revealed.[12] But death influenced potential migrants in other ways, too. Among young couples migrating to the United States together, for example, about a third had lost one or two young infants prior to emigration. Obviously it was easier to migrate without small infants. Still, one suspects that the death of a loved one also loosened ties binding Sicilians to their homeland.

Finally, it seems indisputable that hopes of avoiding military service encouraged men aged eighteen to twenty-two to migrate in large numbers. The proportions of young men who had left Sambuca before their draft call skyrocketed suddenly just before World War I. By contrast, only sons of widowed mothers—a group routinely exempted from military service—were much less likely to emigrate than oldest sons in general.

There is much that we still need to know about selective migration at the individual level. Even if historians can never confidently assess the psychological characteristics of those who left, local sources do contain fascinating clues to how Sicilians made decisions about migration. Much more than economics influenced any individual's decision, and this point must not be forgotten. Nevertheless, economic status and occupation did seriously shape migration from Sambuca. The influence of the two becomes more obvious when we move beyond analysis of migrants as individuals to consider the phenomenon of chain migration and cooperation among the mobile.

Occupation and Destination

Ever since American scholars began using the metaphor of chain migration, historians of Italian migration have emphasized the extent to which village solidarities determined emigrant destinations. Sambucesi went to Rockford while Belmontese traveled to Buffalo; examples like these can be cited by the score. They are assumed to reflect the importance of *campanilismo*—solidarity among those who heard the ringing of the same church bell. This village solidarity, it is believed, allowed migrants to cooperate in forging migration chains. To put it more simply, migrants followed people they knew and trusted—their neighbors who had migrated earlier and established a beachhead in some U.S. city.[13] While a few scholars note the influence of regional networks and solidarities *(regionalismo)* on migration patterns, campanilismo is generally regarded as the most important influence on immigrants' choice of an American destination.[14]

Sicilian sources provide a somewhat different perspective on village solidarity and migrants' selection of American homes and workplaces. Even in the earliest years of migration from Sicily to the United States, villagers rarely chose only one destination. In 1888, for example, Sicilian clerks listed the destinations preferred by Sicilians living in several dozen towns scattered through the region. Emigration to North and South America and to Tunisia was reported. Sicilians in Palermo's immediate hinterland left primarily for New York City. In the central and southern parts of Sicily, however, peasants and workers from any one town might head for any of several destinations. Sicilians going to Argentina, for example, left a narrow band of towns in the neighboring districts of Sciacca and Bivona, while many of their fellow villagers went instead to Chicago or to New Orleans. The center of migration to Chicago could be found slightly north and east of the centers of emigration to Argentina, while migration to New Orleans characterized the wheat-estate towns around Bivona, Sciacca, Corleone, and southern Alcamo.[15]

Sambucesi began migrating to several American destinations almost as soon as migration from the town began. Migration to North Africa and to South America was negligible. Figure 5.1 plots Sambuca's largest migration chains over time. Over 750 residents of Sambuca migrated first to Louisiana; almost 850 traveled to Chicago; over 1,200 settled first in New York; somewhat less than 100 made Rockford, Illinois, their first American home. (See the appendix; destinations for all migrants were not available.) Of the score of other American destinations appearing in smaller numbers in Sambuca's migrant file, only Tampa, Florida, and Kansas City seemed to draw Sambucesi directly from their hometown. Once in the United States, however, small numbers of migrants made Denver, upper Michigan, Boston, southern Connecticut, Texas, southern Illinois, and northern Indiana their second or third points of settlement.

Obviously, village solidarities cannot explain why Sambucesi traveled to so

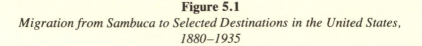

Figure 5.1

Migration from Sambuca to Selected Destinations in the United States,
1880–1935

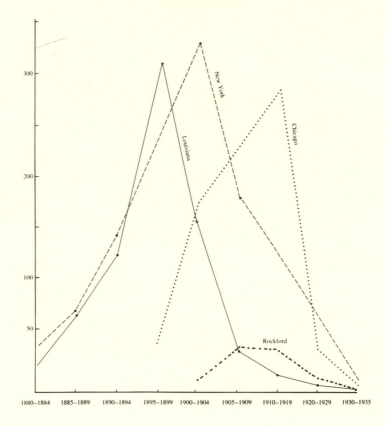

many places in the United States. Regionalismo seems to be a better starting place. Existing regional networks almost certainly encouraged Sambucesi to strike out in certain directions when they decided to leave for the United States. These regional networks also helped guarantee that Sambucesi with different occupations migrated to each American destination. With their superior connections to outsiders, artisans from Sambuca pioneered the way to the United States. But whereas mainly artisans followed the pioneers to New York, only peasants went to Louisiana, and later to Chicago.

The artisans who pioneered the way from Sambuca to Louisiana had been involved in Sicily's agriculture, especially the large wheat-raising estates of their home region. Millers and carters led the way to New Orleans; a small-scale wheat speculator *(mediatore)* and a wine merchant also numbered among the earliest migrants to the southern state. Sambuca's shepherds, whose very livelihood depended upon complex leasing arrangements to pasture lands on large wheat estates scattered throughout southwest Sicily, migrated alongside Sambuca's artisans. Since artisans had long been mobile, and were more likely to marry outside the town than peasants, it is no surprise to find that artisan pioneers had close ties of kinship in the inland wheat towns of Gibellina, Bivona, and Castelvetrano.

Alongside or shortly following the agricultural artisans and shepherds enroute to Louisiana traveled Sambuca's peasants—both middle peasants and poorer sharecroppers and day laborers. Peasants outnumbered artisans traveling to Louisiana from the beginning; even during the 1880s, 70 percent of those migrating to Louisiana had done agricultural work in Sambuca, and of these the largest group came from the poorer families of the town.

By contrast, relatively few peasants migrated to New York in the 1880s; eighty percent of the earliest migrants to New York were artisans. These artisans had pursued many of the more urban trades represented in Sambuca. Shoemakers, barbers, and woodworkers formed the largest groups, but butchers, metalworkers, seamstresses and tailors, pasta makers, and the building trades were all represented, too. Several of Sambuca's earliest migrants to New York also had close kin ties to other Sicilian towns—not to Sicily's interior wheat-raising towns but rather to the coastal commercial town of Sciacca and to nearby towns like Santa Margherita Belice and Menfi.

Once artisans' connections had reached to one American region or another, local occupational networks continued to shape subsequent migration. Table 5.1 summarizes the occupational backgrounds of migrants to the three American destinations Sambucesi preferred: Louisiana, Chicago, and New York. Two-thirds of artisan migrants traveled to New York. Peasants, especially the poorer ones, went either to Louisiana or to Chicago—about one-third to each. By contrast only 15 percent of all peasant migrants went to the artisan stronghold, New York.

Table 5.1

Occupational Backgrounds of Migrants to Louisiana,
New York, and Chicago

	Louisiana	New York	Chicago
Elite	—	9%	—
Artisan	9%	55	12%
Peasant	91	36	88
	100%	100%	100%
Total N	751	1,222	844

In a very real sense, then, it was occupation that determined which American destination a migrant from Sambuca chose. In somewhat different words, occupation forged the links in migration chains. An artisan followed not just any fellow villager but an artisan peer, neighbor, or relative. Peasants followed artisans, too, but to completely different destinations, where they also joined fellow villagers or relatives of similar background.

This is a surprising finding, one that needs further elaboration. Only rarely has occupation or class been considered of much importance in the social organization of migration. Scholars have instead debated the relative importance of labor recruiter and kin in calling migrants to particular American regions or cities.[16] Sambuca's migrant file shows that both labor recruiter and kin were important in organizing migration, but in ways that differed for artisans and peasants. Artisans cooperated with kin and their fellow tradesmen from the very onset of migration from Sambuca, while the labor recruiter sought peasants as laborers until increasing cooperation among peasant kin groups rendered his "services" unnecessary.

One result was that quite different links characterized the chain migration of artisans to New York and the migration of peasants to Louisiana, Chicago, and other cities. Communities of Sambucesi in the United States developed in ways that reflected these differences in chain migration. At the same time, migration to Louisiana and Chicago helped transform social relations in Sambuca. To understand the social consequences of chain migration, including its impact on Sicilian and immigrant labor movements, we must first explore in some detail the social organization of a migration chain.

Forging a Chain

According to most studies, chains of Italian migrants developed in three stages. First, the pioneers ventured forth, mainly as individuals. Birds of passage— young, temporary, male labor migrants recruited by a *padrone*—followed the pioneers. Eventually there was family migration, as brides, mothers, and young children accompanied or followed the birds of passage. Family migration is believed to mark a transition to permanent migration since only families intended to settle in the United States.[17]

This is not a bad model, but it can be refined. Peasants' migration from Sambuca to Louisiana (and, to a much lesser extent, Chicago) did develop as expected. By contrast, artisans migrating to New York early established a different pattern of migration that changed little over the decades. Occupation, kinship, and labor recruitment interacted in the most complex ways among Sambucesi migrating to Louisiana.

The artisans who pioneered the way to Louisiana almost certainly became padrone recruiters of bird-of-passage laborers. Unfortunately not much more than circumstantial evidence documents this development in Sambuca. Sambuca's archive identified only one padrone at work in the town in the 1890s. This man consistently gave his occupation as subagent of emigration, while ten years before, he had called himself a shoemaker. His brother-in-law was one of the earliest artisans migrating to Louisiana. Sambuca's archive also established quite clearly that the town's elite (with the possible exception of one grain merchant) could not have engaged extensively in labor recruitment: Sambuca's civili not only migrated in exceedingly small numbers, they migrated mainly after 1898, and they went almost exclusively to New York City.

Artisans were in a good position to become Sambuca's merchants in flesh. Labor recruitment was essentially a business, for which artisans' entrepreneurial work in Sambuca had well prepared them. That Louisiana's sugar planters encouraged migration from Sicily is also well documented.[18] Their efforts to find a new work force began in the late 1870s, when they turned to the New Orleans Italian community as a potential source of laborers. (This community had developed when New Orleans began importing Sicilian citrus fruits from Palermo and Sicilian sulfur from the southern and central regions of the island.) New Orleans could not meet the planters' requests, probably because the city's Italian peddlers and dockworkers had no financial incentive to undertake the grueling, seasonal, and low-wage work in the sugar fields. Barred by American law from openly sending labor recruiters to Europe after 1885, Louisiana's planters soon came to depend on immigrant middlemen, the padroni, to find workers. Jean Scarpaci interviewed the son of a padrone, a native of Corleone who had recruited workers from towns all over southwestern Sicily, including Sambuca.[19] But no document establishes which men in Sambuca worked as local contacts for padroni like this one.

Nevertheless, one can see in the life histories of Sambuca's migrants to Louisiana the vague outlines of labor recruiters at work. A padrone, like the one Scarpaci uncovered, probably recruited through the occupational networks centered on the large wheat estates and in Sicily's grain trade. Corleone, for example, lay in the center of Sicily's wheat-raising region. This would explain both the predominance of wheat-estate-oriented artisans among Sambuca's earliest migrants to Louisiana and the marked emigration to Louisiana from wheat-estate towns all over western Sicily during the 1880s. Furthermore, the padrone seems to have recruited mainly men who depended for their livelihood on the large wheat estates—that is, the poorest of wage-earning and sharecropping peasants. Poor peasants constituted 60 to 75 percent of all migrants to Louisiana from Sambuca during the 1880s and 1890s. In fact, it seems that only very poor and exploited peasants saw work on Louisiana's sugar plantations as an option worth exploring. Their wealthier neighbors, the artisans, were almost never tempted to migrate to

Louisiana, while Sambuca's middle peasants were more likely to remain at home to inherit a tiny bit of land than to search for work and cash in the American South.

Thus, the artisans who pioneered the way to Louisiana from Sambuca may provide some clues to the social origins and traits of immigrant middlemen padroni. All came from the more prosperous ranks of their trades; two had marital ties to marginal elite families in Sambuca. Padroni undoubtedly were considered ambitious men, intent on upward mobility, men eager to seek out new business ventures. Three owned some land and all possessed substantial homes in the lower town where many artisans lived. All were literate, and appeared on local voting lists after 1882. These were not young men seeking adventure, however, for all were between forty and forty-five in the 1880s. When they migrated, most left wives with two or three children behind them. None remained permanently in the United States. After five to eight years in Louisiana, they returned to their hometown, never to migrate again. (If their children later migrated, as some did, they joined their fellow artisans in New York.) All of Sambuca's padroni lived long lives, dying in Sambuca in their seventies and eighties. All passed on some property to children who remained in Sicily. None, however, acquired civile status. Overall, in fact, padroni did not substantially improve their economic status or the occupational aspirations of their children by becoming merchants in flesh.

The peasants recruited by Sambuca's padroni to work in Louisiana in the 1880s and early 1890s resembled classic birds of passage in many respects.[20] Overwhelmingly male, they migrated temporarily. Ninety percent of the peasants going to Louisiana before 1884 returned; during the next five years, the proportions of temporary migrants fell slightly, to 63 percent. Four out of five peasant migrants were men. Only after 1890 did the permanent peasant migrants outnumber the birds of passage. And only after 1895 did the number of female migrants increase. The Sicilian sources underestimate women's migration to Louisiana, but suggest a female representation of at least one-third by the late 1890s. Scarpaci's study of Louisiana's sugar parishes suggests why temporary male migration persisted so long. As long as men became indebted to padroni during migration, and as long as they found only seasonal employment, few could easily support themselves or save money in Louisiana.[21]

Sambuca's birds of passage differed in one important way from the usual portrait of such migrant workers. Few were young men seeking wages in order to purchase property and to marry. (Young draft-age men did not escape in large numbers to Louisiana.) Instead, most of these migrants had married years before leaving Sambuca, and almost half already owned a simple house. Somewhat younger than the padroni, the typical birds of passage in the 1880s were in their mid-thirties; most left wives with one or two very young children behind them in Sambuca.

It was poor grain harvests during the 1880s that forced so many Sicilian fathers to consider temporary migration. With family subsistence threatened during such years, poor peasants needed additional wages to purchase food. Families with no working children had little choice but to expect husbands and fathers to find wage-earning work elsewhere. Yet only enormous self-sacrifice could have allowed bird-of-passage fathers to send even small amounts of cash from Louisiana to Sicily.[22] Many must have failed to do so.

A number of recent studies have described the American lives of Italian migrant "men without women"; Sambuca's archive tells us more about the women and children the birds of passage left behind.[23] It is obvious that they lived on the edge of starvation when men migrated to Louisiana. Rarely could wives and mothers earn wages, since Sicilian men increasingly claimed wage earning for themselves during this decade. Nor could wives and mothers raise much food, since the families of labor migrants rarely owned even a scrap of land. At best, such women kept chickens and sold or bartered their eggs. The poorest women wandered outside town to exercise the old (but now prohibited) common rights to gather wild plants and snails.[24] In the eyes of the law, of course, they became thieves. Small numbers of migrants' wives also bore illegitimate children during their husbands' absence. Today, informants in Sambuca argue that such children had elite fathers, suggesting that some women exchanged sex for food and money in an effort to feed themselves and their children.[25] Surprisingly, these women did not always suffer social disgrace as a result.[26] Although in one case the wife of an emigrated peasant killed her newborn daughter and fled the town, women more often kept the children; when their husbands returned from Louisiana, additional legitimate children expanded the family.[27]

Obviously, life was difficult for all members of poor peasant families during this period of bird-of-passage migration. A poor peasant man could not afford to migrate without padrone intervention, yet the middleman made it almost impossible for him to achieve the goal (cash) that was the motivation for his departure in the first place. This raises an obvious question: where were the kin of such men? Many scholars have insisted that cooperation among relatives financed migrants' voyages and provided access to homes and jobs for the recently arrived.[28] Such cooperation should have eliminated the padrone and his services.

Cooperation among kin developed slowly among Sambuca's peasants. None of the early peasant birds of passage from Sambuca was kin to an early padrone, and evidence of cooperation among migrant relatives is scanty for the early Louisiana chain. Admittedly, the migrant file did not identify every migrant; this means that kin ties among migrants also could not be estimated with complete accuracy. Still, levels of cooperation among kin seem astonishingly low. No kin migrated together to Louisiana in 1880–1884, and only 10 to 15 percent of migrants traveled with kin or followed a relative during the next five years. Even if the real proportions of

Table 5.2

Sambuca's Migrants to Louisiana, 1880–1904

	1880–1884	1885–1889	1890–1894	1895–1899	1900–1904
Females	—	12%	24%	29%	21%
Artisans	27%	19	15	11	6
Unmarried	—	5	26	43	61
Migrating in nuclear family groups	18	25	21	35	23
Accompanying a relative	—	16	19	53	50
Following a relative	—	3	15	29	60
Returning to Sambuca	93	63	46	26	30

cooperating kin doubled these minimum estimates, many fewer than half of Sambuca's bird-of-passage migrants turned to kin for help in migrating to Louisiana in the 1880s.

This tells us, for one thing, that padroni recruited peasant laborers as isolated individuals, much as estate managers and other employers during the same period sought out day laborers in the piazza labor markets.[29] Padroni looked for laborers among their peasant neighbors. A disproportionate number of peasant migrants to Louisiana lived in the lower town, where artisans migrating to Louisiana had also lived.

About fifteen years after the first emigrants left Sambuca for Louisiana, cooperation among peasants increased, and chain migration began a rapid and startling transition. While peasants still migrated in large numbers to Louisiana, they seemed at this time to break their dependence on the padrone. Migration for Sicilian wheat cultivators became a way of beginning adult (married) life, instead of a search for cash to feed their families. Table 5.2 summarizes some important social aspects of Sambuca's transition from bird-of-passage to family migration.

Artisans and poor married peasant birds of passage made up less than 15 percent of Sambuca's migrants to Louisiana after 1895. The small numbers of artisans who still migrated to the South represented new trades; most settled in and around New Orleans to make or cobble shoes, sell bread, butcher meat, or work in the building trades. Not only did female migration increase after 1895, but fewer male and female migrants returned to Sambuca. Even birds of passage began behaving in new ways in the 1890s, lengthening their sojourns in the United States to over ten years. By 1895, peasants from all sections of Sambuca migrated, not just peasants from the lower town; the peasants living in Sambuca's poorest parish demonstrated a particular interest in migrating to Louisiana after 1895.

This transition is usually seen as the onset of family migration. The term is not completely accurate in this case. Families migrating together did leave Sambuca for Louisiana in greater numbers after 1895; this increase was both modest and temporary, as Table 5.2 shows. Instead, it was the migration of young unmarried men and women and the migration of recently married young couples that produced a rapid increase in total emigration to Louisiana in the late 1890s. Many of the young single men and women who migrated married in Louisiana soon after their arrival; each year, six or seven of these couples sent documentation of their marriages back to municipal clerks in Sambuca. But many more single migrants never bothered to register marriages in their hometown—a hint that they intended their stay in the United States to extend indefinitely.

While migration of nuclear family groups increased modestly, cooperation among kin almost completely replaced padrone-financed voyages about this time. Even assuming that the migrant file identified every migrant during this period (an unlikely possibility), we would find that the majority of migrants to Louisiana after 1895 either traveled with kin or joined kin already living in the state. In fact, it seems likely that every peasant traveling to Louisiana after 1895 did so in cooperation with relatives.

Many factors help explain peasants' sudden liberation from the padroni. It seems obvious that peasants might wish to escape their dependence on the middleman. We also know that grain harvests improved after the early 1890s, easing pressure on the poor fathers who had depended on the labor recruiter in the previous decade. But how did young people avoid turning to the padrone? As a group, after all, they did not come from more prosperous families. One possible answer suggests a change in parental attitudes: perhaps parents had reconciled themselves to the permanency of economic crisis, and had become willing to provide passage tickets in lieu of marriage settlements and dowries. (Passages cost considerably less than did a small house or a sizable dowry, for example.[30]) Thus, emigration came to be a factor in complex parental decisions about inheritance and marriage. Second, peasants living in Louisiana seemed suddenly willing to send for their relatives, and, in all likelihood, to pay for part or all of their passage tickets. (We know that after 1900 most Italians journeyed to the United States on prepaid tickets.[31]) The migrant file showed that one-third of the married men traveling alone to Louisiana after 1895 called for wives and children to join them, although few husbands and fathers had done so before that date. The fact that husbands sent for wives, and that migrants financed the trips of their relatives, indicates that this second explanation for changing migration patterns is related to American conditions.

Bits of evidence suggest that Sambucesi arriving in Louisiana after 1890 began slowly to find alternatives to low-wage seasonal work on the sugar plantations. Sometime in the early 1890s Louisiana's birds of passage began to supplement sugar-harvest work with off-season employment, building and repairing railroads along the Gulf Coast and up into the Midwest.[32] Immigrant bosses controlled access to these jobs; nevertheless, railroad employment provided new sources of cash, so that more migrants worked more weeks of the year. These resources probably enabled peasant migrants of the 1890s to finance passages for relatives, and this in turn allowed later migrants to escape initial indebtedness to a padrone.

To express this change differently, the market for padrone services collapsed. Many padroni simply returned to Sambuca. But new merchants in flesh replaced them. Around 1895, when peasants escaped dependence on padroni for passage money, artisans already in Louisiana and a second, somewhat younger group of Sambuca artisans (mainly masons) again pioneered the way to a new American destination, this time Chicago. These pioneers subsequently attracted small numbers of birds of passage to that city, too.

Significantly, however, chain migration from Sambuca to Chicago did not simply repeat the Louisiana pattern. Return migration from Chicago to Sambuca never reached 50 percent. As bosses and workers moved north along railway lines from Louisiana to Chicago, migration from Sambuca to Louisiana dropped precipitously.[33] Apparently, Sambuca's peasants found wage-earning opportunities on the railroad and in the huge city preferable to work on the sugar plantations. No lengthy bird-of-passage phase was necessary to spur peasants to migrate to Chicago, for kin in Louisiana provided both the incentive and the financial means. The earliest migrants to Chicago (those arriving there between 1895 and 1900) roughly resembled their contemporaries migrating from Sambuca to Louisiana. Not only were their social characteristics similar, but it was primarily kinship that linked them into chains.

While migration to Chicago developed out of the chain migration of artisan patrons and peasant kin to Louisiana, artisan migration to New York was unique from its onset. Artisans migrated in large numbers to the New York area, yet there is little evidence that labor recruiters played any role in encouraging them to do so. Few artisans ever became temporary birds of passage, for example. Artisans' literacy, business skills, cash resources, and traditions of cooperation presumably precluded even an initial dependence on middlemen in the 1880s. Artisans sometimes became padroni; they did not themselves need padroni.

Table 5.3 outlines the social characteristics of Sambuca's New York chain; the differences between migrants to New York and Louisiana (Table 5.2) are striking. Typical birds of passage—married men traveling temporarily and alone—did not constitute even a third of the early migrants to New York. The few married men who did travel alone from Sambuca to New York quickly called for or returned to

Table 5.3
Sambuca's Migrants to New York, 1880–1909

	1880s	1890s	1900–1909
Females	25%	25%	35%
Artisans	70	65	47
Migrating in nuclear			
family groups	55	65	47
Accompanying a relative	17	40	42
Following a relative	5	30	41
Returning to Sambuca	19	15	17

form families, as did Antonino C.'s father. Even in the 1880s, substantial numbers of artisans migrated to New York in nuclear family groups. Female migration lagged behind that of men, but not so markedly as in the Louisiana chain. By the first decade of the century, women probably made up almost one of every two migrants to the city. Artisans often accompanied or followed relatives to the New York area. Finally, it was not large numbers of peasants, but small numbers of elite families from Sambuca who followed artisans to the New York area, especially in the years between 1895 and 1905.

Overall, artisans' migration to New York remained surprisingly constant in its social patterns over a thirty-year period. Undoubtedly this reflects superior opportunities for skilled men and women and petty entrepreneurs in New York's burgeoning industrial and commercial economy. Nevertheless, two related changes can be noted. New York occasionally attracted the butchers, millers, carters, and flour merchants of Sambuca; these were the men who probably functioned as labor recruiters in Louisiana. Agricultural artisans made up about a quarter of the artisans traveling to New York in the early 1880s. Relatively few arrived there during the following ten years, but from 1895 to 1910, their numbers again increased. Migration of peasants to New York City followed the pattern of the agricultural artisans almost exactly: while poor peasants made up one-fifth of all migrants to New York in 1880–1884, their representation dropped to a low of 11 percent in the 1890s. After the turn of the century, their numbers increased three-fold, and in the years after 1910, peasants for the first time constituted a majority of the Sambucesi arriving in New York. It is impossible to assess the precise significance of these variations. It seems likely, however, that Sambuca's potential padroni failed to make connections in New York with significant employers of unskilled labor gangs in the 1880s. (Their failure is puzzling, for such employers clearly existed.[34]) After peasants had freed themselves from padrone dependence in Louisiana and Chicago, a new generation of millers and carters returned to try their luck again in the eastern city. This time, peasants followed them there.

To summarize, the evidence from Sambuca's migrant file shows that one model cannot describe all migration chains. The migratory sequence of pioneer, padrone and bird-of-passage, and family migration describes peasant migrations to areas of the United States demanding unskilled male labor. By contrast, New York's more diverse job market attracted the skilled, the professional, and the female for almost thirty years. Artisans and civili had no need of padrone assistance. Occupation and class status, not village solidarity and kinship, explain the very different character of chain migration from Sambuca to Louisiana and to New York.

Chain Migration and Labor Movement

It is indeed ironic that J. S. MacDonald—whose work encouraged American historians to see migrants as rejecters of collective action—also introduced them to the concept of chain migration.[35] For more than fifteen years, historians of migration have documented how cooperation linked migrants into chains. In fact, attention to chain migration has encouraged an important revision in our understanding of the migration experience. No longer do we view migrants as uprooted from their homelands; they were, instead, "transplanted," a far gentler process.[36]

Was migration a form of collective action? And, if it was, what does this tell us about other alternatives like movements for economic, political, and social change? Clearly, individuals decided to migrate, chose destinations, and assembled resources through consultation with others, within and outside of their immediate families. Occupations, regional networks, and kin groups all cooperated during migration. If we define collective action as "the application of pooled resources" to a struggle over other resources, or more simply as a "substantial number of people acting together," then chain migration must be viewed as a minimal form of collective action.[37] Artisan padroni and peasant birds of passage did not pool resources, but one might argue that they acted together. Artisans traveling to New York pooled resources; at least on a limited basis, they shared information and money among themselves. So, too, did groups of peasant relatives and neighbors migrating to Louisiana and Chicago after 1895. While not voluntary associations, most migration chains became organized movements resting on some pooled resources.

It is sensible, then, to compare migration to other forms of collective action. The most obvious difference between migration chains and peasant protest (or Socialist Party section) would seem to be the motives and intentions of participants in each movement. Many scholars have described migration as familist or individualistic, not because migrants traveled randomly or in isolation, but because they sought change primarily for themselves and their immediate families.[38] By contrast, we generally assume that crowds, protesters, and Party members seek structural change—not just for themselves but for all like themselves. Recent studies of peasant rebels, however, reject this dichotomy, claiming that peasant rebels are rarely motivated exclusively by ideology or collective aims. In fact, any sensible revolutionary hopes, among other things, to benefit individually from structural change.[39] Individual/familial and occupational/class interests do not always conflict; nor are individuals motivated simply by one or the other. Differing motives can be a point of investigation. But it is not safe to assume from the outset that migrants and activists differed significantly in this respect. (Obviously, the systematic and largely quantitative sources used in this chapter do not shed much light on this issue.)

Furthermore, some scholars have shown that migration could and did result in structural, collective transformations—whether that was the intent of migrants or not. This view enjoys much support among Italian students of the mass migrations. Francesco Renda reminds us, for example, that contemporaries described migration as a kind of strike, a relatively effective alternative to workplace protest.[40] Migration did achieve some of the goals sought by workers through voluntary association in the workplace or the political arena. By reducing the number of available laborers, mass emigration sometimes pushed local wages upward; this could encourage large landowners to abandon unproductive lands and agricultural practices. When migrants returned with cash earned abroad, they also drove land prices higher, tempting the owners of extensive but ill-cultivated land to sell.[41] In fact, Antonio Gramsci concluded that emigration from southern Italy had introduced a "passive revolution."[42] European scholars have continued to use and revise Gramsci's concept.[43] Thus, even if we see migration and rural militancy as conflicting strategies, we can admit that the two sometimes accomplished similar ends. This is how sociologist Pino Arlacchi has described the importance of both in rural Calabria: "What emigration did on the economic plane, class conflict tended to do on the political . . ." even if "they tended to exclude the other [so that] when there was one, there was less or none of the other."[44]

The case study of chain migration presented in this chapter adds flesh to these somewhat spare theoretical portrayals of migration and militancy as strategies for social change. Four points stand out in the histories of migration and militancy in Sambuca. First, the rhythm of chain migration paralleled in suggestive ways the development of labor militancy in the town. Second, migration patterns contained hints of changes in peasant motives and consciousness—changes which easily could have affected peasants' organizational and political behavior. Third, the relations of artisan labor recruiters and migrating peasant clients helped change the social foundation for Sambuca's politics in the twentieth century. Finally, the distinctive migration patterns of artisans and peasants guaranteed that only some of Sambuca's New World settlements would enjoy close ties to the militants of their hometown. This would seriously affect any transplantation of Sicilian traditions of labor militancy to immigrant settlements.

Turning points in the history of labor militancy and in the history of migration from Sambuca often occurred contemporaneously. For example, individual artisans began leaving for the U.S. just as the towns' artisans began to distance themselves from local elite leadership in autonomous mutual benefit societies. Ten years later, as strike and protest rocked many towns in western Sicily, a new generation of peasant migrants from Sambuca more quietly succeeded in changing conditions in their international workplace—they escaped the padrone's "services." Socialist artisans who consciously tried to broaden their support and attract peasant members after 1900 could not have been unaware of the effects of migration. Since almost every young artisan reaching maturity from 1880–1900 spent at least some time in the United States, artisan Socialists might have perceived their numbers falling while those of their elite enemies remained unreduced by migration. Sambuca's artisans could never influence local politics while the numbers of artisan voters fell. Was this why they began to see peasants as potential allies? And was this change in any way related to the rapid increase in peasant migration to New York shortly thereafter? The sources, of course, cannot speak directly to these questions. Nevertheless, it is immensely suggestive to outline the parallels. Migration seems to have brought artisans and peasants into closer contact in Sambuca.

Events of the 1890s also hint at changes occurring among Sambuca's peasants. Two cultural traits are often attributed to South Italians, both with quite different implications for their behavior as migrants or as militants. On the one hand, South Italians are said to be natural conservatives who, as migrants, desire to shore up an old way of life or who, as militants, refer persistently to a past period of social harmony.[45] On the other hand, they have also been called adventurers and millenarians with a passionate desire to reject old injustices for a better life, either through revolt or through exodus.[46]

While both portraits are exaggerated, the second more nearly fits Sambuca's artisans, men who had been moving about in search of individual and familial improvement for decades. Artisans' search for family economic advantage had not prohibited them from intermittently organizing or revolting, nor had it prevented them from seeing structural change or new rulers as solutions to their problems. It is probably revealing that when Sambuca's artisans migrated, they more frequently left in family groups and became permanent settlers. In fact, overall, artisan Sambucesi returned in far lower proportions than did peasant migrants from the town.

Sambuca's peasants, by contrast, more nearly fit the first portrayal—at least, before the tumultuous 1890s. One element of the unrest of the 1890s was peasants' desire to reclaim some feudal privileges as well as the communal lands usurped by the new elite in the early nineteenth century. Similarly, their migration patterns throughout the 1880s and early 1890s reflected a reluctance to leave their hometowns permanently. Birds of passage migrated primarily to shore up an old way of life through wage earning in the United States.

By the mid-1890s, however, something was almost certainly astir. Sambuca's peasants, unlike many of their near neighbors, did not turn to either millenarian or "modern" revolts, but as migrants they did abandon hopes of shoring up past lives. Like artisans since the 1880s, peasant migrants after 1895 seemed to look for a new life when they went to the United States. Fewer returned, for one thing.

More importantly, like artisans, peasants began cooperating with their peers in order to migrate. Were migration and new American resources shaking old conservative or familist ways of viewing the world in peasant Sambuca? At least one student of the fasci revolts believes that by the 1890s the long-standing migration of peasants from wheat-raising towns had freed Sicilian agriculturalists to perceive the injustices they experienced, and to act to change them.[47] Emigration could not introduce capitalist development, but it could tear away traditional blinders. Similarly, the suppression of the fasci revolts could not kill peasant protest in Sicily, but it may have encouraged younger peasants to consider seriously beginning new lives for themselves far away from home.

It is speculative, but probably desirable, to think about cooperation among migrating kin in this context. It may be that peasants simply put existing kin ties to new purposes after 1895.[48] It is also possible that conflicts with padrone labor recruiters encouraged migrants to perceive kinship in a new way, as a basis for cooperation.[49] After all, Sicilian peasants had, in the past, seemed less familiar with cooperation, even among kin, than their artisan neighbors. Peasant brothers could have traveled together to Louisiana. But they did not initially do so. Instead, like peasants described by modern-day anthropologists, birds of passage probably saw their own brothers as competitors for scarce resources.[50]

My own conclusion is that younger peasants migrating in the 1890s did cooperate with kin in new ways, in order to avoid dependence on the padrone. Circumstantial evidence points in this direction. Elsewhere in Sicily, cooperation in general had been increasing among peasants since the 1880s, most notably in the formation of mutual benefit societies and fasci. Furthermore, the peasant migrants who cooperated with kin to travel to Louisiana represented roughly the same age cohort as the early artisan Socialists. Unlike the Socialist artisans, who were concerned with local taxes and politics, peasants may have come to perceive injustice during migration; their enemy was the padrone.

Thus the relationship between padrone and peasant migrant, while limited and short-lived, is probably central to any understanding of chain migration's impact on the development of labor militancy in Sambuca and in many western Sicilian settlements in the United States. Louisiana's Italian communities were deeply shaped by exploitative artisan/peasant ties. Ironically, padrone-induced migration both brought artisans and peasants together into new social relationships and forced them into inevitable conflict with each other. Sicilian settlements in the United States and in Sicily reflected opposite aspects of these complex ties of dependence and exploitation.

For Sambuca's peasants in the 1880s and 1890s, the oppressor appeared in a form unknown to the artisans of the town—the wheat-estate manager and the padrone labor recruiter. In some cases, both enemies were actually one, for agricultural entrepreneurs could move easily from one role to the other. Using new American resources and their kinsmen's help, peasants did break their dependence on the labor recruiter. But in doing so, they may have complicated the work of Sambuca's labor militants as they sought peasant supporters in the years after 1900. While padroni did not usually exercise the same trades that supplied Sambuca with most of its first labor activists, there was always some occupational overlap of padroni and Socialists (carters appeared in both groups, for example). Did tensions inherent in the padrone/bird-of-passage relationship color peasants' views of Sambuca's activist artisans during these years? We cannot know. While peasants familiar with estate managers and padroni could easily grasp the concepts of a Marxist ruling class or of class struggle, peasants' understanding of kinship solidarity may have offered a poor symbolic bridge to the vocabulary of collective action and structural change used by Sambuca's Socialist artisan activists.

Artisans' recruitment of peasant laborers for work in the United States did have another side, however. In Sambuca prior to the 1880s, peasants and artisans represented two distinctive status groups, with relatively few reasons for cooperating. Poor peasants knew artisans mainly as marketers of goods—wily men of the marketplace. Most peasants did not farm artisan lands; most did not go to school with artisans. The two groups did not intermarry. Chain migration instigated by artisan padroni was a new and regular, if ambiguous and difficult, social tie between individual artisans and peasants in Sambuca. However exploitative their relations, patrons and clients did form a kind of social network, one with special strength in the lower town, where artisan militancy had originated in the 1880s and 1890s. The use of patron/client ties in municipal politics was a long tradition in Sambuca. Just as one social network of artisans had acquired political content and produced most of Sambuca's early Socialists, so, too, returned patrons and clients formed a network that had the potential for politicization.

By contrast, chain migration from Sambuca separated most artisans and peasants who settled permanently in the United States. Links between hometown artisan activists and American settlements varied tremendously as a result. The artisans who migrated to Louisiana (carters excepted) had learned trades peripheral to artisanal activism in Sambuca. (Agricultural artisans figured more prominently, instead, in the development of Sambuca's local mafia.[51]) After the early 1890s, and even more decidedly after 1900, migrating artisans might have served as a conduit for hometown labor traditions as they traveled in small numbers to Chicago, Tampa, or Rockford. Ties between artisan activists in Sambuca and Sambucesi in New York were, of course, strengthened by continuous arrivals of new artisans from the hometown. Since Sambuca's early militants migrated as enthusiastically as the artisan population as a whole (their migration rate was 50 percent), their choice of destination also shaped contacts between hometown militants and New World settlements. Significantly, every one of the Socialist artisans who migrated went to New York City, primarily in the years between 1905 and 1915. If, as some scholars have argued, labor activism among immigrant workers initially developed out of European experiences, ideals, and traditions,[52] then we should expect to find the clearest echo of Sambuca's developing labor militancy in New York.

Conclusion

This chapter has carried the reader a long distance from the individual lives of the four Sambuca migrants introduced at the beginning. Their lives revealed the connectedness of one migrant to another, while also pointing to a certain amount of overlap in the personnel of labor and migratory movements.

Obviously, migrants and militants were not distinctive subgroups in a town like Sambuca. Occupation, sex, generation, and family factors influenced self-selection in both movements. Artisans' outside contacts brought them early to socialism, and made them important as migrant pioneers. Peasants followed artisans in both movements, but always for reasons of their own.

Peasants' options as immigrants were always more limited than those of artisans. Many could not avoid dependence on a padrone. Few escaped recruitment for the least desirable jobs the New World had to offer, a fact that would color all their subsequent experiences in the United States.

Still, the onset of migration became a significant turning point for Sambuca's peasants. Children gained new autonomy, and kin practiced the intricacies of cooperation, reaping tangible results, during these years. However lowly their U.S. jobs, peasants acquired new resources and new social ties to their artisan peers. Considerable evidence suggests that peasants' understanding of power, of the past and of the future, changed as they became migrants. The next chapters explore some of the consequences of these changes, first in immigrant communities in the United States, and then in Sicily itself.

Chapter 6
Immigrant Workers: Louisiana and Chicago

For twenty years, historians have revised our understanding of the experiences of immigrants, portraying them as rational, risk-taking individuals surrounded by supportive communities of friends, neighbors, and kinsmen from the homeland. The theme of many of these studies has been the transplantation of older cultural traditions and ways of life onto American soil.

There are still some significant gaps in our understanding of this transplantation process, however. While we know something of the European-rooted political cultures of urban Germans and Jews of Europe, we know much less about the political traditions of rural migrants from southern and eastern Europe.[1] This is especially true of Italians, largely because study of this group focuses—often obsessively—on family life.[2] Attention to family life is not misplaced, for family and kinship were important to south Italians. But family loyalties overlapped with and did not always weaken other forms of solidarity. Nor did they necessarily inhibit the spread of political ideology among southern Italians, as earlier chapters showed.

Chapters 2 through 5 identified a number of factors which could have influenced the rooting of Sicilian political traditions in the soil of the United States. The fact that Sicilians varied considerably in their experiences with rural rebellion, and that artisans and peasants often shared unequally in modifying rural forms of protest, complicates the search for New World developments. Chain migration undoubtedly introduced other complexities. Among Sambucesi, migration first transformed social relations among the mobile, and then altered migrants' connections both to activists at home and to potential activists in their number. Obviously, description and analysis of New World developments can take these factors into account.

Fortunately, we have some clues about where to begin. Between 1884 and 1914, over 600,000 Sicilians from the western provinces of Trapani, Agrigento, and Palermo applied to migrate; the vast majority of those who actually left their island homes journeyed to the United States.[3] Like Sambuca's migrants, western Sicilians rarely sought new homes randomly; because of chain migration, Sicilians were not evenly distributed across the United States. Their presence in American Little Italies varied considerably from city to city, and from region to region. Chain migration from Sambuca provided a fair, if small-scale, introduction to the destinations Sicilians preferred.

Like Italians in general, Sicilians tended to settle in large cities in the northeast and midwest.[4] By 1910, they made up almost half of the huge Italian-born populations of New York and Chicago.[5] Each of these two cities could claim distinctive Little Sicilies within their boundaries. More than half of the Italians in Buffalo, and even higher proportions of the Italians in Kansas City, originated in Sicily. By contrast, continental south Italians migrated in large numbers to Philadelphia and to Boston.[6] Sicilians formed over 90 percent of the Italian population of Tampa, Florida, but only 7 percent of the Italian-born residents of Utica, New York.[7] Sicilians sometimes migrated to places other south Italians ignored: Louisiana, with its population of Sicilians in New Orleans and the sugar parishes provided the clearest case of this.

Even this rather rough accounting of Sicilian settlement in the United States suggests where and how one might sensibly study the transplantation of Sicilian political traditions. Fortunately, migrants originating in Sambuca lived in almost every one of the major Sicilian settlements in the United States. This meant that the case study begun in previous chapters could be extended to the other side of the Atlantic, and that Sambucesi could again be compared to other western Sicilians, rather than standing as isolated and perhaps aberrant individual cases. The focus of this chapter and the next is Sicilian immigrant workers, including migrant Sambucesi, living in New York, Illinois, and in the South. Settlements in Tampa, Louisiana, and Brooklyn are explored in some detail, while some information about Illinois communities is also included.

There were good reasons for choosing these particular settlements for study. Peasants traveled to Louisiana, Tampa, and Illinois, while artisans went to New York; patterns of chain migration also differed considerably among Sambucesi traveling to each destination. Sicilian communities developed throughout the South and Midwest as migrants initially working in Louisiana began to seek permanent work and more remunerative jobs elsewhere. Thus Sambucesi who had first gone to New Orleans and the sugar plantations began to travel along railroad lines to Chicago and to Tampa during the mid-1890s; after the turn of the century, they ventured in small numbers to Kansas City, St. Louis, Texas, and Denver.[8] San Francisco's Sicilian settlement also originated in the migration to New Orleans.[9] Many of the residents of Sambuca stopped in southern Illinois mining towns on their way to Chicago. While Chicago became a permanent home for many of them, others went on to Rockford or moved to the industrial suburbs of the big city. Beginning about 1904, Sambucesi traveling to Chicago began entering the United States through New York rather than via New Orleans; thereafter, a tiny but ongoing exchange of residents developed between New York and Chicago. In general, however, the South/Midwest and the New York area became distinct rather than overlapping migration fields. This variation allows analysis of the influence of social and occupational background and the migration process itself on traditions of workers' organization and militancy.

Of equal importance in the choice of these settlements was the fact that Louisiana, Brooklyn, Chicago, and Tampa offered distinctive "opportunity structures" to the Sicilians seeking jobs and homes in the United States.[10] Like the migrants leaving Sambuca, Sicilians in general went to the United States to earn wages, to pursue their trades, or to continue their work in petty commerce. Many believed themselves and proved in fact to be temporary labor migrants. Of those who settled permanently or semipermanently in the United States, especially after 1900, most found urban and industrial work.[11] The type of work Sicilians took changed over time, but even more significantly, it varied from region to region. Theorists have long postulated, and detailed studies often show, that working conditions, industrial relations, and the skill and wage levels of workers heavily influenced their behavior as labor activists and as citizens.[12] In the United States, as in Sicily, some types of laborers were far more likely than others to organize or to strike, to become involved in electoral politics or radical workers' movements. Since Sicilians earned their living in quite different ways in places like Tampa, New York, Louisiana, or Chicago, the impact of the American environment and workplace on the Sicilian heritage of protest and politics must also be assessed.

Settlements of western Sicilians in the South, in Illinois, and in the New York area differed in their histories and patterns of development, and in their occupational and social structures. By sorting out the influence of Sicilian experiences, migration patterns, immigrant community structures, and occupational opportunities in the United States, we can begin to understand the variable behavior of Sicilian workers in Brooklyn, Tampa, Louisiana, and Chicago. Sicilian roots occasionally survived the trip across the Atlantic, but only under special circumstances. This chapter examines two Sicilian settlements that failed to develop a labor movement drawing on European traditions. Chapter 7 then explores two cases of successful transplantation—in New York and, even more notably, in Tampa.

Migrant Workers: Louisiana's Sicilians

The chain migration of poor peasants from Sambuca and other Sicilian wheat towns to Louisiana was described in considerable detail in chapter 5. In many ways, it is easier to study Sicilian migration to Louisiana than it is to establish the quality of migrants' experiences once they got there. A particular problem is that census takers in Louisiana at the turn of the century did not (and probably could not) enumerate temporary migrant workers laboring in Louisiana. Fortunately, Jean Scarpaci's excellent account of Louisiana's Italians is now available. Although the group still has not attracted the attention it deserves, several other recent studies shed light on Louisiana's Italians.[13] When supplemented with data from Sambuca's migrant file, the contours of Italian life in Louisiana begin to emerge. However tentative this combination of sources may be, it points clearly in only one direction. Almost no legacy of Sicilian labor militancy could be found in Louisiana.

As chapter 1 showed, explanations for passivity among foreign laborers abound, but they conflict with each other. The backgrounds of immigrants, the migration process, the characteristics of the communities they form, their rates of geographic and economic mobility, their intention to stay or to return home, conditions of labor in the United States, and native prejudice have all been mentioned as important influences on the behavior of immigrant workers. We already know a great deal about the backgrounds of Louisiana's Italians. First, most were Sicilians. In addition, most came from wheat-raising towns, both before and just after the revolts of the 1890s.[14] Most had worked as peasants, and (among Sambucesi at least) poor peasants outnumbered landowners. Especially before 1895, male birds of passage outnumbered women. After 1895, potential migrants rarely depended on the padrone, but instead turned to relatives and friends to ease the move from Sambuca to Louisiana. We know that Sambuca's labor activists never went to Louisiana, and that most peasants migrating from Sambuca could have had little experience with voluntary association and labor protest. This was not true of all Sicilian migrants to Louisiana, however, since the wheat-raising towns numbered prominently among the most militant in the 1890s. Furthermore, peasants on the wheat estates had formed mutual benefit societies as early as 1880. Migrants arriving in Louisiana may have been among the poorest of Sicilians, but they were not necessarily the most passive in tradition and experience.

Any effort to understand the subsequent lives of Sicilians migrating to Louisiana must recognize one important source of variation in their American experiences. The Italian settlements in New Orleans and in the sugar parishes developed in rather different ways, and must be considered as somewhat separate settlements. Map 6.1 identifies the most important sugar parishes stretching south and west of the Crescent City. Rural and urban Italians' settlements were in no way isolated one from the other; in fact, most migrants probably lived at some point in both, since laborers on the sugar plantations often used New Orleans as a home base between harvests.[15] Despite this exchange of population, however, New Orleans and sugar-parish populations grew in alternating spurts, attracted somewhat different migrants, and offered them vastly different occupational opportunities.

The first Italians who arrived in the American South settled in New Orleans, a city which housed proportionately more immigrants than any other southern city except Tampa, Florida. Italians in New Orleans in the 1880s and 1890s labored on the docks, controlled the lucrative fruit trade (both as corporation heads and as humble peddlers), organized the vast "French" market of the city, and operated countless small shops and stores.[16] New Orleans probably also attracted considerable numbers of skilled and entrepreneurial migrants from Sicily. In 1900, for

Map 6.1
Louisiana's Sugar Parishes

example, all the Sambucesi in New Orleans census listings came from artisan families, and most either worked at the trade they had learned in Sicily or ran grocery stores. From an original settlement around the wharves, the New Orleans Italian community grew to encompass substantial sections of the old French quarter of the city. Termed Little Palermo (the port city that sent sailors and fruit traders to become New Orleans' first Italian residents, and from which most Sicilians continued to depart in the 1880s and 1890s), the neighborhood expanded and contracted seasonally as agricultural laborers destined for the rural parishes arrived, tried to find work to support themselves through the off-season, or passed through the city enroute to jobs elsewhere.[17]

As planters sought harvesters for their plantations after 1877, the Italian settlements of the sugar parishes gradually surpassed the New Orleans Italian community in size and importance. Many migrants landed in New Orleans, but soon left for the cane fields; others traveled directly to the plantations from their ships. In the 1880s and 1890s, Sambucesi married, died, and baptized children mainly in the three sugar parishes closest to New Orleans.[18] By 1900, however, Sambuca's peasants had scattered. Eventually they came to prefer parishes far to the south and west of New Orleans. While only 15 percent of Louisiana's Italian-born residents lived in sugar parishes in 1880, and only 47 percent did so in 1890, by 1900 almost 90 percent of the state's Italian residents lived there. Most probably were of peasant background; not a single skilled man from Sambuca lived in the sugar parishes in 1900.

Work in the sugar parishes was even more important for Sicilian migrants than census figures suggest, because harvest laborers were excluded from the enumerators' count of the Italian population. Beginning around October 15 each year, 60,000 to 70,000 Italian laborers arrived in the sugar fields to cut and grind cane. A typical 800-acre plantation required about 200 temporary laborers for the three-month harvest and grinding season. A strong worker harvested several tons of cane daily, and received a wage of ninety cents to a dollar for a twelve to fourteen-hour day. Italians rarely found jobs as foremen or supervisors; they did not work in any skilled capacity in the cane factories. They made up 60 percent of the harvesters, however. In early January, the migrant laborers departed for the New Orleans docks, for their homes in Sicily, New York, or Chicago, or (after 1890) for construction jobs along the Gulf Coast or in the Mississippi Valley. Most harvesters had little choice but to find additional work, since a man could scarcely survive the year on the seventy-five to one hundred dollars earned during the cane harvest. Thus, the Italian settlements of the sugar parishes were temporary phenomena at best, especially during the 1880s, when harvesting was the only plantation job open to Sicilian workers.[19] In fact, it would probably be false to call these settlements communities at all. Gang laborers may have been linked together in migration chains, but their communities were not geographically based ones.

Originally recruited only as harvesters, small numbers of Sicilian migrant laborers did eventually become year-round employees and tenants on the sugar plantations, where they made up about 12 percent of the permanent work force by 1900. (The majority of full-time employees were Afro-Americans, former slaves and their children.) Scarpaci estimated that a typical plantation needed only seventy permanent hands, of whom perhaps eight were Sicilians. For most of the year, full-time employees planted, cultivated and weeded cane rows, earning sixty to seventy cents daily. The pace of work was more leisurely than during the harvest season; bad weather guaranteed many unpaid days. Besides wages, year-round laborers received rough housing, free fuel, and a quarter-acre subsistence plot.[20] Unattached Sicilian men lived in dormitories or—according to census listings for 1900—in three- to four-man cooperative households. Census listings also suggest that plantation owners preferred families as permanent employees: families (occasionally with a boarder) substantially outnumbered the all-male households in sugar parishes by 1900.

Observers emphasized the frugality of the Sicilian families of the sugar plantations. They purchased little except cloth and flour. Women raised gardens and
goats, but worked for wages only irregularly (as droppers and planters during the
sowing season). Men earned wages more regularly, cultivating and weeding under
the supervision of a French, native-born, Irish, or German foreman.[21] For the
small groups of Sicilians who formed the permanent core of these tiny sugar-parish
settlements, subsistence production had again become the primary means of
survival. They saved their small cash earnings to finance the passages of kin, to
purchase land, or to accumulate capital for a small business.[22]

While studies like Scarpaci's have described the organization of work on the
sugar plantation, far less is known about the social characteristics or social life of
sugar-parish communities. Ethnic loyalties seemed to prevail; while Italians
maintained neutral relations to the Afro-Americans among whom they lived and
worked, the two groups always constituted separate communities, marrying and
socializing among themselves.[23] Compared to Italian settlements in many American cities, those of the sugar parishes seemed relatively homogeneous, at least
within ethnic boundaries. Most Italians who worked in the sugar parishes were
Sicilians from the western provinces, and most came from wheat-raising towns.
Regional and local loyalties worked a certain influence, of course. Both Sambuca's
birth and marriage records and the American manuscript census listings for 1900
reveal concentrations of Sambucesi in St. Mary and Terrebonne parishes around
the turn of the century. The Sambucesi of Terrebonne made up about a quarter of
the 500 first-generation Italians living permanently in the parish; in St. Mary's they
formed only a visible minority. Elsewhere they lived without sizable numbers
of their fellow villagers as neighbors.[24] Despite this fact, relatively few of the
marriage records forwarded from Louisiana to Sambuca revealed matrimonies
linking residents of Sambuca to Sicilians from other towns. And no document
records a marriage between a Sambuca resident and a native-born American.

Whether they lived among a few people from their hometowns or from other
western Sicilian towns, migrant workers in Louisiana shared at least a roughly
common dialect and broadly similar customs based on centuries of regional interaction in Europe. Louisiana's Italians could communicate with ease and without
the barrier of fierce provincial jealousies. This was not always the case, for
example, among the Neapolitans, Genoans, and Sicilians who jostled for living
space in Lower Manhattan's Little Italy during the same years.[25]

Sicilians living in Louisiana's sugar parishes in 1900 may also have experienced
for the first time an Italian social world without clear class distinctions. The
poorest residents of these settlements—the harvesters—may not have figured in
the community at all. Furthermore, the plantations seemed to provide little opportunity for advancement beyond the status of year-round employee, and thus little
possibility for the emergence of an immigrant middle class. The sugar planters did
not hire Sicilians as foremen or skilled workmen.[26] This means that plantations

provided few opportunities for padroni to become bosses or permanent members of the parish community. Some padroni joined the community as small business-men, of course. The Louisiana padrone described in chapter 5 worked primarily as a peddler and importer, selling olive oil and some foodstuffs to the Sicilians labor-ing on the plantations.[27] A year-round population of subsistence producers could not support a sizable middle class, however. Census listings for 1900 confirmed the almost classless character of the sugar-parish Italian communities. One planta-tion supported one Italian grocer or peddler; barbers or other tradesmen rarely appeared. Only two Sambucesi identified in the sugar parishes in 1900 avoided agricultural labor—one sold produce and the other operated a plantation store. Finally, plantation owners seemed reluctant to sell land to any Sicilian migrants who succeeded in saving enough money to buy it; this, too, guaranteed that the upwardly mobile left the sugar parishes rather than form a resident middle class in the migrant community.[28] The bosses and the rich—familiar enough characters to any migrant from west Sicily—still existed, of course, but they lived outside the immigrant social world, either because they were Anglo and French planters or because, as labor recruiters, they worked out of cities and did not accompany and supervise their clients as railroad bosses did.

The sugar-parish communities were in constant flux as residents moved in and out. Data from Sambuca's migrant file show that few Sicilians remained more than a few years. Migratory labor was not limited to unattached men; even the year-round employees of plantations moved frequently, threatening the tenuous Italian communities of the rural parishes. Scholars have always known that birds of passage moved about constantly, but the mobility of Sambuca's families in Louisiana was unusual. Of families that could be traced over a ten-year period, the typical one moved every year or two, even after 1900. They lived much like the D. family, introduced in chapter 5. From New Orleans, a family traveled first to one sugar parish, then to another; often they returned temporarily to New Orleans or moved onward to Chicago after five or six years. Why they moved so fre-quently is not clear. Their mobility is not so surprising, given what we know about later generations of Hispanic migrant workers in the agricultural fields of the Southwest. But it is interesting because it modifies our understanding of family ties as demobilizers of long-distance migrants like Sicilians.

Studies of chain migration have viewed the departure from Europe of women and family groups as symbolic of the onset of permanent migration and settle-ment.[29] Obviously, Sambuca's migrants behaved in more complex ways. Consid-erable numbers of sugar-parish laborers actually returned to Sicily, even when they had worked year round in the United States in family groups. It is true that rates of return migration from Louisiana dropped in the years after 1890, as the migration of women increased. This did not mean, however, that either women or family groups always settled permanently in the United States. In fact, the Sambucesi who migrated to Louisiana in family groups constituted over a third of all returners to Sambuca. That family groups returned home is documented further by the fact that almost a third of the returners were children born in the U.S. Almost a quarter of the couples and family groups migrating to Louisiana eventually returned to Sambuca; this rate of return was not much lower than that for the Louisiana migrant population as a whole after 1890. Even young men and women who married in the southern state without bothering to send a marriage certificate back to their hometown sometimes returned to Sambuca, bringing several American-born children with them and registering their births after their return.

While life in a nuclear family did not necessarily tie Sambuca's migrants to any particular New World workplace or sugar parish, village and kinship ties—life in a community, that is—sometimes did. The Sambucesi listed in Louisiana manuscript census documents for 1900 had, on average, many more kin ties to other migrants in the state than did those who had moved on to Chicago or returned to Sambuca. Furthermore, the Sambucesi who lived where their fellow villagers clustered, in St. Mary and Terrebonne parishes, tended to remain in Louisiana longer than those who lived among strangers. As was true of potential migrants from Sambuca, family ties could sometimes bind.

Proportionately more migrants returned from the sugar parish to Sambuca in the 1880s than in later decades, but new migrants constantly arrived to replace them. In the long run, however, more migrants moved out of Louisiana's sugar parishes than came to seek work there. This trend is clear both in Sambuca's migrant file and in the population histories of Louisiana's rural parishes. Figure 6.1 charts my estimates of the rise and decline of Sambucesi in the state. After growing slowly before 1890, the population of Sambucesi in Louisiana quadrupled between 1889 and 1895. Crises in the world market for sugar in the mid-1890s affected Sicilian migrant workers immediately; for example, between 1895 and 1897, the number of Sambucesi in the state actually dropped to about 225. Economic recovery attracted large numbers of new migrants, and by 1904 about 650 migrants from Sambuca lived in the southern state. Departures from Louisiana, however, increased markedly after 1900, and the depression of 1907 permanently ended the migration of Sambucesi to Louisiana, with departures continuing and even accelerating. The result was that by 1920 no more than 250 former residents of Sambuca remained in Louisiana. Today, family names common in Sambuca cannot be found in the sugar parishes, although they appear occasionally in New Orleans telephone listings.

Census figures also reflected the sudden exodus of Sicilians from the sugar parishes. The Italian population of Terrebonne declined from 550 in 1900 to 194 in 1910. Most of Louisiana's sugar parishes experienced similar or even larger declines during these years. By 1910 only 35 percent of the state's Italians lived in the sugar parishes.

Perhaps the temporary nature of Louisiana's sugar-parish settlements explains why a once very sizable immigrant population received almost no scholarly atten-

Figure 6.1

Estimated Population of Sambucesi in Louisiana, 1880–1915

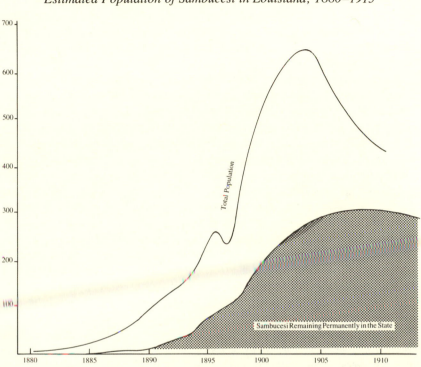

tion for so long. For much the same reason, residents of Sambuca today have al-most no memory of migration to the southern state. Although at one time children born in Louisiana formed the largest group of foreigners living in Sambuca, only one of dozens of persons asked told me that "peasants used to go to New Orleans." And even that comment is a revealing slip of memory, since it was artisans and not Sambuca's peasants who lived in the southern city. While scores of informants told of migrants digging for the railroad or sewing pants, not one mentioned cutting or grinding cane as a typical American job for a migrant in the United States.

Italian communities in and around New Orleans proved to be more permanent, and often grew as sugar-parish settlements declined. In many other respects, too, they differed from the sugar-parish communities. During the years when thousands of Sicilians found work in the cane fields, the permanent Italian population of the Crescent City scarcely increased. But as Italians left the sugar plantations by the thousands, New Orleans attracted at least some of them. Scarpaci found that Si-cilians remaining in Louisiana left the cane fields to purchase truck farms in

Tangipahoa parish or to operate small businesses in and around New Orleans.[30] Relatively little is known about New Orleans Italians after 1900. It seems likely, however, that the settlement was never as homogeneous as the sugar-parish communities: wealthy Italian businessmen and poor Italian longshoremen had already attracted notice by 1880; unlike the rural parishes, the city offered migrants ample opportunities for petty enterprise. That, in fact, seemed part of the city's appeal to the more prosperous Sicilians leaving the sugar parishes after 1900.

As might be expected, Sicilians in the sugar parishes and in New Orleans also behaved differently as workers in the years between 1880 and 1910. New Orleans Sicilians began to build almost immediately on homeland labor precedents. By the mid-1880s, they had organized a number of mutual benefit societies which, in their diversity, resembled contemporary Sicilian experiments in mutual aid. Several societies limited membership to Sicilians from a particular town, while the shoemakers of New Orleans admitted any Sicilian to membership. Sicilians from Palermo organized a confraternity-like society that financed a yearly festival in honor of Saint Rosalia, the patroness of their hometown.[31] Like many nationalist Italians of the 1880s and 1890s, New Orleans Sicilians seemed otherwise indifferent to religion and to the Catholic Church. None of their mutual aid societies, for example, was connected with a church. Both the skilled backgrounds of the New Orleans Sambucesi and the American experiences of petty entrepreneurs and artisans undoubtedly encouraged the early development of voluntary association in this Italian community.

Sicilian wage-earners' efforts to organize are harder to classify, largely because padroni often controlled access to their jobs, especially on the docks. One account of the complex events leading up to the murder of Police Chief Hennessey in 1890 (and the subsequent lynching of eleven Italians accused of the crime) mentions the existence of two rival labor groups among Sicilian longshoremen. (One of these groups may have been involved in seeking illicit police protection from Hennessey.) Richard Gambino termed the Provenzano and Matranga dock groups "gangs" and "labor cliques"—factions presumably organized and controlled by two competing padroni. He compared their feuds to the labor violence of the docks in the twentieth century.[32] Like trade unions, of course, such padrone factions attempted to limit the numbers of unskilled laborers competing for wages on the wharves. Unfortunately, Gambino could say nothing about the ideology or identities of Sicilian padroni like Provenzano or Matranga; we do not know if one or both thought of themselves as bandit leaders, civile bosses, or working-class leaders—all role models familiar from the rural rebellions of their Sicilian homelands in the early 1890s. That gangs like these might have perceived themselves pursuing workers' interests becomes more plausible when we remember that existing longshoremen's associations excluded Sicilians during the 1890s, and, in the wake of the lynchings, attempted to exclude them from the wharves entirely.

We do know that some of the peers of the New Orleans padroni thought of themselves as radicals by the late 1890s. Police rounded up "anarchist" Italians on several occasions; New Orleans and a number of other coast cities claimed small sections of the Italian Socialist Federation.[33] Most were short-lived. In New Orleans, one dedicated man, S. La Nasa, tried to rejuvenate the section which "had been languishing for some time" in 1905.[34] He organized May Day parades, welcomed visiting left-wing Italian-American dignitaries like Arturo Caroti, collected money for the imprisoned Carlo Tresca, initiated a campaign against the absentee and aloof Italian consul in New Orleans, and publicized lynchings and incidences of violence (frequent enough) against migrant workers in the sugar parishes.[35]

Still, New Orleans never became an important center of Italian-American radicalism. A study of a small group of radicals in nearby Texas offers one possible explanation: the author found their discussions completely abstract, with only limited understanding of the significance of wage earning and wage earners in the class struggle. Scattered evidence about the occupations of immigrant radicals in the area reveal a Sicilian pattern: these men were petty entrepreneurs, musicians, macaroni importers, and shoemakers. Like Sambuca's militants in the early twentieth century, they seemed to have few ties to the sugar parishes, the cane harvesters, or even the wharves. It is certain that men like La Nasa never succeeded in appealing to the wage earners of the city or countryside. Perhaps this was too much to expect given the violence with which southern vigilantes censured migrant worker behavior: La Nasa's sons—"prosperous businessmen" in one sugar parish—found themselves run out of town by a mob of enraged natives threatening violence on at least one occasion.[36]

The sugar parishes provide even fewer examples than New Orleans of immigrant workers organizing in pursuit of collective goals or self-interest. It is not possible to identify any one factor that satisfactorily explains the passivity of Sicilian agricultural workers in Louisiana. Clearly, the organization of work on the sugar plantations hindered worker solidarity. The use of a huge population of temporary Sicilian harvesters and a small group of year-round, predominantly Afro-American employees divided the plantation workforce in important ways, and undermined the emergence of a working-class community there. Perhaps, too, we do finally find in Louisiana a relatively clear case of mobility undermining militancy. As temporary migrants, Sicilian harvesters may have had more incentive to tolerate poor conditions and pay than to protest them.[37] As year-round employees, they could count on feeding, sheltering, and warming themselves. Thus the more stable parts of the community gained a sense of security they had recently lost in Sicily, leaving them with the very real impression of having made gains simply by migrating. As illiterate, unskilled, and seasonal workers, sugar-parish workers had special reasons for caution: no Sicilian could be ignorant of the lynchings and other acts of violence against Italians that marred Louisiana history after 1890.

Racial divisions in the workforce proved crucial in undermining worker solidarity. Sicilians began arriving in Louisiana just as black plantation workers intensified their efforts to obtain better wages. In fact, the recruitment of Sicilian workers in the 1880s reflected planters' fears that their former slaves had become too contentious and aware that they could leave Louisiana if frustrated in their demands. (Striking black plantation workers during the 1880s carried banners threatening "A Dollar a Day or Kansas.") The Knights of Labor became active in the state at this time, but mainly among black workers. In 1886 and 1887, scattered strikes (some of which resulted in violent confrontations between Knights of Labor strikers and white vigilantes) occurred in most of the sugar parishes then attracting Sicilian workers. Sicilians seem not to have participated in them; whether they feared violence, hoped to scab, or simply remained ignorant of Afro-American labor initiatives is not known.[38] A recent study of labor activism on Louisiana's sugar plantations does not even mention the thousands of Sicilians working in the fields during this period.[39]

Although Sicilians rarely organized or struck together with Afro-Americans, they did sometimes act collectively, especially in the 1890s. Harvesters were the most likely to stage workplace protests, and when they did so they drew as much on the old Sicilian tradition of peasant jacquerie as they did on the newer protest forms of the fasci. Scarpaci found only a few cases of organization among harvesters, but she found considerable evidence of sabotage and efforts to menace foremen or employers and to destroy property. Several groups of harvesters struck spontaneously, but their strikes rarely lasted long. One ended when grinders in a cane factory demanded higher wages, stopped work, and then left the plantation to seek work elsewhere when their demands were not met. One resourceful Sicilian migrant and his peers organized the American equivalent of a peasant *latifundium*, leasing a plantation together and dividing it up among themselves.[40]

It is understandable that labor activism among Sicilians in the sugar parishes peaked in the 1890s, as thousands of arrivals during that decade had recently experienced unrest in their own hometowns. But it would be unwise to overestimate the extent of this echo. Scarpaci concluded that Sicilian labor militancy never matched the intensity of that found among Afro-American workers ten years earlier. Plantation workers in Louisiana did not organize in large numbers until the mid-twentieth century, and then they did so primarily with help from activist Roman Catholic priests.[41] Nowhere in the United States did migrant agricultural workers of any background form a strong labor movement before that time. Perhaps, like agricultural wage earners in Europe, Louisiana's sugar harvesters controlled too few resources to risk or undertake a prolonged struggle. Obviously, the organization of American workplaces seriously affected the behavior of migrants as workers.

By contrast, Sicilians in Louisiana's sugar parishes did eventually join together in mutual aid, although the societies they formed resembled Sicilian precedents in limited ways at best. Italians in ten sugar parishes organized mutual benefit societies, mainly in the years after 1900, when small but stable ethnic communities had formed and reached their peak populations. Considering the relative newness of mutual aid and voluntary association among Sicilian peasants, peasant laborers in Louisiana organized a surprising number of such societies. (Western Sicily in the 1890s, for example, had one society for roughly every 4000 Sicilians, while Louisiana in 1910 had one for every 1000 Italians.) Most striking was the complete absence in Louisiana of the kinds of connections between mutual aid and labor movement which had been obvious in Sicily by the early 1890s.[42]

The men who joined together in mutual aid in rural Louisiana seemed to care less about shared occupation (a common basis for solidarity in Sicily) than about a shared national and religious identity. Only one sugar-parish mutual benefit society mentioned the occupation of its members in its name, although this had been common practice in Sicily. By contrast, four societies took religious names or were initiated by Italian-speaking parish priests. Another four societies took the names of Italian royalty or historical figures, signaling their ethnic nationalism and general patriotism. Somewhat closer to the complex Sicilian tradition of mutual aid were two Christopher Columbus societies. Unlike their Sicilian counterparts, Louisiana societies served quite limited functions, providing life insurance and sponsoring a yearly banquet or social event.[43]

The fact that mutual aid had come detached from its earlier entanglement with Sicilian labor militancy did not reflect the impact of narrow village solidarities, as is sometimes assumed; all but one of the Louisiana societies welcomed Italians regardless of home origin. Instead, it reflected the new nature of leadership in sugar-parish communities. In Sicily, peasants had turned quite late toward voluntary association and labor militancy, and then primarily with the encouragement of their increasingly radical artisan peers. In Louisiana, peasant immigrant workers had almost no peers of artisan background and almost no lower-middle-class neighbors. Other men—primarily priests—encouraged them to augment their familial and kin loyalties through mutual aid. Clerical activism of this sort had Sicilian precedents but remained a rare phenomenon in Europe. When priests urged peasants to organize in Europe, they led them toward a type of mutual aid narrower in focus than that of most workers' societies in Sicily in the 1890s. The same type of organization occurred in the United States, and perhaps even more easily, since not all the parish priests working with sugar-parish workers were either Italian or Sicilian. While Scarpaci noted religious indifference among New Orleans Sicilians in the 1880s and 1890s—a predictable outgrowth of the anticlericalism of most Italian socialists and nationalists of the era—the Church and Roman Catholicism, and not the anticlerical artisan labor activists, were providing the basis for ethnic organization by 1910.[44]

The history of Louisiana's Italians introduces in outline the difficulties inherent in transplanting a Sicilian labor movement to the United States. While family and kin loyalties provided Sicilian migrants with a "flexible tradition," traditions of protest, organization, and workers' activism proved less flexible.[45] In Sicily, they flourished mainly where artisans and proletarianized wheat cultivators came to see one another as allies in a common struggle. Migration made that alliance unlikely. Migration splintered the two groups and rarely allowed them any common ground in the United States, even though the country offered work opportunities to both. Thus, it is impossible to separate the independent influence of Sicilian backgrounds and American workplaces on migrant workers' behavior, largely because chain migration guaranteed that American workplaces attracted either peasants or artisans. In Louisiana, where peasants lived and worked among themselves as cane harvesters and agricultural employees, no significant labor movement emerged. By contrast, in a city like New Orleans, Sicilian traditions took root, only to atrophy rather quickly among a population of small businessmen. (The next chapter shows that small businessmen could remain carriers of the Sicilian artisanal traditions of radicalism, but only under other conditions.) In New Orleans, where artisans and wage earners lived or worked together, the tensions inherent in patron-client dependencies made transplantation quite unlikely. The Provenzano and Matranga gangs provided one example of this complex problem. The next section examines several other cases of peasant migration, drawing on some data about Sambucesi and other Sicilians in several Illinois locations.

Construction Sites, Mines, Factories: Illinois' Sicilians

Illinois' Sicilians rarely remained as unorganized as Louisiana's, but in the Midwest, too, migrants seldom formed a labor movement drawing directly on Sicilian roots. By the time peasants began to leave for Illinois, they no longer needed the help of a padrone middleman to finance their passages or guide them to jobs across the Atlantic. Still, padroni were instrumental in redirecting peasant migration from Louisiana to Illinois, largely as foremen, labor agents, and recruiters of labor gangs for the railroads. Among Sambucesi, a new and younger generation of men became padroni after 1895; while some still resembled the Louisiana recruiters occupationally (most still were carters), others worked at nonagricultural trades, especially in construction, as masons and carpenters. Unlike the earliest padroni, these younger men who headed for Illinois left Sambuca after the artisans' "turn to the left" in the mid-1890s; they formed a potential link between hometown activists and migrant communities in the upper Midwest. Bosses like these men channeled Sicilian workers into jobs that also promised to make the experiences of workers in Illinois unlike those in Louisiana: industrial workplaces, construction sites, and mines all supported small but growing (and often multi-ethnic) labor movements by the 1890s. Finally, Chicago and, to a much greater extent, smaller Illinois cities and towns became areas of second settlement. In such places, we can see the effects of years of American residence on migrant workers' organization and activism.

Studies of Illinois Italians have focused on Chicago, but many of the smaller cities of the state also attracted considerable numbers of migrant workers. The town of Rockford, Illinois, drew particularly large numbers of Sicilians from Sambuca. People in Sambuca today claim that more people from their town live in Rockford than in Sicily. They exaggerate: nevertheless, over 500 families in Rockford today probably do trace their origins to Sambuca.[46]

Rockford in 1900 was a town of just over 30,000 residents. Located sixty-five miles northwest of Chicago, it had grown steadily since the 1850s, attracting mainly Swedish immigrants, who made up over 40 percent of the population. Rapid growth and development began after 1890, when Illinois Central Railroad tracks connected the town to a vast transportation network. Rockford in 1900 enjoyed a mixed economy with a strong industrial base. Local companies had manufactured agricultural implements since the 1850s; Swedish immigrants had strengthened a native furniture industry with their own skills in woodworking. Newly established hosiery plants, foundries, machine-tool plants, and pump manufactories survived the crises of the 1890s into the twentieth century.[47]

Migrants from Sambuca began arriving in Rockford in 1904–1905. Railroad maintenance work—and immigrant middlemen bosses with their gangs of laborers—brought them to the town.[48] (Besides the Illinois Central, stations of the Chicago and Northwestern; Chicago, Burlington and Quincy; and Chicago, Milwaukee, St. Paul, and Pacific railroads stood along the town's main street.[49]) Rockford's Italian population grew rapidly between 1900 and 1910, and by that date Sambucesi made up somewhat more than 10 percent of the Italian residents of the town.

The early history of Sambucesi in Rockford demonstrates the diminishing role of the padrone or middleman in a predominantly peasant immigrant community. Existing evidence suggests that a padrone from Sambuca tried to "bring socialism" to Rockford, just as the shoemaker Michele B. had brought socialism from a Sicilian jail to his hometown ten years before. In 1905, not long after the first Sambucesi arrived in the town, a group of Italians ("workers," they called themselves) wrote to the New York City paper *Il Proletario*.[50] (This paper became the official organ of the Italian Socialist Federation, and after 1905 it kept close ties to Italian activists in the I.W.W., with emphasis on syndicalist rather than political action.) The Italian workers of Rockford had collected money for the defense of Carlo Tresca, the well-known immigrant activist who was in prison at this time. Near the top of the list of signers appeared Rosario M., a carpenter from Sambuca. At least one person in Sambuca identified Rosario M. as a railroad boss. Near the bottom of the list were the names of two poor peasants from Sambuca.

Five years later, a second group of Italians from Rockford wrote to *Il Proletario*, announcing the formation of a Socialist section, "among the most honest and intelligent workers of the city."[51] Three of five officers of this group hailed from Sambuca: one was a miller; another was a middle peasant whose cousin in

Sambuca would later found their hometown's Communist Party section. At their first meeting, the Rockford radicals discussed anticlericalism, "Christ as the First Socialist," antimilitarism, and "economic questions." The group reported enthusiastically that "At last the sons of free thought, raisers of the red flag and followers of Karl Marx have organized themselves in this town." They committed themselves to doing "the possible and the impossible" in order to enlarge their group and to carry civic culture *(civiltà)* to all the "honest Italians" working in Rockford.

When Sambuca's migrant activists expressed their hopes, they chose words that reflected fifty years of Sicilian workers' initiatives. The earliest Sicilian mutual aid societies in the 1860s had criticized capitalist lust for profits when they called themselves associations of "honest" workers. The Sicilian mutual benefit societies of the 1880s had often dedicated themselves to raising peasants' and workers' cultural levels, so that they might vote. Indeed, education of the illiterate had been the main goal of Sambuca's Socialists since 1900. The image of "Christ as the First Socialist" had been a popular one in the fasci revolts of the 1890s. Obviously, these migrant activists had also moved beyond a local or purely Sicilian orientation in their political understandings, for antimilitarism was probably the single most important issue for Italy's Socialist Party in 1910–1911. Similarly, the words "possible and impossible" signaled the migrants' hopes of transcending quarrels between reformers (the possibilists) and revolutionaries, quarrels which repeatedly split Italian leftists after the turn of the twentieth century.

Il Proletario never heard again from the Rockford Socialists, nor did the group simply switch allegiances to the Italian reform socialists centered in nearby Chicago. Like many other radical organizations, this society of immigrant workers in Rockford disappeared without leaving a trace. Clues to its failure and disappearance might be sought in many places. The early padrone activist Rosario M. had moved out of Rockford within five years, and at least one of the 1910 Rockford radicals returned to Sambuca. At least as important were the absence of either a lower middle class in Rockford's early Italian community or a multi-ethnic labor movement in the town.

Even in 1910, many migrants arriving in Rockford had escaped from the immigrant boss, and from the railroad and construction jobs he controlled. This was certainly the case among Sambucesi living in the town; of almost 100 migrants listed in manuscript census materials for 1910, only a quarter of the employed men were railroad or construction laborers. Most of these men were single and lived in boardinghouses. The typical migrant from Sambuca, by contrast, was a family member. The men found year-round jobs, working either as city laborers, or for the interurban railroads, or as laborers in local foundries and tanneries. Smaller numbers of young men, usually the sons of migrants, had taken semiskilled positions in factories manufacturing pumps, agricultural implements, stockings, and socks. (Few Sambucesi or Italians in general worked in Rockford's furniture factories, which remained Swedish strongholds. Informants in Sambuca report a strong move in the 1920s and 1930s into the foundries and agricultural-implements, tool, and pump manufactories of the town. This is, of course, an interesting development, since as late as the 1890s Sambuca itself had been a minor center of metalworking, with several semicapitalist foundries.) The daughters of Sambuca families also worked for wages in 1910, primarily in the knitting mills; wives rarely worked outside the home, but some cared for a boarder or two at home. Overall, relatively few Sambucesi needed padrone help to find a job in 1910.

One reason that the padrone found few clients in Rockford by 1910 was that most of the Sambucesi living in the city had come there from other locations in the United States, rather than directly from Sicily. Of these, the largest group had lived in Louisiana, for an average of ten years. Migrants continued to come directly from Sambuca to Rockford, of course, right up until the 1960s. Primarily, however, Rockford became an area of second settlement, a town that attracted migrant workers already seasoned by life in the United States or looking for a town that could provide work not just for laborer fathers but for more American-ized sons and daughters in factories. In the 1920s in particular, considerable numbers of Sambucesi left Chicago to make new and permanent homes in Rockford.[52]

Nor was there much evidence of a flourishing class of immigrant small businessmen to serve as a connection between Old World militants and Sicilian workers in Rockford in 1910. Not a single Italian in Rockford listed himself as a steamship agent or banker, although numerous Italians ran large boardinghouses, as well as a few saloons. Among Sambucesi, only two (of thirty) households engaged in business, and neither of these families had backgrounds or migration patterns typical of Sambuca's padroni. A barber headed the first family; he had moved with his family to New York in the 1890s, returned to Sambuca, and remigrated to Tampa after the turn of the century; this family had arrived in Rockford from Tampa in 1909. A grocer headed the second family. The son of a peasant in Sambuca, he was related to a family of butchers living in New Orleans, where he had originally migrated with his family. His own young son worked as a butcher in the family's grocery business in Rockford in 1910.

Settlement patterns in Rockford also hint that migrants who could find jobs for themselves consciously segregated themselves from those who still depended on the labor or railroad boss. Migrant families that had long been in the United States or had arrived from other American locations actually separated themselves spatially from what remained of the immigrant boss and his gang laborers. The men giving railroad laborer, section hand, railroad agent, or boardinghouse keeper as occupations in 1910 lived clustered around Rockford's four railroad stations. Most were men in their thirties and forties, and most were relatively recent arrivals. The real heart of Sambuca's settlement was quite some distance away. There, clustered along three adjoining streets, laborers and factory employees lived in family groups in the small wooden houses characteristic of the town. Rockford's permanently settled families had visibly withdrawn from the highly transient world of patrons and clients. They were a closely knit group; even in 1910, every family had at least one tie of kinship to another family. It is quite possible that padrone militants like Rosario M. or the miller writing to *Il Proletario* in 1910 had little contact with this part of Rockford's community of Sambucesi.

The history of Sambuca's early settlement in Rockford shows that artisan middlemen could not easily bring socialism to peasant fellow villagers in the United States. It was no easy task in Sambuca; it was an almost impossible one in the United States. For many years, kin networks remained the primary form of cooperation among Rockford's Italians. Men from Sambuca did later organize a mutual benefit society, and like Italian-Americans elsewhere, especially in the 1920s, they joined the Sons of Italy.[53] Since increasing numbers of Rockford's Italians and their children worked in industry, they did often become union members during the C.I.O. organizing drives of the 1930s. By then, however, most ties to Sicilian radical traditions had long since been severed.

Ironically, perhaps, Rockford was governed by a succession of labor mayors beginning in 1912, primarily as a result of successful mobilization among a sizable group of left-wing Swedes. And in 1921, Swedish-born Socialist Herman Hall-strom, a bricklayer, became mayor of Rockford as the result of a Swedish write-in campaign. He held the position for five consecutive terms.[54] There is no evidence that the Sicilian backgrounds of Rockford's Italians or the efforts of militants from the homeland influenced elections of mayors sympathetic to labor. Not surprisingly, padroni had proved poor conduits for Sicilian traditions of labor militancy.

The escape from the padrone did not always result in a community of immigrant familists, however. In other Illinois cities, labor activism among migrant workers developed, and in two distinctive forms. Although my research on Sambucesi in the United States did not focus in as great detail on those living in south Illinois mining towns and in Chicago, nevertheless the behavior of migrant workers there was distinctive enough to warrant at least a brief comparison to Rockford.

In contrast to Rockford's Italians, the immigrant workers of southern Illinois organized early, and as workers. In towns like LaSalle, Cherry, and Joliet, one can see how an active and unbiased American labor movement could successfully appeal to migrant workers of peasant background. Like syndicalists in Sicily, American trade unionists appealed to Sicilian miners in their workplaces. An American movement could do so in part because a considerable proportion of the Sicilians working in the mines had already lived for a number of years in the United States; they were not new arrivals, recruited by padroni or unable to speak any English. In many respects, the miners of southern Illinois more resembled the militant Italian workers of South America, studied by Samuel Baily, than they did their neighbors in Rockford, even though their backgrounds were much the same.[55] The presence of labor organizations eager to work with immigrant workers clearly made a difference.

When Sicilians found their way into the coal mines of Cherry, La Salle, or Spring Valley, they usually found northern Italians already at work there. These northern Italians probably served as a mediating group between the new arrivals and American institutions like labor unions. In only a few towns did northern and southern Italian migrants organize separate mutual benefit societies as they did in other American locations; organizationally, at least, the two groups of Italian migrants merged with relative ease. (I found, however, no evidence of intermarriage in the documents forwarded to Sambuca's town clerk.) Both Sicilians and North Italians also quickly joined the United Mine Workers once that union began organizing drives among foreign miners, around 1905.[56] Clearly, American workplaces influenced the behavior of Sicilian workers; so did the appeal of an American labor movement that focused on workplace problems. The main difference between Rockford and the mining towns seems to have been that Rockford's heavy industries did not yet support unions that could have influenced migrants' subsequent Americanization.[57]

Sicilians in the mining towns not only became good trade unionists; many supported Socialist initiatives as well. While originally formed as sections of the Italian Socialist Federation, most groups eventually became foreign-language locals of the reform-oriented Socialist Party. Italian miners in Illinois often became social democrats, while the syndicalist philosophy of the I.W.W. seemed to hold more appeal for Italian miners in Pennsylvania (where the U.M.W. also remained weaker).[58] In these mining towns, immigrant radicalism died hard, in the aftermath of World War I and the Red Scare.

The most complex example of the difficulties of transplanting a Sicilian labor movement to the New World is that of Chicago's well-studied community of Italians.[59] Unlike Louisiana's or Rockford's Sicilians, Sicilians in Chicago organized as ethnic nationalists, as immigrant citizens, and as workers. But charges of corruption and illegalities plagued the histories of Sicilian mutual benefit societies, ward political clubs, and many Italian labor unions in Chicago. It is worth considering the possibility that crime and corruption was the final part of the legacy of the padrone or immigrant middleman's influence in a community of immigrant workers. The vague outlines of padrone corruption which surfaced on New Orleans wharves in the 1890s are much clearer in Chicago.

Unlike Rockford or the mining towns—areas of second settlement—Chicago continued to attract substantial numbers of peasants traveling directly from Sicily.[60] Almost 200 Sambucesi went from their hometown to the Windy City in 1900–1904, and the number of new arrivals grew yearly until World War I. While the migration to Chicago never resembled the temporary bird-of-passage migration to Louisiana, still some similarities point to continued roles for immigrant middlemen in Chicago. Carters, millers, and masons continued to migrate from Sambuca to Chicago throughout the early twentieth century: 22 percent of the migrants in 1895–1899 were artisans or petty merchants; after 1910, the proportion finally dropped to about 10 percent. Although rates of return migration from Chicago never matched those from Louisiana, nevertheless men looking for unskilled work always dominated in this migration chain. The poorest peasants made up 65 percent of the Sambucesi migrating to Chicago in 1895–1914; women never constituted more than 20 percent of the migrants during any five-year period.

Recently arrived unskilled male migrants probably kept the demand for middleman services high in Chicago, even after the end of what Humbert Nelli termed "the padrone era" (the 1890s). Proportionately more of Chicago's Italians found poorly paid and unskilled jobs than in most other American cities. Almost three-quarters of Italian men over sixteen worked as unskilled and usually casual laborers according to one study.[61] Chicago, noted Hull House's Grace Abbott, remained "a clearing house for the seasonal laborers of the country."[62] Padroni continued to channel Sicilian migrants into excavation, construction, railroad, and street work. Their influence probably explains the fact that Italians rarely found jobs in meat packing, for only outdoor work employed gangs of laborers under the supervision of their boss.[63] The skilled Italian construction worker, especially the mason or bricklayer, often held the key to hod-carrier jobs on construction sites, and thus became first a minor boss and later a construction contractor. The immigrant banker/steamship agent remained a fixture of most Chicago Italian neighborhoods as late as World War I.[64] The important point is not that the majority of Chicago's Sicilians depended on a boss at any one time, but rather that most migrants entered Chicago's job market with some form of initial middleman's help. As a result, Sicilian life in Chicago was shaped by internal tensions as immigrant middlemen strove to institutionalize leadership of their communities.

Unlike peasants in Louisiana's sugar plantations, Sicilians in Chicago organized in mutual assistance early—in fact, almost as soon as they entered the city. The first Sicilian mutual benefit society, the Trinacria Fratellanza Siciliana, appeared in 1892. A few years later the Unione Siciliana united a score of existing village-based societies; it grew into a sizable federation open to all Italians.[65] It is very likely that efforts on the part of early middlemen explain the early appearance of Sicilian voluntary association in Chicago. (Similar men in New Orleans had also organized promptly.) Nelli denies that the Unione had ties to the labor movement comparable to those typical in Italy; he instead emphasizes the social functions of the mutual aid societies.[66] But he also documents that leaders of the Unione often had led specific unions with large Sicilian memberships, and this establishes that at least personal ties existed between mutual aid and labor movement.[67] While the Unione formed an early anticrime "White Hand" society, its leaders after 1910 also commonly associated with criminals or had criminal records. By the twenties, well-known criminals competed for control of the Unione, which reorganized and changed its name as a result.[68]

The same names that appear as corrupt leaders of the Unione Siciliana reappear in Nelli's account of politics and trade-union activism among Chicago's Italians. Because naturalization papers opened the door to jobs on city construction contracts, Sicilians probably resembled Chicago's Italians as a whole in becoming citizens more quickly and in higher proportions than Italians in most other American cities.[69] In politics, too, bosses reigned, building careers on the votes of laborer citizens.[70] Many of these unskilled voters were fellow villagers of ward leaders, since Sicilians in Chicago formed fairly dense (if ever-changing) neighborhood clusters. Sambucesi, for example, clustered in the Gault Court/Milton Avenue area on Chicago's near North Side. Among them, the son of a carter rose to modest prominence as a ward political leader.[71]

The impact of immigrant bosses is also suggested immediately when we contrast the histories of Chicago unions of gang laborers (those most likely to have been recruited by middlemen) and those formed by semiskilled and skilled Italian workers in industry. Sicilians in Chicago quickly joined unions, particularly the Hod Carriers' and Building Laborers' Union (organized in 1903 as an A.F. of L. affiliate) and the Sewer and Tunnel Workers' Union.[72] Both unions had close ties to the Unione Siciliana, sharing some of its corrupt leaders, several of whom died gangland-style deaths just before World War I.[73] Far different was the case of Chicago's Italian garment workers, whose well-known strike began in 1910 when a Sicilian girl led other female employees out of the shop in protest over wage cuts.[74] The Amalgamated Clothing Workers of America (organized in 1914 when rebellious Chicago garment workers became dissatisfied with their A.F. of L. affiliate) included a significant group of Sicilian activists, many of whom had close ties to the Italian Socialists of the city.[75] The A.C.W.A.'s Italians never attracted charges of either corruption or ties to criminals.

Chicago also became the center of Italian support for the Socialist Party in the United States, even before Italy's social democrats departed from the revolutionary-dominated Socialist Party in the homeland. Italians in Chicago's 19th Ward organized a Socialist Party foreign-language local in 1907; in 1908, they began publishing *Parola dei Socialisti* (later *Parola del Popolo*).[76] The Socialists waged constant war on the padroni, the *prominenti* (immigrant elite), and the ward bosses whom they knew enjoyed great influence in many immigrant communities.[77] They themselves had little influence in the boss-dominated unions, and little success in drawing street-laborer voters away from their ward patrons. Their strength was in the A.C.W.A., some smaller craft unions of skilled immigrant workers, and in Illinois mining towns. Chicago's Socialists resembled those in Louisiana and in Sicily in many respects: many were small businessmen, skilled workers, and intellectuals.[78] Ideology aside, their attack on the bosses made perfect sense, since they wanted to replace the bosses as leaders of immigrant communities united by class, not patron/client ties. Chicago's Socialists dreamed of themselves as middlemen, too, linking militant migrant workers to American unions and to the Italian-speaking branch of the Socialist Party.

Eventually, of course, most individual Sicilians in Chicago escaped dependence on the boss, just as had Rockford's Sambucesi. In doing so, Sicilians in Chicago often abandoned both the neighborhoods and institutions founded and dominated by the immigrant bosses. By the 1920s, an Italian-American middle class of upwardly mobile immigrants slowly formed in Chicago: the grandson of a peasant from Sambuca became a University of Chicago sociologist; another ran a success-ful can manufactory.[79] It is hard to imagine men like these taking over commu-nity institutions founded in 1890–1910: the Unione Siciliana and Italian ward clubs were suspect because of their ties to organized crime; the Socialist Party and the unions had become suspect as unAmerican organizations. Nelli's work shows quite clearly that the upwardly mobile disappeared into the anonymity of the suburbs, while only those who had succeeded in crime or politics remained tied to inner-city neighborhoods with the less successful and the more recently arrived.[80] Nelli's work strongly suggests that pride in Mussolini, loyalty to the Church, and participation in the newer ethnic organizations like the Sons of Italy characterized their lives.

Conclusion

Sicilians' migration to the South and the Midwest developed from agricultural practices and social networks on western Sicily's wheat estates. In Sicily, perhaps no individual had been hated as much as the *gabellotto,* the agricultural entrepre-neur who leased large wheat estates, hired day laborers in the piazza marketplace, carried a gun as he supervised harvesters' work in the fields or their meals in the estate courtyard in the evening, and cheated sharecroppers out of grain each harvest. In Sambuca men like these, with their carter, miller, shepherd, and butcher associates, often became the local mafiosi. The network of local strong men was never completely isolated, either socially, occupationally, or culturally, from the local Socialist militants, although (in Sambuca at least) these ties rarely resulted in corruption or crime among the leftists. There was also always consider-able conflict between militants and mafiosi in Sicily. Many of the peasant protests of the 1890s aimed at limiting the abusive power of the gabellotto or eliminating his position altogether; mafiosi often attacked Socialist activists, especially after the turn of the century. But some Sicilian strong men repeatedly sought power within the workers' societies of the same period, in an effort to use existing organizations for their own ambitions.

In the South and Midwest of the United States, the troubled history of Sicilian agricultural entrepreneurs and impoverished day laborers continued, but developed in varying ways. Padroni proved quite useful in directing laborers to American employers. Nevertheless, not all American employers organized production in ways typical of the large Sicilian wheat estates. Sugar planters seemed uninterested in leasing estates or in hiring immigrant middlemen to supervise Sicilian harvesters. Mines and most factories rarely sought gangs of laborers, let alone gangs complete with a supervisor boss. Thus, American workplaces limited immigrant middlemen's opportunities to reproduce their power and influence over poor peasant migrants. Cooperation among kin helped peasant migrants avoid turning to padroni to finance passages, but it was the organization of American workplaces that allowed acclimated migrants to escape bosses and their exploitative supervision permanently. Fleeing the padrone, peasants often cut their main link to the militants of their hometowns, and sometimes they found themselves with no ties to any labor movement. This is what occurred in the sugar parishes and in Rockford. In doing so, however, peasants also escaped the crime, divisions, and corruption that could accompany boss leadership of the immigrant community. And in a few cases, notably Illinois' mining towns, peasant migrants found a place in an American and Italian-American labor movement on their own.

In a very few important instances, however, American workplaces did reproduce the organization of labor typical of Sicily's large wheat estates, usually through some form of labor contracting. The most obvious case was railroad construction and maintenance work, where gangs of workers traveled long distances from their homes to work at temporary jobs for wages and food (also provided by the labor-agent boss). Even Chicago's construction sites and excavations showed some of these characteristics, especially bosses' prerogatives to pick and to supervise their own laborers. The results in Chicago resembled those in some Sicilian towns in the 1890s. Laborers sometimes revolted against their bosses; bosses also sought power within workers' institutions and as leaders of workers' movements. Some, like Rosario M. or the activists of Rockford's short-lived Socialist section, may have been militants in Sicily before becoming migrant middlemen. Many more simply followed an elite tradition of boss politics, typical of Sicily's provincial towns. The rough division between mafiosi agricultural entrepreneurs and the more urban-oriented artisans of Sambuca's Socialist Party had fascinating parallels in Chicago, where sewer excavators and garment workers developed separate and mutually incompatible labor movements. Padroni could not simply build a labor movement drawing on Sicilian precedents. Only more detailed studies of the origin of labor "rackets" and the social relations of unskilled laborers, small businessmen, and garment workers in Chicago's Sicilian settlements can reveal why immigrant Socialists and trade unionists failed to challenge successfully the bosses of their communities as they sometimes did in Sicily.

Chapter 7
Immigrant Workers: Tampa and Brooklyn

While peasants had migrated to Louisiana and Illinois, artisans and petty merchants from Sambuca more frequently chose to seek new homes on the East Coast of the United States. In the Immigration Commission's survey, only 31 percent of South Italians in New York City claimed to have worked as farmers in their homelands.[1] Skilled Sicilians probably preferred cities like New York where they could find work in shops and factories or in small businesses of their own, rather than entering the U.S. job market as unskilled and seasonal laborers as their peasant peers did. The many studies that have traced Italian's occupational choices in New York show fewer Italian immigrants engaged in pick-and-shovel work than was true in Chicago.[2]

Furthermore, evidence from Sambuca's migrant file revealed no evidence that artisans journeyed to New York as birds of passage or padrone clients. How typical the Sambucesi may have been is, of course, open to question, especially in the 1880s and 1890s. Still, there is some reason to believe that the patrons controlled proportionately fewer jobs in New York. For one thing, most East Coast cities differed from Chicago; they were not so exclusively railroad and transportation centers. And the occupational figures mentioned above also suggest that New York's subway excavation, wharves, and construction sites were not the sole employers of gangs of laborers, as they were in Chicago. This does not mean that there were no prominenti or immigrant middle classes in such cities, only that padroni and immigrant middlemen made up a smaller part of the immigrant elite outside cities like Chicago.

This chapter explores two American cities, Tampa and Brooklyn, that resembled New Orleans in attracting skilled migrants from Sicily. The resemblance ends, however, with the similar backgounds of migrants to the three cities. In New Orleans, transplanted Sicilian labor institutions atrophied among the petty merchants, labor agents, and grocers of the French Quarter. In Tampa and in New York, the outcome was quite different: artisan migrants struggled to apply their Sicilian experiences and build an immigrant labor movement in the United States. In both cities, skilled migrants became intimately involved in the problems of wage earning in industrial workplaces. This probably explains much of their continued activism. In Tampa, family ties linked small businessmen and industrial wage earners in a shared struggle against capital for over twenty years. In New York, by contrast, small businessmen and wage earners sometimes found themselves on opposite sides of the class struggle, or in opposing factions within the Italian-American labor movement.

Cigar Makers and Small Businessmen: Tampa

Although a southern settlement, Tampa presents a striking contrast to the history of Sicilians in Louisiana. In Tampa, one finds the clearest case of Sicilian labor traditions transplanted to an industrial setting in the United States. In fact, Tampa's Sicilians have attracted considerable attention for their labor militancy.[3] The cigar industry of Tampa and nearby Ybor City experienced persistent strikes and labor unrest during the first decades of the twentieth century. And it was in Tampa that an artisan from Sambuca rose to local prominence as a working-class leader. Giovanni Vaccaro did not work among his own fellow villagers, for Tampa never attracted substantial numbers of migrants from Sambuca, yet his role in Tampa's labor movement clearly reflected Sicilian traditions easily transferable to a settlement like the one formed by Tampa's Italians.

The first Italians to migrate to Tampa came from Louisiana; groups of laborers found work around the city in the late 1880s.[4] A few Sambucesi began to migrate directly to the city around 1890, but most who traveled to Tampa did so in the ten years after 1895. At its peak the population of Sambucesi in Tampa numbered only forty (or roughly one percent of Tampa's Italian-born population in 1910). There is no ready explanation for the fact that few Sambucesi went to Tampa. The first migrants from Sambuca to the town were carters, the men who played an important role in initiating mass migrations to other locations. These carters arrived in Tampa just before some of their fellows ventured to Chicago. Perhaps the Tampa carters lost out in a competition for peasant laborers with their Chicago counterparts. More likely, they simply failed to find the kinds of jobs they could offer peasant migrants: work in Tampa's major industry, cigars, required skills that few poor peasants had, and the area otherwise offered few options for unskilled laborers to work with pick and shovel as they did on the railroads and in Chicago.[5]

Tampa's Italian community began as a spin-off from Louisiana, but the small numbers of Sambucesi who migrated there little resembled their fellow villagers in the sugar parishes. For one thing, women outnumbered men among the Sambucesi traveling to Tampa. Even more strikingly, artisans and middle peasants, not the poor, predominated. Artisans were 47 and middle peasants 25 percent of the Sambucesi in Tampa. A small cluster, these men and women seem to have come as settlers, for only one in ten ever returned to Sambuca. (About a third, however, eventually moved on to Chicago, Rockford, or New York, both during the depression of 1907 and during the 1920s.) Finally, the Sambucesi in Tampa were a closely knit group. Over half were close kinsmen, the children of three sisters, women whose father had been a shepherd from the Sicilian town of Santo Stefano Quisquina.

It was this Santo Stefano connection that brought Sambuca's carters, middle peasants, and artisans to Tampa. Pozzetta and Mormino found that 60 percent of Tampa's Italian residents originated in Santo Stefano, while 5 percent hailed from four nearby towns, Alessandria della Rocca, Bivona, Cianciana, and Contessa Entellina, Sambuca's neighbor to the north.[6] Unlike Sambuca, all these towns had numbered among Sicily's more militant in the early 1890s, just as migration to Tampa began in earnest.[7]

It is likely that migrants from Santo Stefano and other towns well represented in Tampa resembled Sambuca's migrants in coming from middling or artisanal and industrial backgrounds. Cianciana, for example, was a sulfur-mining town, and Bivona and Santo Stefano both had some local industry and more middle peasants, proportionately, than did Sambuca.[8] (Only in Contessa Entellina did large wheat estates completely dominate the local economy.) In any case, Sicilians coming to Tampa from these towns, like Sambuca's artisans, seem to have come with little help from labor recruiters. Mormino and Pozzetta found no lengthy period of sojourner (or bird-of-passage) migration into Tampa.[9] Neither did the occupational structure of Tampa's Sicilian settlement reveal any clear-cut division between a small prominenti group and a majority of unskilled and seasonal laborers, such as was found in Chicago.[10]

The work history of Tampa's Sicilians instead suggests that those settling in the town built upon considerable homeland experience with petty commerce, reproducing in important ways the lives they had known in Sicily. Lacking knowledge of cigar making, and blocked initially by suspicious Cuban factory owners, Sicilian men moved instead into truck farming and dairying; into marketing milk, fruits, and vegetables; and into small businesses and street trades. At the same time, they bought land, and their wives and small children raised goats and most of their families' food in backyard plots.[11] Still, Pozzetta and Mormino report, Sicilians settled in small business "with an eye to the cigar factories"; industry and industrial jobs seemed important to them as a stepping stone. Apparently, they saw wages as a means of accumulating capital to establish their petty enterprises on a firmer and more secure basis.[12]

Considerable evidence suggests that it was the sons, daughters, and wives of Sicilian families who accumulated the capital required by small-businessmen fathers. In 1900 about half of Tampa's adult Italian-born citizens worked in the cigar industry.[13] There were more jobs for women than for men, explaining perhaps why women from Sambuca migrated to Tampa in greater numbers than men. Wives and daughters worked in about equal numbers in the cigar factories, mainly as strippers. In contrast to Rockford or Chicago, where mainly unmarried women worked outside the home, fully half of the Italian female cigar workers in Tampa in 1900 were married.[14] Most of the Sicilian men who entered the cigar industry did so as youngsters, after learning the trade informally from Spanish or Cuban workers; apparently Sicilian small businesses could not employ most family members profitably.[15] One result of the entrance of boys into the cigar factories was that men outnumbered women in the cigar industry by 1910. By that date, almost 80 percent of the working-age Italian population of Tampa earned wages making cigars.[16]

Overall, migration and settlement in Tampa enhanced the likelihood that Sicilian traditions of labor militancy would prosper there. The timing of migration to Tampa (just after the fasci revolts) was propitious; the most organizationally experienced and radical occupational groups migrated there; many migrants came from towns with labor unrest. Unlike Louisiana, Tampa offered Sicilians skilled and semiskilled jobs in industry, the economic sector central to most contemporary American trade-union organization. Tampa also provided options for experienced artisan/petty merchants and middle peasants; their economic niches provided the same independent resources and flexibility they had in Sicily.

While the Italian population of Tampa was undivided by provincial loyalties, the cigar industry itself employed a diverse workforce of Cubans, Spaniards, and Sicilians. The potential for ethnic antagonisms was high; nor was such antagonism unknown. Pozzetta and Mormino emphasize, however, that for the years 1900 to 1920 cultural differences rarely divided workers, at least in the workplace.[17] When Sicilians began to take their places in the cigar factories, Spanish and Cuban militants already enjoyed an audible presence there, electing their *lector* (reader) who read aloud from the labor press each day. Although each group of cigar workers had its own traditions of labor militancy, activists of all three backgrounds seemed to share roughly the same vocabulary of protest, class, and exploitation, as well as broadly "Latin" customs.

It is not necessary to retell the story of Tampa's labor movement in order to complete this tale of a Sicilian labor movement in the United States. According to Pozzetta and Mormino, at least twenty-seven labor disturbances occurred in Tampa cigar factories between 1895 and 1920. The years around 1900, 1910–1912, and 1916–1919 were particularly tumultuous. After the "ten-month strike" of 1920, Italians began to leave the industry, the men often returning to the small businesses begun by their fathers, the women experimenting for the first time with Italian-American domesticity. During the previous twenty years, however, Sicilian participation equaled or surpassed that of the other immigrant groups in the cigar factories. Within a Latin environment, Sicilian men and women created a radical subculture of their own. For the men, this represented a continuation of past experiences; for the women, a new (and apparently temporary) political education.[18]

At the very center of Tampa's radical subculture was Giovanni (John) Vaccaro, born in Sambuca in 1882, the son of a carpenter. Like many of the other Sambucesi in Tampa, Vaccaro had ties to Santo Stefano Quisquina, the town that sent so many residents to Tampa.[19] His mother was one of the shepherd daughters from Santo Stefano, mentioned above. Before leaving Sicily he had been often in Santo Stefano, and had been influenced by events there in the 1890s. Vaccaro was to have become a priest, but his father's early death caused a loss of faith—and perhaps also a loss of income—that encouraged his subsequent migration, first to an older brother in New York City, and then to his mother's relatives in Tampa.

Through visits to his mother's hometown in the 1890s Vaccaro—like many of the migrants from Santo Stefano—became a follower of Lorenzo Panepinto. Panepinto, a local schoolteacher and member of the minor gentry, committed his life to working with Sicilian peasants and changing Sicily to meet their needs. He had begun in the 1890s by organizing a workers' fascio, and became one of Sicily's best known rural Socialists. By the time Vaccaro would have been elibible for the draft, roughly at the time his artisan peers in Sambuca organized their workers' school, he had left for the United States. Almost immediately, he found work and became recognized as a leader among Sicilian cigar workers.

Like his idol Panepinto, Vaccaro was variously characterized as an anarchist, a syndicalist, or a revolutionary socialist. In Tampa, the activist from Sambuca worked primarily in the local affiliate of the A.F. of L. Cigar Makers' Union. He had far closer ties to Eugene Debs' Socialist Party (of which he was a member) than to the I.W.W., although this group, too, attracted an Italian following in Tampa. Vaccaro probably considered himself a reform Socialist, as did many of Sicily's artisans and urban workers by World War I. Had he remained in Sicily, close to Panepinto, his political loyalties might have developed quite differently.

Vaccaro was no inflexible sectarian, a characteristic he apparently shared with most of Tampa's Italian radicals, regardless of their ideological leanings. He quarreled openly with anarchists and syndicalists, whom he accused of disrupting the local Socialist Party section, but he corresponded regularly with *Il Proletario*, and he also worked closely with revolutionaries, anarchists, and syndicalists during cigar-worker strikes or in Italian community institutions. Vaccaro's age, his birth in Sambuca's lower town, his religious skepticism, his premigration politicization, and his rather catholic approach to working-class solidarity can be seen as representative of the Sicilian labor movement of the 1890s. What distinguished Vaccaro in Tampa from many of his artisan peers in Sambuca was his new status as a wage earner, and, related to this, his trade-union activism.

Mormino and Pozzetta's study of Tampa clearly demonstrates that Vaccaro and other Italian labor militants became the leaders of a united Italian community in the southern city. In Tampa, labor militants did not compete with prominenti, with the Church, or with ethnic/nationalist leaders for that honor. This was so because the labor militants themselves built the institutions of the community, shaping Italian ethnic culture in Tampa into their own vision of a working-class community. Tampa remained an anticlerical stronghold into the 1930s. The Italian community actually began in the mutual benefit society formed in Tampa by small businessmen (the *Unione Italiana*); in later years it was usually led by labor activists. Unlike Louisiana's mutual benefit societies, or Chicago's Unione Siciliana, the Unione Italiana in Tampa closely resembled its Sicilian counterparts. Not only did it enjoy close ties to the labor movement, it provided a broad range of services: medical care, insurance, entertainment, meeting rooms, social facilities, social celebrations, and education. (Panepinto himself organized a workers' school during a visit to Tampa shortly before his death.) Even ethnic nationalism assumed a new meaning in Tampa. This became particularly clear in the 1920s; Tampa became and stayed belligerently anti-Fascist.[20] John Vaccaro, in fact, left Tampa and trade unionism for New York, where he opened a small cigar store with his sons and dedicated most of his time to working as press agent for the Anti-Fascist Alliance of North America.[21]

Pozzetta and Mormino emphasize the pragmatic character of labor militancy in Tampa, arguing that radicalism among Sicilian cigar workers became primarily a means to accomplish their original goal of capitalist enterprise. Once the capital was earned, Italians left the cigar factories, and radicalism, behind —mainly to become small businessmen.[22] In Sicily, the relation of petty enterprise, independent workplaces, and radical ideology had been a complex one: control over one's work and independent resources had been the foundations for modern labor militancy. The same was true in Tampa, but only initially. Young men and women in the cigar factories had been able to strike, in part, because small-businessmen fathers, goats in the back yard, and extensive kitchen gardens fed them during strikes. The decline of labor militancy and the departure of Sicilians from the cigar factories reflected many factors, but of obvious importance were structural changes in the cigar industry and a nationwide assault on immigrant radicals, which placed men like John Vaccaro under constant surveillance in the years during and after World War I. Severing their ties with the factory, Sicilians severed their ties with the labor movement. For a short period, however, Tampa had become a New World counterpart to the militant Sicilian towns in the 1890s and the Sicilian red towns developing after 1900.

Barbers and Shoemakers: Brooklyn, New York

If traditions of Sicilian labor militancy could be carried to the New World, then New York City seemed an even more likely place for successful transplantation than Tampa. Artisans traveled permanently in large numbers to the New York area; so did half of Sambuca's early Socialist activists. The migrants arriving in New York enjoyed firm ties to homeland militants, through shared occupation and kinship. Furthermore, New York itself seemed to offer an environment conducive to the growth of an Italian-American labor movement. In New York's high-density housing, Italian immigrants tended to live in relatively homogeneous enclaves.[23]

Figure 7.1

Estimated Population of Sambucesi in New York, 1880–1935

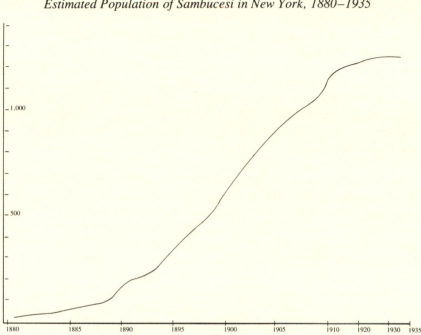

Many of the trades and some of the industries that employed Italians supported trade unions prior to Sicilians' arrival. Many more industries entered the ranks of the American labor movement during the years of mass Sicilian immigration.[24] Finally, New York early became one of the most important centers of Italian-American radicalism in the United States, providing newly arrived and provincial militants with a ready and relatively visible reference point in their new homes.[25]

Yet Sicilian radicals in New York remained at best an important minority. They did not shape the ethnic community, as they did in Tampa. They maintained a visible presence, but never established hegemony in the immigrant community. The transplantation of Sicilian traditions of labor militancy to New York must be judged at best a moderate success. No one single factor satisfactorily explains this. Three related variables can be mentioned as especially important: the position of independent craftsmen/small businessmen in the immigrant community, their educational aspirations, and their relations to the wage earners of the community. In all these respects, Brooklyn's Sicilians differed from Tampa's.

With time, more Sambucesi lived in the New York area than in any other city or region in the United States. Figure 7.1 outlines my estimates of the number of migrants from Sambuca living in New York in 1880–1935. Most Sambucesi who came to New York remained in the metropolitan area: relatively few (under 10 percent) came to New York after living first in some other American city. And comparatively few returned to Sambuca.

The New York area is, of course, a sizable one, and it is unlikely that all Sambucesi migrating there arrived as parts of one single migration chain. Migrants from Sambuca headed for distinct neighborhoods, not simply to New York. For many years, in fact, little evidence suggests that Sambucesi in New York formed a community rooted in any particular neighborhood at all.

In the 1880s, the small number of Sambucesi who could be traced to specific addresses in American or Sicilian sources lived mainly in lower Manhattan or Brooklyn: two in Brooklyn's Navy Yard/Fort Greene neighborhoods, three in Red Hook, and three on the Lower East Side or the Fourteenth Ward Little Italy in Manhattan.[26] (See map 7.1 for the New York area and the location of neighborhoods preferred by Sambuca's migrants.) All the Sambucesi living in Brooklyn in the 1880s were artisans: several shoemakers, a musician (whose father was a peasant, but whose mother was the illegitimate daughter of a civile gentleman), a stonecutter, and a carpenter. Half of Sambuca's migrants in Manhattan, by contrast, were of peasant background.

As migration from Sambuca to New York increased in the 1890s, migrants from the town scattered even more widely. No more than 18 percent of the fifty Sambucesi located in U.S. sources during this decade lived in any one Brooklyn neighborhood. Sambucesi made their homes all over northern Brooklyn (Navy Yard, Fort Greene, Bedford-Stuyvesant, Greenpoint, Williamsburg, and Bushwick), in South Brooklyn (Red Hook, Park Slope), in Manhattan (Elizabeth Street, East Harlem, the Lower East Side) and in Hoboken, New Jersey. Almost all these migrants came from artisanal families; most worked at trades and small businesses in New York, and in most cases, these were trades the migrants had learned in Sicily. Shoemakers and barbers formed the largest group, although carpenters, bakers, iron workers, musicians, grocers, stonecutters, and painters were also represented. The only traceable migrant of peasant background lived in Manhattan's Little Italy. (City directories rarely listed laborers in the 1890s.)

This dispersed pattern of settlement did not change much after 1900. In the years between 1900 and 1908 Brownsville/East New York housed the largest group of Sambucesi, about one quarter of the total traceable in U.S. records. Migration to other neighborhoods also increased. And the patterns of the past continued: migrants of artisanal backgrounds preferred Brooklyn and New Jersey (although there, they now traveled further to Union City, Newark, and Elizabeth), while the smaller number of peasant migrants from Sambuca settled in Little Italy in Manhattan.

Obviously, migrants from this town did not form a densely clustered Little Sambuca immediately upon their arrival. They did, however, live in neighborhoods of the city which were attracting other Sicilians and Italians. In fact, the early migrants seemed well connected to Sicilians from outside their town: most

Map 7.1

New York Area, Showing Neighborhoods Preferred by Sambucesi

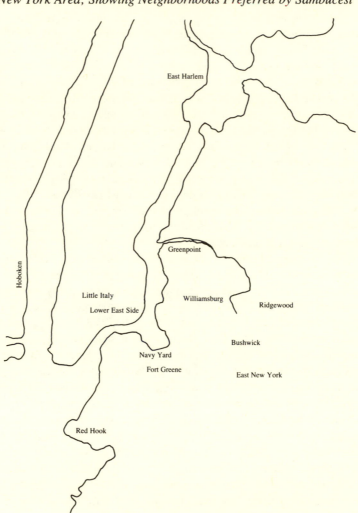

of the American marriages reported to Sambuca's city clerk were with non-Sambucesi.

Sambuca's early migrants scattered because most of them had come to the United States seeking markets for their artisanal and entrepreneurial skills. Unlike fish or produce peddlers, who settled in distinctive market areas, Sambuca's bakers, cabinetmakers, barbers, or shoe repairmen could not have plied their trades or wares successfully had they all settled together. In this respect, artisanal migrants from Sambuca resembled, on a smaller scale, the German Jewish migrants of the nineteenth century, who had also dispersed in search of markets.[27]

Artisans from Sambuca seem, nevertheless, to have formed a community, even if it was without a clear geographical center. By 1889, they had organized a religious confraternity, which celebrated the festival day of Sambuca's patron saint, Maria dell'Udienza. (Whether this should be considered a religious organization is unclear: typical of anticlerical artisans, these early migrants often omitted religious ceremonies when they married, sending back to Sambuca copies of New York City marriage licenses instead.) The festival was held in the Fort Greene area, but the male organizers of the festival included artisans living in several different Brooklyn neighborhoods.[28] Unlike their peers in Sambuca, the shoemakers, carpenters, and barbers of Brooklyn did not experiment with organizations newly popular in Sicily (the mutual benefit societies) but returned instead to an older artisanal form of voluntary association.

One can only speculate about their reasons for doing so. In Sambuca, artisans had organized in the early 1880s, at about the time that their peers began migrating to New York, and just as some artisans became voters. The joining together in mutual aid in Sambuca had been political; artisans attempted to address their status grievances in an elite-dominated local government. Perhaps migration had eliminated these motives for pursuing mutual aid. As recently migrated aliens, Sambuca's artisans did not feel themselves to be potential actors in local Brooklyn politics. Furthermore, the source of many artisanal grievances—the civili—were nowhere to be found in Brooklyn in the 1880s and 1890s.

In other respects, however, early Italian voluntary association in New York followed Sicilian patterns more closely. Edwin Fenton has catalogued early mutual benefit societies formed by Italian migrants in a number of American cities, including New York. Most were associations of skilled or semiskilled workers, and many were founded by socialists (from northern Italy, according to Fenton).[29] Fenton did not note whether groups like the New York City Barbers or Shoe Workers (founded 1883 and 1886, respectively) or the Pastry Cooks (1882), Masons (1886), Musicians (1891), or Woodworkers (1896) admitted both independent craftsmen and wage earners, but in Sicily, where such societies became common around 1880, that had often been the case. It seems unlikely that early Italian mutual benefit societies like these had no ties at all to the American labor movement, since sizable Knights of Labor and (in the 1890s) American Federation of Labor unions grew in most of the trades where Italian workers were well represented. By 1891, to give only one example, 5,600 of New York's 7,000 carpenters belonged to a union, and Italians were among them.[30] A somewhat different offshoot of Old World experience was the organization by Brooklyn's Sicilians of the "Fasci Siciliani," a group about which little is known.

By the years around 1910, when their numbers had reached almost 1,000, migrants from Sambuca had begun to cluster more noticeably. Over a third of the

200 migrants located in American sources for 1909–1913 lived in Williamsburg, in north Brooklyn. Fifteen percent lived in adjoining Bushwick, and another 10 percent in Greenpoint, which also bordered on Williamsburg. Williamsburg and Bushwick grew as peasants from Sambuca arrived in ever larger numbers after 1905. In Bedford-Stuyvesant and Greenpoint, by contrast, more of Sambuca's migrants came from artisanal families. This Little Sambuca, it is important to note, was shared with many other west Sicilians, a sprinkling of Calabrians, and, in parts of Bushwick and nearby Bedford-Stuyvesant, with Russian Jews, Poles, and Germans.[31] Sambucesi during this period became less likely to marry migrants from other villages, but when they did marry out, they almost always chose Sicilian spouses. Only two young men of artisan origin departed flamboyantly from this pattern—one by marrying a woman born in North Dakota and the other by choosing a Jamaican woman as his bride.

Although Brooklyn prided itself on being "the city of homes," it had also become a major industrial city by this period.[32] It was probably the industries of Williamsburg and Bushwick that attracted Sambucesi to Little Sambuca. Williamsburg alone claimed almost a third of the garment and shoe factories of Brooklyn; in addition, small furniture and piano factories, metal shops, and bakeries dotted the area. A mix of industries and residences (small tenements, converted private homes, and occasional single-family houses) could be found, if not on every block, then within any neighborhood.[33] Brooklyn's housing, however, was generally superior to that of Lower Manhattan: lower in density, newer, and less expensive.

Socially, the population of Little Sambuca differed considerably from that of a Manhattan Italian neighborhood like Little Italy in the Fourteenth Ward. For one thing, migrants from Sambuca usually shared their block (although not always their tenements) with immigrants from a variety of backgrounds. Boardinghouses scarcely existed; nor was boarding or the doubling up of families as common in Little Sambuca (under 15 percent of all households) as in Manhattan's Little Italy at this time (40 percent).[34] Overall, the residents of Little Sambuca in 1910, at the time of the federal census, were older and longer resident in the United States than those in Manhattan. At first glance, then, Little Sambuca resembled an area of second settlement, although the evidence does not suggest that this actually was the case. (I found, for example, not one case of a migrant settling first in Manhattan before moving to Little Sambuca.)

Because the Sambucesi who migrated to Brooklyn often had come to the United States with skills, the occupational distribution of Sambuca migrants both in Little Sambuca and in Brooklyn as a whole little resembled New York's general population of immigrant Italian workers or the communities founded by their fellow villagers in Chicago or Rockford. Table 7.1 summarizes the work experiences of male and female migrants from Sambuca in 1900–1913.[35] Only about 10 percent of the men worked as laborers. (By contrast, almost half of male Italians living on

Table 7.1

Occupations of Sambucesi in Brooklyn, 1909–1913

	Men	Women
Laborers	10%	—
Semiskilled shop and factory employees	19	82%
Proprietors, small shops and stores	57	5
Lower white collar	4	13
Business and professional	10	—
	N = 188	N = 62

Elizabeth Street, the Sicilian street in Manhattan's Little Italy in 1905, did this kind of work, and the proportions of New York's Italians as a whole were not much different.[36]) Less than a quarter of the men earned wages in shoe and garment factories, in metal- and woodworking shops, and in barbershops, while over half ran small and independent craft shops (mainly as barbers or shoe repairers), or they operated small stores (selling shoes, groceries, dry goods, musical instruments, and so on). Almost 15 percent of Sambuca's male migrants circa 1910 worked as clerks, professionals, or substantial businessmen (real estate and insurance brokers, macaroni manufacturers, a flour merchant and importer, a banker, etc.) On Elizabeth Street in Manhattan, the comparable figure was only 3 percent.[37]

Women migrants from Sambuca more nearly approached the general New York pattern for South Italian employment. They worked less frequently than their husbands and brothers, and when they did work for wages, they concentrated heavily in the garment industry. Women from Sambuca probably could take up the more skilled aspects of garment work when they arrived in New York (tailoring, sewing seams, finishing, buttonholes) since many had worked in Sambuca as seamstresses or ladies' tailors or had mothers who had done similar work there.[38] Furthermore, women's employment among Sambucesi was just as completely limited to garment making as it was among New York's general South Italian population. (Ninety-four percent of employed women on Elizabeth Street worked in the garment industry.) Two midwives and three independent dressmakers, as well as thirteen female white-collar workers (mainly bookkeepers, clerks, and saleswomen) appeared in households originating in Sambuca. Female workers like these were almost unknown in Manhattan's Little Italy.[39]

The occupational distribution of Sambucesi more closely resembled that of New York's Jews in 1910 (or Chicago's Germans in the 1880s) than it did that of their Italian conationals in the city or in the United States as a whole. In general, Brooklyn seemed to attract skilled South Italians both directly from Italy and from other parts of the New York region. Skilled and entrepreneurial workers were over-represented in Brooklyn in 1905.[40]

The Sambucesi who made their homes in Little Sambuca were less skilled than their fellow villagers elsewhere in Brooklyn. A somewhat higher percentage were of peasant background, and considerably more (almost 50 percent of those in Bushwick and Williamsburg, for example) earned wages as factory operatives. By contrast, white-collar workers and professionals from Sambuca were particularly likely to live outside Little Sambuca, even in 1910.

The Sambucesi of Brooklyn formed a migrant community unique in its class dynamics; their differences from the Sambucesi of Chicago, Rockford, and even Tampa are obvious. For one thing, Brooklyn, unlike any other American settlement of Sambucesi, attracted a small group of Sambuca's elite. The importance of commerce and trade in New York City's economy also undoubtedly encouraged the early move of skilled Sambucesi and their children into white-collar and professional work. Finally, in Brooklyn—again, unlike any of Sambuca's other settlements in the United States—migrant entrepreneurs sometimes directly employed other migrants, usually of peasant background, as wage earners. Briefly put, class divisions in Little Sambuca were less marked than in Chicago, but considerably more complex and pronounced than in Rockford, Tampa, or Louisiana. Furthermore, potentially divisive class tensions were not mediated by patron/client ties (as in Chicago), nor were they always assuaged by ties of kinship between wage earners and small businessmen (as in Tampa).

Although Sambuca's elite migrated late and in small numbers, they almost always headed for Brooklyn, where they ultimately became 9 percent of the Sambucesi living there. Data on twelve civile families from Sambuca living in Brooklyn around 1910 suggest why relatively few substantial landowners migrated to the United States: too few could expect to benefit from Old World privileges once there. One elderly gentleman from a family of wealthy landowners found himself living in a Williamsburg tenement apartment, supported by a wife who finished pants at home and children who worked in garment and shoe factories. A son of a civile family in Sambuca became a junk man in Brooklyn; another earned wages in a barbershop. Migrants with a profession fared somewhat better: two pharmacists from Sambuca pursued their work in Park Slope and South Brooklyn; two physicians from the town served immigrants in Williamsburg, as did a civile jeweler/watchmaker. In addition, a few enterprising men from elite families founded businesses oriented toward immigrant needs and purchases: three sold life insurance and sewing machines, and one operated a small factory manufacturing cheap parlor furniture.

Clearly, no civile migrant easily assumed his accustomed position of power over his fellow migrants or enjoyed the prestige he had in his hometown. At best, he could hope to sell humbler migrants a service or a product; at worst, he became occupationally indistinguishable from former artisans and peasants, undoubtedly a painful experience for a status-conscious Sicilian. This small group of civile migrants did not exist in Tampa; neither were they the equivalents of Chicago's bosses, with their considerable influence as labor and political brokers. Brooklyn's civili lacked economic clout; they saw their status slipping away; their effort to assume their accustomed position as leaders of their community proved difficult. I will argue that their efforts contributed to the considerable social fragmentation that came to characterize Brooklyn's Sicilian communities.

Unlike the Sicilian in Tampa, a town with a primarily industrial economy, a migrant in Brooklyn seemed to imagine more for his children's future than taking over and continuing the family business. In 1910, almost half of the sons of migrant Sambucesi were still in school at age 16. Daughters, too, were far more likely to be in school in Sambuca's families than in South Italian households in New York City as a whole.[41]

Every one of the young men and women working in lower white-collar positions in 1910 had fathers of artisanal or petty-merchant backgrounds, most of whom had become small businessmen in Brooklyn. Typical was the B. family, headed by a shoe repairman with his own shop in downtown Brooklyn. B.'s oldest son was a barber. His second child, a daughter, worked as a saleswoman in a dry-goods store, while his younger son clerked in an office. Somewhat more successful was the R. family; R. himself operated a macaroni store (his parents in Sambuca had been *pastai*, too). In 1910, R.'s oldest son worked as an electrician—he would later become a general contractor. Two younger sons were studying: one would later go to law school, and the other was preparing to become an architect. A fourth son, also in high school, worked as an operator in a moving-picture show. While oldest sons or daughters frequently became wage earners, younger sons and daughters trained for white-collar work, in a pattern more usually associated with Williamsburg's Russian Jews than with South Italian migrants. This pattern is not surprising, however, given the background of Sambucesi in Brooklyn or the occupational dynamics in Sambuca, where a jealous elite had monopolized higher education, white-collar work (primarily in municipal offices), and the free professions.

Finally, Brooklyn's Sambucesi, like those in Tampa, included both industrial wage earners and small businessmen. The children of Brooklyn's small businessmen rarely worked in their fathers' shops and stores. Shops were simply too small to justify the practice. Instead, many children became wage earners, as they had in Tampa, to provide capital for their fathers' businesses or for their own future enterprises. In most, cases wage earners probably shored up marginally profitable shops with their wages, guaranteeing fathers the independence that Sicilian artisans valued. Most oldest sons and daughters from small-business families became wage earners, often in an industry connected to their fathers' trades. Typical were the families of shoe repairmen B., whose sons in 1910 worked in woodworking and garment shops and in a shoe factory; shoe repairmen C., whose daughter was a saleswoman in a dry-goods store and whose sons incuded a journeyman barber and an office clerk; and carpenter V., who had among his older children an independent shoe repairman, a daughter sewing shortwaists in a garment factory, and a son earning wages in a shoe factory. Fathers who were shoe repairmen especially seemed to view wage earning in the shoe factories of Bushwick and Williamsburg as a kind of apprenticeship.

Unlike the wives of Tampa's Sicilian small businessmen, the wives of Brooklyn's barbers, shoe repairmen, and grocers rarely reported wage earning or occupations to census takers. This may have reflected only the census takers' unwillingness to consider seasonal work at home in garment production an occupation worth mentioning. Wives of grocers are always called housewives in Brooklyn census listings, yet it would be absurd to conclude that none of these women worked in their husbands' stores, especially since store and home usually adjoined. (Only 10 percent of the small businesmen of Little Sambuca worked at an address different from their residence, according to city directories.)

Unlike Tampa, however, New York's small proprietors and wage earners were not always linked by close family ties. Arriving in Brooklyn in ever greater numbers after 1900, and becoming the majority of all new arrivals by 1910, Sambucesi of peasant background more often became laborers and factory workers than did the migrants of artisanal backgrounds or their children. For this reason, as noted above, laborers and factory workers tended to concentrate in Little Sambuca, a neighborhood offering many jobs of this type. This means that Little Sambuca replicated in new ways some of the class divisions that had separated peasant from artisan in the hometown.

The institution that would eventually divide Little Sambuca and other immigrant communities most sharply was the barbershop. This was an important Italian small business, and a significant employer of Italian wage earners.[42] Master and journeymen barbers together made up almost 30 percent of the male Sambucesi working in Brooklyn in 1910, and this proportion may not have been atypical for Brooklyn as a whole. Barbering was the trade most readily open to Sambuca's peasant migrants if they attempted to leave behind unskilled labor or the shoe, garment, and metal factories of Brooklyn. Independent barber schools trained barbers quickly and in great numbers.[43] By contrast, master barbers with independent shops seemed not to encourage their own sons to follow in their trade. Only one of roughly thirty master barbers from Sambuca in 1910 had a son also working as a barber. Becoming a barber often meant working for an Italian, but it rarely entailed work for one's own father or in a family-oriented shop. The potential for class conflict within the immigrant community, hardly imaginable in Tampa, was quite real in New York City.

Social and structural patterns like these had a perceptible, if perhaps not determining, impact on the transplantation of Sicilian labor traditions to Brooklyn. One intriguing example is the rather belated development of village-based mutual benefit societies in Brooklyn. In cotrast to Chicago, where village-based societies organized by padroni appeared immediately, mutual aid societies based on shared village origins developed in Brooklyn only after fifteen to twenty-five years of migration from the home towns, usually between 1900 and 1910. Migrants from over half of the towns in the west Sicilian province of Agrigento and from three-quarters of the towns in Trapani province formed village-based mutual benefit societies during these years.[44]

In this respect, migrants from Sambuca were typical. In 1904, men from the town organized Concordia, a society with club rooms on Myrtle Avenue. The society provided medical services (through contract with a doctor), a place for meetings, burial insurance, and a yearly banquet or celebration (usually in May, which is the time of the Maria dell'Udienza festival in Sambuca.)[45] However common village-based societies like Concordia became in Italian immigrant communities, their belated organization requires some explanation. Sambucesi had lived in Brooklyn for almost twenty-five years without seeming to need a *paese* society. Since no written records of Concordia survive, the reasons for its establishment in the twentieth century must remain, in part, conjecture.

Migrants from Sambuca organized Concordia at a time of considerable change in their settlement. As Figure 7.1 reveals, the number of migrants arriving from Sambuca increased rapidly in the years after 1900; for the first time, significant numbers of peasants and gentry landowners were among them. So were four of Sambuca's Socialist founding fathers. Also during these years, a geographically centered community, Little Sambuca, developed. These changes may provide some clues to the emergence of mutual aid among Sambucesi in Brooklyn.

Significantly, Concordia opened its club rooms in Little Sambuca. This alone suggests that the emigrated Socialists did not provide the moving force for its organization: those four men were all scattered elsewhere in Brooklyn. (Thirty years later, when published information about Concordia became available, the Socialists and their sons did not number among the leadership of the group.)[46]

Instead, Concordia may have appealed to the many peasants arriving in Little Sambuca from 1900 to 1909. But another explanation is also possible. Newly arrived civile professionals and aspiring businessmen undoubtedly viewed a village-based mutual aid society as a means to establishing their leadership and ensuring their livelihood in Little Sambuca, even if they did not always live there themselves. Such men served as the "social doctors" for mutual aid societies; they also sold the insurance which the mutual aid societies provided. Furthermore, their primary allies in organizing Concordia seem not to have been recently arrived peasants but rather small businessmen of artisanal background. That, at least, is what the leadership of Concordia thirty years later suggests: of twenty-two men of known background, nineteen were of artisanal background and two had civile fathers.

Concordia appears to have been apolitical from its establishment, which made it quite different from the mutual aid societies founded by artisans in Sambuca. In this respect, too, it was typical of many of the mutual aid societies formed in Brooklyn in the early twentieth century.[47] The local political quarrels that had divided civili from artisans seem to have become irrelevant in Brooklyn, especially as many civili fell occupationally, and as artisan sons and daughters began entering white-collar work and the professions. (A surprising number of these younger Sambucesi, it is interesting to note, became salesmen of life insurance.) Unfortunately, scanty documentation does not reveal anything about the relations of civili or artisans to the growing population of peasants and wage earners in Concordia. Since the membership of the club peaked at about 400 (well under half of the Sambucesi living in the New York area by the 1920s), it is possible that peasants never joined the society in large numbers. Certainly, they did not appear among its leaders in the 1930s, when only one activist was of peasant background. The problems of former peasants, either as illiterate migrants or as industrial wage earners, may never have been a matter of concern for Concordia. If this is so, then mutual aid separated artisan from peasant and broke a connection which in Sicily had been essential for the development of labor militancy.

Not all mutual benefit societies founded by Sicilians in the early twentieth century remained completely apolitical or distant from the labor movement. In fact, political quarrels often divided fellow villagers into several mutual benefit societies.[48] Immigrants from a number of militant towns in the province of Trapani organized two or more societies, and the names of the competing groups suggested the divisions among them. Migrants from Marsala, for example, could join "Liberty and Labor" (a labor-oriented group), "The United Brothers of Marsala," or the "Marsala Civic Association." (After the rise of Mussolini, migrants from this town formed two additional societies.)[49] Personal quarrels and factionalism also frequently divided fellow villagers in their mutual aid societies.

Labor activists in the twentieth century repeatedly discussed the desirability of "boring from within" by working with the mutual aid societies. The brothers of several Socialists from Sambuca joined Concordia, without apparent result, as did Giovanni Vaccaro when he left Tampa for Brooklyn and anti-Fascist activism there in the 1920s. One cynic observed that the radicals before World War I limited their organizing efforts to yelling "'long live the workers' revolution' . . . shortly after having danced with the patroness" (the queen of the yearly ball).[50] Syndicalists generally rejected the mutual aid societies as too narrowly patriotic and too dominated by aspiring elite immigrants, the prominenti. Social democrats seemed somewhat more sympathetic, although no more successful with a strategy of boring from within. As a result, only a small group of mutual aid societies in Brooklyn, in great contrast to Tampa, considered themselves firmly within the labor movement.[51]

Overall, Brooklyn's immigrant labor movement developed independent of the mutual aid societies. Drawing on the same mixture of industrial wage earners and small businessmen as in Tampa, Brooklyn's radicals were nevertheless more sharply divided. Conflicts between Socialists and syndicalists marked the critical ten years between 1905 and 1915. A vaguely defined group of immigrant free-thinkers and anarchists often attempted to bridge the gap between the two, but for much of this ten-year period autonomous radical societies and migrant activists dedicated to organization and action in the workplace went their separate ways, while carrying on a bitter war of words. The newspaper *Il Proletario* clearly points to the Little Sambuca area in Bushwick and Williamsburg, with its heavy repre-sentation of wage earners in shoe and garment factories, as one of the most active of Brooklyn's Italian neighborhoods in the years before World War I. A look at its radicals offers insight into the complex relations of small shopkeepers and factory wage earners during the period.

Founded sometime in the early twentieth century, the Williamsburg Socialist circle undoubtedly provided continuity from Old World to New for recently arrived Sicilians, especially those of artisanal backgrounds.[52] The group drew membership from all over North Brooklyn, and at least one of its members was a shoe repairman from Sambuca. Whether or not independent craftsmen like him dominated the group is not clear, although its program suggests this was the case. Like Socialist circles in Sicily, the Williamsburg group offered meeting rooms, and thus a social alternative to the mutual aid societies; its headquarters was in Greenpoint.[53] It also opened a workers' school which, following American cus-toms, was called a Socialist Sunday School. Its home was in Bedford-Stuy-vesant.[54] While *Il Proletario* regularly carried notices of the group's meetings, little evidence exists that these Socialists considered themselves syndicalists or trade unionists, or that they agitated in industrial workplaces. (*Il Proletario* carried notices of such initiatives in Manhattan, but not in Brooklyn.) Neither did the Socialist circle become involved during this period in electoral politics, even though reformers in Sicily's Socialist circles had often done so. If Sambuca's small businessmen were typical of the membership of Williamsburg's Socialist circle, the reason for this is obvious: relatively few became citizens. Only one in three of Sambuca's long-time U.S. residents had become naturalized by 1910.

Closer to the heart of north Brooklyn's network of Sicilian radicals was Club Avanti, located at 202–204 Bushwick Avenue. Founded by free-thinkers, Club Avanti offered a broad program, although scarcely one focused on organizing wage earners in their workplaces. Like the Socialist circle, it supported education, sponsoring lectures on peace, religion, and sexual and family questions, on wo-men's emancipation, nationalism, imperialism, major immigrant strikes, the Mex-ican revolution, the problems of political prisoners in Italy, and, more generally, current events.[55] It gave classes in Italian, the natural sciences, and "social questions." Club Avanti also published a small newspaper, *La Luce*, probably named after a journal written by Bakuninists in Sicily's Agrigento Province in the 1870s.

Club Avanti attempted to build a family-centered alternative culture which linked Italians to other immigrant groups in the neighborhood.[56] While all of its regular activists were men (and artisan family names common in Sambuca appeared repeatedly in its programs), women occasionally attended lectures and, on a handful of occasions, presented talks. The club organized a yearly harvest festival and occasional family entertainment evenings with films, lectures, and dancing. It also sponsored a theatrical group—the "subversives' philodramatic." Finally, it sponsored various protests, from gathering money for strikers to attempting to lower rents; frequently it acted in conjunction with Spanish-speaking and Jewish groups in the neighborhood.[57]

Only with the organization of the I.W.W. did workplace agitation increase in Brooklyn. This occurred at about the same time that large numbers of peasants began arriving from Sambuca in Brooklyn. From 1905 onward, I.W.W. supporters began to work actively in the area that included Little Sambuca. According to *Il Proletario* reports, these early supporters seem to have been men employed in Brooklyn's shoe factories, where short strikes occurred repeatedly during 1905–1909.[58] Some of Brooklyn's Italian Wobblies probably had participated in the Williamsburg Socialist circle, for in 1911, during a major but factionalized strike of shoe-factory employees, syndicalist dissidents withdrew from the circle to form their own group (in Bushwick)—the Industrial Workers' Club.[59] Differing work experiences of small-businessmen fathers and wage-earning sons probably fed this conflict, which was in part a generational one. In fact, the key organizer of the dissidents seems to have been the son of one of the reform leaders, a man who remained active all his life in the Socialist Party.[60] But not all wage earners in Bushwick had small-businessmen fathers, as we have seen. The conflict between Socialists and syndicalists, which in Sicily took on urban/rural dimensions, in Brooklyn reflected class divisions between migrants of artisanal and peasant background in communities like Little Sambuca.

Throughout this crisis, Club Avanti functioned as a mediator and supporter of united-front coalitions among immigrant radicals of all stripes. Responding to an earlier local conflict, the club's correspondent had reminded readers that "here, there is no majority or minority, no six and three; we exist, united in one fascio, to change society and make it better for the malnourished, the beggars, and the nationless."[61] In 1911, Club Avanti stubbornly continued its policy of broadmindedness. It opened its doors to reformers and to syndicalists, attempted a reconciliation meeting, which failed, and persisted in supporting the subsequent protest activities and financial appeals of both groups.[62] The club, like Tampa's radicals (and like Sicilians in the 1890s) tolerated considerable diversity—and even contradictions—among its supporters. From 1905 onward, its easy-going attitude toward ideological and strategy disagreements was useful, because conflicts between reformers and revolutionary or syndicalist Socialists increasingly threatened to destroy the national Italian Socialist Federation and most local networks of rdicals as well.[63]

The differing organizational histories of immigrant shoemakers, garment workers, and barbers suggest much about the origins of reformer/syndicalist splits and accommodations in communities of factory wage earners and independent craftsmen like Little Sambuca. Clearly, wage earners had the greater incentive to move beyond mutual aid or radical educational initiatives to unionize and confront their employers. It is also quite easy to understand the anger and frustration that many young men must have felt toward reformers' apparent disinterest in workplace action: many of these men had learned the language of class struggle from their Socialist fathers, but they found the I.W.W. more appealing than either the Williamsburg Socialist circle or the trade unions of the American Federation of Labor. At the same time, only a few independent craftsmen or reform-minded Socialists had any material reason for ignoring or opposing wage earners' efforts for very long. Family ties still linked considerable numbers of small craftsmen and wage earners in Brooklyn, as in Tampa, so that both groups could expect to benefit from the unionization of factory employees. In Brooklyn, as in Tampa, many Socialist artisans from Sicily must have come to appreciate the principle of trade unionism only after arriving in the United States.

As one might expect, the barbershop threw conflicts between wage earners and small businessmen, between fathers and sons, and between those of artisanal and peasant background into the sharpest relief. The 1913 strike of 10,000 Brooklyn barbers proved the most divisive labor conflict immigrant Italian neighborhoods experienced before World War I, largely because both employers and employees came from the same communities. Members of the Italian Barbers Benevolent Society (which admitted both wage earners and small owner/operators), were pitted against each other.[64] The strike began as an I.W.W. initiative organized by Calabrian Leonard Frisina; in the course of the strike, Frisina and his followers enraged I.W.W. supporters by abandoning syndicalist principles to sign a contract. This, however, did little to repair relations between master and journeymen barbers.[65] Even Club Avanti reeled in the aftermath of this strike: its notices in *Il Proletario* disappeared for several months, and when the club broke its silence, it did so with a plaintive appeal: "Se si senta compagno, si faccia vivo" ("Those who are still our comrades, please show up.")[66]

In sharp contrast to the barbers, reform-minded independent tailors and shoe repairmen came to see the advantages of workplace activism, especially the unionization of shoe and garment factories. Brooklyn's shoe and garment workers struck without much initial help from the reform Socialists.[67] But I.L.G.W.U. and A.C. W.A. successes in the women's and men's garment industries followed quite quickly as reform-minded Socialist Jews and Italians turned their attentions to the workplace in 1909–1914.[68] A similar development occurred among shoe workers. Independent shoe repairmen organized a union in 1913; their union subsequently provided needed resources for organizing the largest and most successful strike of Brooklyn's factory shoe workers in 1919.[69] Italian immigrant syndicalists and reform Socialists continued to attack each other verbally in the years before World War I, and to pursue organization independently, but at least they were at work in the same fields by then.

One result of this tactical rapprochement among Italian radicals in New York was that Italian labor militants came temporarily within reach of assuming leadership of their communities in the years just before World War I—as they had done more than ten years earlier in Tampa. The Lawrence strike and the defense of Wobblies Ettor and Giovanitti drew support from scores of mutual benefit societies and Italian community institutions outside radical circles.[70] Radicals seemed well aware that emerging nationalist sentiment lay behind this change; they had been criticizing the rise of such sentiments—and blaming the prominenti for it—for several years.[71] They pressed their advantage, nevertheless, hoping to seize ethnic enthusiasm from prominenti hands and make it the basis for labor activism instead, as it had been in Tampa.[72] The radicals scored some successes; for example, the Sons of Italy by-laws, written in 1911, included strong support for trade unionism, promising to censure any member who scabbed.[73] But radicals' gains melted away as first World War I and then Mussolini changed Italian immigrant communities forever. The wartime isolation of the I.W.W. and the postwar Red Scare were felt in every Brooklyn community. In New York, probably more than in any other state, nativist sentiments fed the antiradicalism of the Red Scare, so that even relatively minor immigrant radical groups found themselves under investigation in the postwar years.[74]

The years following World War I exacerbated the organizational fragmentation and intracommunity conflicts that had characterized Brooklyn's Sicilian settlements since 1900. Like many immigrant enclaves, Little Sambuca did not persist indefinitely. By the early 1930s, when almost 100 families from Sambuca could be positively identified in city directories for Brooklyn, Manhattan, and Queens, less than a third lived in the Williamsburg/Bushwick/Greenpoint neighborhoods. Many Sambucesi living in Bushwick moved into nearby Ridgewood (Queens), a neighborhood that would attract a fresh wave of migrants from Sambuca after World War II.[75] In general, however, Sambucesi scattered in small family and kin groups, not as village chains. Thus, while brothers or parents and children still lived close together in the 1930s, Sambucesi lived all over western Long Island—from Long Island City to Bay Ridge, and from South Ozone Park to Whitestone.

By the 1930s, the Sambucesi of Brooklyn and Queens had changed jobs in predictable ways; the results of small businessmen eductating their sons and daughters were particularly obvious. Table 7.2 summarizes the available data. If anything, the community was more sharply divided than in the past between a growing group of white-collar, business, and professional workers (mainly of artisanal background) and a growing group of factory wage earners (mainly of peasant origin). Small business had declined in importance since 1910. Even more remarkable were changes in women's work. Daughters had easily made the transi-

Table 7.2
Occupations of Sambucesi in Brooklyn and Queens, 1933–1934

	Men	Women
Laborers	10%	—
Semiskilled shop and factory employees	38	29%
Proprietors, small shops and stores	32	7
Lower white collar	10	46
Business/professional	10	18
	N = 219	N = 28

tion from factory to office.[76] Teaching and, to a lesser extent, pharmacy and medicine had also attracted daughters of Sambuca's artisan families.

Factional quarrels between Fascists and anti-Fascists, declining interest in mutual benefit societies, and increased interest in American politics all marked organizational life in Brooklyn's Sicilian communities in the 1920s and 1930s. In a sense, quarrels between supporters and opponents of Mussolini simply replaced those between prominenti and radicals and between reformers and syndicalists fifteen to twenty years earlier. Of course, the participants in the new opposing factions had changed somewhat. Many prominenti, predictably, supported Mussolini, as did many nationalist and smaller mutual aid societies, including (for a time) the Sons of Italy, which had refused to enforce its anti-scab statute as early as 1917.[77] Opposition to Mussolini came from labor circles, of course, especially Italians in the A.C.W.A. and I.L.G.W.U., and from trade unionists associated with the Socialist Party, like Giovanni Vaccaro.[78] But considerable numbers of labor supporters also became enthusiasts of fascism, following the path of Mussolini himself from socialism to revolutionary syndicalism to nationalism and fascism. One prominent New York City Fascist had been an I.W.W. activist, and the Brooklyn mutual benefit society that was decorated by Mussolini for its support had been a syndicalist stronghold in 1905.[79] Neighborhoods of occupationally and socially mobile Italian small businessmen, white-collar workers, and professionals supported scores of Fascist groups, according to Gaetano Salvemini; there were three in Ridgewood alone.[80] This suggests that in Brooklyn many reform Socialists had also joined the ranks of Mussolini's Italian-American supporters during the 1920s.

At the same time that Mussolini's nationalism attracted wide support in the Sicilian communities of Brooklyn, younger Sicilians began turning their eyes away from Italian and toward American politics. Young men from Sambuca families rallied around Pietro Giambalvo, a young lawyer born in a town near Sambuca; Giambalvo's law offices adjoined Concordia's meeting room.[81] Throughout the early 1930s, many young American-educated lawyers of Sicilian descent began to build niches and careers for themselves in northern Brooklyn's Democratic Party.[82] *Il Corriere Siciliano*—Brooklyn's Sicilian newspaper—generally supported the Democrats, although for iconoclastic reasons. The New Deal drew most Italian votes in New York during this era, but in some sections of Brooklyn it was the Republican Party that attracted ambitious young Italian migrants like Giambalvo.[83] Men like these sponsored political clubs, which appeared in surprising numbers among New York Italians in the late 1920s and 1930s. One study of New York political clubs found 130 Italian clubs of which 110 were Democratic compared to only 31 clubs formed by Jews. This is not evidence that Italians were more politically active than Jews, but rather a clue to the small and personalistic nature of the Italian clubs, and of immigrant politics in general.[84] By contrast, in north Brooklyn only one Socialist candidate, an aging activist of the Williamsburg Socialist circle, continued to run for office in the early 1930s.[85]

Fascists, anti-Fascists, and Democrats tried unsuccessfully to influence or capture the loyalties of the only community institutions which had persisted from the pre-Fascist era—the mutual benefit societies. But most of these village-based societies remained adamantly apolitical. By the 1930s, they seemed less concerned with Italian or American politics than with their own survival: the children of the migrants and the younger generation in general showed little interest in the banquets feting new doctors or lawyers, or in the fixed traditions of speeches, patronesses, and toasts at annual balls.[86] Even the appearance of American musical groups like Barney's Virginians, the Original Bell Hop Entertainers, and the Georgia Rhythm Kings at balls failed to attract young Sambucesi, for example.[87] A few of the mutual benefit societies formed junior and women's auxiliaries in the hope of luring new members; the former attempted to begin scholarship funds to support young members, but both groups soon foundered.[88] Concordia finally closed the doors of its club rooms in 1934, although it continued to hold an annual ball for several more years.[89] Instead of participating in Concordia, Italian-Americans of Sambucese descent formed a number of smaller social and recreational clubs in their new neighborhoods–the Sambucese Forum, the Silver Knights Club, and the Fairmont Club.[90] A federation of Brooklyn's Sicilian mutual benefit societies, formed in 1932, never succeeded in finding a program that inspired members to action.[91] Eventually national organizations like the Sons of Italy or its anti-Fascist counterparts and Church-linked fraternals like the Knights of Columbus attracted the second generation.[92]

Thus while the personnel and issues had changed by the 1930s, the organizational life of Brooklyn's Sicilian communities remained contentious and fragmented. Artisans in Brooklyn, unlike those in Sambuca, found they could become *prominenti*; those who remained committed to labor traditions or who became trade unionists or syndicalists in the United States found themselves pitted against former artisanal colleagues and friends or relatives. Only in some cases, and then with some difficulty, could Brooklyn's small businessmen ally themselves long-term with industrial wage earners, as they did in Tampa or in Sicily's militant towns. Fascism and Americanization added further sources of fissure in the already cracked Sicilian communities of Brooklyn. Unity and harmony eluded Brooklyn's Sicilians in the 1930s as they had thirty years before.

Conclusion

The earliest studies of Italian migrants as workers emphasized that South Italians lacked both a native communal traditon of protest and experience with wage earning and modern, class-conscious labor movements. As a result they became, at worst, scabs, and at best, passive bystanders in urban industrial conflicts. While a few early studies, like those of Edward Fenton or Samuel Baily, clearly pointed out that South Italians could quickly become labor activists under specific conditions, this more positive view of Italian migrants never fully replaced the older more negative one.[93] Recently, students of Italian workers have countered the negative view with one of Italian migrants as preindustrial jacqueristes—rural people who brought with them into their American workplaces the communal protest traditions of moral economy, and tax and food riots. In a 1976 article that drew together most existing work on Italian immigrants as workers, Rudolph Vecoli summarized these two interpretations of Italians as "padrone slaves and primitive rebels."[94]

Is this a fair summary of the experiences of the Sambucesi described in the last two chapters, at work in cane fields, railroad and construction sites, cigar factories, shoe-repair and barbershops, grocery stores, shoe or garment factories, pharmacies, and butcher shops? Obviously, the Sambucesi who migrated to Louisiana, Rockford, Chicago, Tampa, and New York did include padrone slaves and primitive rebels among their numbers. What existing interpretations have underestimated, however, were the other items in migrants' cultural baggage— especially the deeply rooted traditions of voluntary associations with ties to the emerging labor movement, substantial experience with "modern" forms of labor protest, and a not inconsiderable commitment to class-conscious ideologies, especially among middle peasants and craftsmen from the Sicilian countryside. These more modern traditions of labor militancy could have been transplanted to the United States, but successful transplantation was the exceptional, not the typical result.

Cane harvesters in Louisiana and railroad or construction workers in Chicago seem the most likely candidates for the label padrone slaves, since these migrants actually found their way to the States or worked under the auspices of an immigrant labor agent. Yet it is hard to see their dependence on the labor agent as the most important source of a failed transplantation. Like the Italians in the early negative view, the peasants who migrated to Louisiana sometimes lacked much experience with modern politics, voluntary association, or labor protest, but they were intimately familiar with primitive rebellion. Their passivity in Louisiana was the result of isolation from the middle classes of their home communities and seasonal migratory labor. Their work almost never brought peasants into sustained contact with an American labor movement. (Similar types of harvesters organized in increasing numbers in Sicily after the 1890s, however, a clue that the context in which peasants worked significantly influenced their behavior as wage earners.) Chicago's Sicilians, on the other hand, cannot properly be classified as passive padrone slaves at all, even though the labor agent continued to operate far longer in Chicago than in the cane fields. Albeit in distinctive (and to many eyes, including my own, questionable) forms, the padrone slaves of Chicago became active trade unionists and regular voters in American elections, often years before their more politically "modern" and experienced artisan peers in Brooklyn.

Nor is it accurate or particularly revealing to characterize the Sicilian labor militants of Tampa and Brooklyn as primitive rebels. Such an interpretation ignores the European experience of the middle peasants and craftsmen of these settlements. Worse yet, it ignores or dismisses as trivial the small-scale and local yet remarkably persistent and widespread efforts of ideologically aware and committed individual labor militants. Such men were at work in most immigrant settlements that included any artisans—even, on occasion, when those artisans functioned as padroni. Particularly striking in the case studies examined in the last two chapters was the almost complete absence of female rioters in the United States; this was true even though women in the 1890s had become the primary bearers of Sicilian communal traditions of protest.[95] Italian women emerged briefly in both Tampa and Brooklyn as strikers and trade unionists, apparently with the support of their families; at least some women became involved in the work of groups like Club Avanti as well. The absence of female jacqueristes and the presence of Italian immigrant women on picket lines provide evidence of the passing of older traditions, not their transplantaion to the United States.

Obviously, communal traditions of protest did not simply disappear as Sicilians migrated to the United States, any more than they simply disappeared in Sicily. Tampa's cigar workers provide an excellent example of an immigrant community on strike.[96] The same was probably true of the Italian miners of southern Illinois. But in other settlements in the United States, Sicilians united as communities only with difficulty, whether on strike or not. Brooklyn provides the best example of how European backgrounds, selective migration patterns, and American workplaces interacted to create immigrant communities split by class tensions, conflicting ideologies, and alternative hopes for the future.

When immigrant workers confronted capitalism in the United States, they viewed their experiences through lenses colored by class dynamics in the Sicilian communities they knew best—those of the homeland and those of the immigrant settlement they had chosen in the United States. An immigrant Sicilian worker who thought about "the rich" or "the ruling class" might recall European experiences with an arrogant landlord, a more recent conflict with a banker or labor agent, or the peremptory dismissal of a work companion by a disliked Irish or American foreman. A radical paper like *Il Proletario* blasted immigrant prominenti (and of course the Church) with much the same vituperative language it reserved for American capitalists; in fact, it sometimes seemed more incensed by the former.[97] How Little Sambuca's lower-middle-class "elite" of Socialist small businessmen and white-collar workers in Brooklyn responded to such language, we do not know; we can only guess what the Socialist padroni of Rockford thought of such attacks. That prominenti sometimes protested that they, not Carlo Tresca or Joe Ettor, were "the real Socialists" is documented.[98] The position of these "real Socialists" is even understandable, given their European experiences. Immigration complicated migrants' understanding of class, and diminished the likelihood that a Marxist analysis of "rich and poor" would make immediate and intuitive sense to a migrant, as it sometimes had to Sicilians in the 1890s.

The consequences of class dynamics in immigrant settlements varied place to place. In Rockford, immigrant workers eventually participated in the labor movement, but only after a lengthy period of Americanization. In Chicago, the result was labor corruption. In Brooklyn, conflicts among several varieties of labor activists, new prominenti and their insurance societies, and Fascists actually prevented the formation of a unified community. Conflict undermined the very ethnic institutions that in cities like Tampa had been a necessary foundation for workplace militancy. Overall, there were many ways in which transplantation could fail; far fewer ways for it to succeed. In their political culture, many migrants must be considered uprooted, not transplanted.

Only where wage earners and lower-middle-class small businessmen and independent craftsmen lived together and in social harmony did Sicilian traditions take root and flourish in the United States. One-class communities of Sambucesi did not support a strong labor movement. In Louisiana, wage earners in 1900 seemed demobilized and without leadership or ties to homeland militants. In Brooklyn in the 1880s and 1890s, small businessmen from Sambuca reverted to a pattern of voluntary association quite unrelated to the workers' societies they had known in western Sicily. Tampa's small businessmen and cigar workers and Brooklyn's shoe repairmen and factory operatives provide the best examples of the two groups living close together and in relative social harmony. In both cases, family ties and needs unified lower-middle-class fathers and wage-earning wives, sons and daughters. In both cases, sending children into factories to earn wages was a temporary family strategy. And so was the labor militancy that resulted.

While it would be folly to underestimate the disastrous impact of the Red Scare and governmental repression on the Italian-American labor movements of Tampa and New York in the years after World War I, other factors obviously played a role, too. The abandonment of wage earning by immigrant artisans' children reproduced again in the New World the sharp status and financial distinction that had separated artisans and peasants in the Old World. Depression in industries typically providing employment for such children, the smearing of labor radicalism as unAmerican, the maturation of the second generation, and the nationalism awakened among immigrant elites before and after Mussolini cannot easily be separated to measure their independent influences. All helped guarantee that the labor militancy sprouting from Sicilian roots in some American cities became a passing phenomenon, forgotten, and often denied, by the children who had lived closest to it, in their fathers' houses.[99]

Finally, immigrant workers' perception that their European political experience was irrelevant must be mentioned as a critical hindrance to labor militants who hoped to build on Sicilian roots in the United States. This was especially the case for migrants from middling backgrounds, for whom local politics had frequently been the path to radicalization. The policies of the Italian nation-state and the taxes imposed by local government, as well as a general desire for the democratization of local and national governments, had driven such groups to labor militancy in Sicily. Unlike Sambuca's artisans, immigrants experienced class either as exploitation in the workplace, or as nativist scorn, or as resentment of lower-middle-class success; politics was an American arena. Migrants' contact with American politics usually remained quite limited for many years: most workers were not taxpayers or, outside of Chicago, voters. And, in any case, the United States already was a republic; even immigrants, once naturalized, were not excluded by birth from political privileges like voting. Many immigrant workers retained an initial interest in hometown politics, but radicals in the United States could put these interests to little use. One Sicilian correspondent from Chicago reported to *Il Proletario* about the defeat of Catholic activists in his hometown, only to be ridiculed by the editors for "wasting his time with such nonsense." He was instructed "to write of more important events." Not surprisingly, he stopped corresponding with the paper altogether.[100] The problem was not that this immigrant worker was narrow and provincial politically, but rather that neither he nor the radical journalists, who weekly proclaimed their internationalism, could see any clear connections between political struggles in peripheral and industrialized nations. The praxis of migration had far exceeded the radicals' theoretical understanding of class relations in an increasingly unified world economy.

Chapter 8
Rural Conflict in Sicily after 1900

Sicilians on both sides of the Atlantic remained linked through ties of kinship and friendship, but the experiences of the two groups diverged increasingly after the turn of the century. Of course, one can also point to some similarities. In both North America and in Sicily, more Sicilian laborers than in the past depended entirely on wages for their livelihood; proletarianization was a common experience, whether one remained in Sicily or left for the United States. So, too, enthusiasm for independent work continued to characterize both groups. Disagreements and conflicts between immigrant syndicalists and reform-minded Socialists also had parallels in Italy and in Sicily in the early years of the century.

Overall, however, it is the growing divergence of Sicilian immigrant experience that is most striking. Significant numbers of Sicilians in the United States became increasingly nationalistic in the years around World War I, while in Sicily, a regional separatist movement still enjoyed considerable support in the years after World War II. One could even plausibly argue that Mussolini enjoyed greater popularity in many Italian-American communities than he did in most Sicilian towns in the 1920s and 1930s. Finally, in the years after World War II, large numbers of Sicilians quickly recovered older labor traditions and turned to the parties of the left, while their relatives in the United States—Republicans, Democrats, and the unnaturalized—wrote letters to Sicily, warning kin against such dangerous behavior.[1]

Twentieth-century Italian history seems fragmented by a series of deep ruptures; Sicilians perceived many of these changes as imposed from the outside. Never in the twentieth century did Sicily regain a position center stage in national events such as it had in the 1890s: the important events and the sources of change—from Italy's sudden development into an industrial power to the end of free migration, the rise of fascism, Mussolini's fall, and the American invasion—originated "outside." Sicilians reacted to each, and with each reaction they broadened the cultural distance between themselves and their Sicilian-American kin, friends, and fellow villagers.

This chapter examines one measure of the distance that had separated the two groups by the 1950s, focusing again on the development of Sicilian red towns. The last chapters showed that traditions of Sicilian labor militancy rarely survived transplantation to the United States or, when transplantation occurred (as it did in New York or Tampa), that such traditions rarely persisted beyond World War I.

Those same traditions continued to evolve in Sicily, however, and ultimately survived mass emigrations, return migrations, Fascist government oppression, and American disapproval. How and why labor militants sometimes succeeded in Sicily—while they almost always failed in the United States—is the theme of this chapter.

Peak Migrations; New Rebellions

Emigration from western Sicily had climbed rapidly in the years after 1900, to equal migration from other South Italian provinces. Not only did emigration from towns with long histories of transatlantic migration increase, but towns previously untouched by migration fever also began losing residents for the first time. Emigration actually began after 1900 in one west Sicilian town in five; in another one in five emigration began again after a hiatus of ten to fifteen years.[2]

Chapter 4 demonstrated generally that this twentieth-century increase in emigration did not lead directly to a collapse in peasants' and workers' initiatives. In particular, the years 1901 to 1905 saw a rebirth of organization and activism at the local level. The countryside again became quiet between 1905–1919, as it had during other intervals in the past century. As in the past, too, this interval of peace ended in new rural revolts, which immediately preceded Mussolini's rise to power.

Many observers noted that the Sicilian rural protests of 1901–1905 lacked the fervor of the fasci revolts of the previous decade.[3] The Italian state did not even tremble during this period of unrest, and national leaders seemed more concerned with the growing rebelliousness of workers in Italy's expanding northern industries than with Sicilian protests. Still, it is worth exploring what observers meant by the lack of fervor during these years, for the Sicilian unrest of the early twentieth century did differ from the fasci revolts in important ways.

Gone, for example, were the tax protests, the mobs of women, the spontaneous destruction of property, and the land occupations of the previous decade.[4] Few deaths occurred, although arrests were common and private and public security forces were freely used. An orderly strike of sharecroppers—organized in peasant leagues or cooperatives—or a spontaneous strike of sulfur miners or transport workers was the typical form collective action took in 1905. Rural Socialist activists and Catholic priests organized cooperatives during these years; both groups succeeded in collectively leasing large wheat estates in several towns. Catholic and Socialist activists often competed for support in the same towns.[5] But their competition for a peasant following was often more apparent than real, since Socialists and Catholics tended to organize among somewhat different groups. Only in two towns, for example, did Catholic organization attract much support from miners. Catholic peasant leagues and cooperatives found more support among middle peasants, and this probably encouraged priests to experiment, as they did, with the foundation of Catholic rural credit associations. By contrast, Socialist cooperatives and leagues drew their members from the sharecroppers, especially in wheat towns. By 1907, peasants had organized eighteen cooperatives in Palermo (with 5,600 members), 13 cooperatives in Trapani (with 3,700 members), and 11 cooperatives in Girgenti (with 3,700 members).[6]

The spread of cooperation and various forms of Catholic and revolutionary syndicalism among Sicilian peasants belies any notion that Sicilians universally rejected collective action as they began to migrate in large numbers. In fact, more towns experienced strikes in the early years of the century than during the fasci revolts. The strike, viewed as an important means to improved working conditions, wages, or harvest division, was no longer restricted to sharecroppers and wage-earning harvesters on wheat estates. Strikes also became common in a wide range of wheat-exporting towns, especially where sharecropping on the small to medium-sized civile-owned plots dominated, and in large parts of Trapani where phylloxera had destroyed vines, rendering peasants again dependent on wheat crops. In a few cases, grape cultivators also struck for better contracts in 1900–1906.[7] Overall, strikes in distinctly noncapitalist workplaces had become commonplace. While the disappearance of the tax protest after 1894 lowered western Sicilian rates of protest, the strike nevertheless continued to grow in popularity among Sicily's cultivators.

Some evidence points to the possibility that both emigration and strikes became common strategies for peasants generally during these years, much as they had been for wheat-raising peasants in the 1890s. More than 50 percent of the west Sicilian towns where emigration began late (the "late-starters"; see Map 4.2) experienced strikes or other forms of labor unrest at this time. The evidence from Sambuca also suggests that the town's middle peasants—the group that in other towns became increasingly militant after 1900—also began migrating in large numbers after that date. After a last series of violent and unsuccessful strikes in Sicily's sulfer towns, miners, too, began emigrating to the United States, usually after 1905.[8]

While existing sources sketch Sicilian workplace activism at least in rough outline, the history of local politics and of the island's Socialist Party during these years is less well documented. Chapter 4 mentioned tensions between urban and artisan reformers and rural, often syndicalist, leaders like Bernardino Verro, Nicola Barbato, and Lorenzo Panepinto; these conflicts paralleled those in Brooklyn at least superficially. But there were important differences. Immigrant Italian reform Socialists rarely became actively involved in electoral politics in the United States; instead, many, like Sambuca's Giovanni Vaccaro in Tampa, turned more quickly to workplace activism than did their counterparts in Sicily. Furthermore, in Sicily no family ties linked generationally divided reformers and syndicalists as they often did in Brooklyn.

The changing constellation of political tendencies within Italy's Socialist Party after the 1890s was thus not precisely the same one found in immigrant communities like Tampa or Brooklyn. Unfortunately, only election data allow an (admittedly inadequate) glimpse into regional developments among Sicilian Socialists during these years.[9] After the broadening of the Italian franchise in 1882, the numbers of Sicilians voting reached a peak during and just after the fasci revolts. Even before the advent of the fasci, Napoleone Colajanni, a reformer interested in the social question, had gleaned one vote in ten in Girgenti and parts of the city of Palermo. After the fasci revolts, when fascio and Socialist activists sometimes gained local office, rural activists like Nicola Barbato and Bernardino Verro also enjoyed considerable support in regional elections—although their supporters came primarily from Palermo and not the countryside (where peasant rebels typically could not vote).

The repression of the fasci and increases in emigration during the 1890s and twentieth century led to a real decline in the size of Sicily's electorate. Even after the Italian state lifted restrictions on workers' organization after 1901, 10 to 20 percent fewer men voted in districts like Sciacca or Corleone. Peasant activism in the early years of the twentieth century did result in modest increases in rural Socialists' participation in the election of 1904. But the subsequent mafia murders of Verro, Panepinto, and others, the continued disenfranchisement of most Sicilian peasants, and the rural activists' inability to convince their urban comrades of the necessity of workplace initiatives, left Sicily's Socialist Party largely in the hands of urban reformers. Socialists like Tasca di Cutò or Aurelio Drago focused almost exclusively on building electoral support for the Party. They enjoyed some success, too, receiving 30 to 50 percent of the votes in some districts (including Sciacca, parts of Palermo, and Cefalù) in the elections of 1904 and 1909. As these results suggest, not all their supporters lived in big cities, but many probably were artisans and marginal members of the landowning elite.

The enfranchisement of most peasants in 1913 and 1919 did not immediately undermine the reformers' advantage. In 1913, reform and independent Socialists and social democrats earned clear majorities in several districts where they had long enjoyed support; they attracted voters in a number of new districts as well. Only in Calatafimi did the revolutionary Socialists (the "maximalists") draw significant support. Overall, in western Sicily in 1919, 11 to 12 percent of the vote went to reform Socialists, while about 5 percent went to the maximalists. The reformers grew in strength after World War I. Social democrats and Unitary Socialists together earned 44 percent of the Sicilian vote in 1924. Italy's Communist Party inherited maximalist supporters after the war, with 5 percent of the vote that year. Thus, while the numbers of Sicilians voting tripled after 1913, and significant proportions of new peasant voters did not vote at all, those who did vote gave their support to the urban reformers, not the revolutionaries.

The failure of poor peasants to vote in large numbers scarcely reflected their passivity; nor did peasant voters' apparent support for reform Socialists and social democrats signal any rejection of workplace activism. In the economic crisis that followed World War I, Sicilian peasants again struck and occupied lands, and in larger numbers than at any time since the 1890s. Organizations of veterans, Catholic or Socialist activists, and/or cooperatives led some of those who occupied the land. In other cases, groups like these worked mainly to incorporate spontaneous revolts into their own initiatives.[10] In a few cases the leaders "lost control" of the revolt; in Ribera, the result was "four days of Bolshevism."[11] No systematic study of the postwar revolts exists, so it is difficult to compare this period of unrest with earlier ones. Overall, it seems that the same towns that had experienced strikes in 1900–1905 again saw peasants marching—and this time with more fervor.[12] One study notes that peasant agitations were constant during 1920–1923 in the province of Agrigento, while in Trapani a broad spectrum of peasants rebelled, as they had in the 1890s.[13] Surprisingly, the revolts of the postwar period seemed to produce local-level gains for reformers in the early 1920s. Thus, while quarrels between maximalist and reform Socialist leaders intensified during these years, leading to the formation of Italy's Communist Party in 1921, ordinary peasant voters in Sicily's countryside seemed to see no contradiction in storming their workplaces while voting for Socialist reform of the state.

Sicilian women, too, re-emerged from the shadows as peasant activists in the years prior to and after World War I. In these years, as in the 1890s, women focused on different enemies—the state rather than employers. Spontaneous groups of women in wheat-raising and sulfur towns protested Italy's entrance into the war in 1915 and 1916. Only in rare cases did these protests originate with Socialist Party support. Newspaper accounts of the growing women's antiwar movement did highlight the existence of a local female Socialist Party section in one town, but whether this group had existed before the protests or whether it came into existence as Socialist men attempted to gain control of women's spontaneous protests is not known. (The women of this town, Piana degli Albanesi, formerly Piana dei Greci, had also protested spontaneously against taxes in the 1890s.) As the war continued, groups of women throughout western Sicily aimed their antiwar demonstrations at schools and schoolteachers—agents of the state whom they saw as violating mothers' wishes by inculcating children with militaristic and patriotic values.[14]

Even before the war ended, Sicilian women also joined together to protest in the marketplaces of many Sicilian towns. They demanded food, bread, and grain.[15] That food riots developed in Sicily in the twentieth century seems surprising, since such protests in Europe were usually associated with state formation and consolidation of national markets—events of the eighteenth and nineteenth centuries.[16] In most of Europe, too, food riots had been urban events. Food riots in grain-raising rural regions in Sicily point to the much diminished importance of subsistence production for peasants by the twentieth century.

The rise of fascism and Mussolini's ascent to power ended the postwar wave of

Sicilian unrest, just as it ended the rebellions that occurred all over Italy during these years.[17] Factory takeovers and red peasants in the Po Valley seemed far more threatening to Mussolini, and Italian nationalists generally in the 1920s, than did rebellious Sicilian peasants. The Sicilian rebellions failed to produce a strong Fascist backlash locally; Fascist attacks on Socialist Party, union, peasant league and cooperative offices occurred, but were relatively few, given the extensive protests of the period.[18] Sicilian landowners had no incentive to encourage or support Fascist reprisals in order to protect themselves or their property—mafia effectively served that purpose, murdering two well-known rural Socialist activists in the early years of World War I and several more in the early 1920s. Nor did Mussolini's subsequent antimafia campaign encourage Sicilian landowners to support him with enthusiasm. Regional loyalties also seem to have rendered Sicilian deaf to Mussolini's nationalist appeal. If anything, regional and separatist sentiments had grown among Sicilians since the 1890s.[19] Only in the United States, where Italian nationalism met distinctive immigrant needs, could Mussolini expect an enthusiastic audience among Sicilians.[20]

Had emigration shaped the political and workplace initiatives during these years? Electoral support for Socialists remained low but stable from 1890 to 1909; it increased suddenly and noticeably from 1913 to 1919. But it is impossible to know if declines in the Sicilian electorate during 1895–1904 reflected emigration or simply rural withdrawal from electoral politics during a period of state repressions; the two were obviously linked. Emigration almost certainly artificially lowered the proportions of peasants who voted in 1913 and 1919, but other factors must be mentioned, too. The failure of all groups of new voters to exercise their franchise is well documented, quite independent of mobility.[21]

Emigration seems most clearly responsible for the disappearance of the tax protest, once the most common protest form for artisans and middle peasants. It is very likely that emigration provided hard-pressed peasant marketers of grapes and citrus fruits with cash, either from remittances or as savings brought to Sicily by returning migrants. This cash could buy land or pay taxes. It is also likely that, as a result, enfranchised small-scale producers abandoned tax protests for electoral politics.

By contrast, emigration had almost no impact on the rhythm of workplace organization or protest among peasants. Peasants organized to demand contract and wage changes and improved access to land in increasing numbers, from the first agricultural mutual benefit societies of the 1880s to the league of Sicilian peasants founded in 1919. The incidence of strikes and land occupations, taken together, increased from the 1890s to the first decade of the twentieth century and remained steady in the years after World War I. Even the fourteen years of peace in the countryside (1905–1919) cannot easily be interpreted as the effective operation of the emigration safety valve. Such periods of peace had characterized the Sicilian countryside since the late eighteenth century. If anything, intervals between rural rebellions grew shorter during the peak years of emigration from Sicily.

In 1924, Sicilians were about to experience another decline in labor militancy. No new emigration surges occurred, for the United States effectively blocked mass emigration at about this time. Like some of the peaceful periods of the past, this one was imposed by the state, in the form of Mussolini's strong hand. As in the past, the state could count on assistance from cynical Sicilian collaborators, the ever-flexible and wealthy landowners.

Return Migration and Labor Militancy

Mobility in Sicily during the first twenty years of the twentieth century meant more than moving to America. It could also mean moving to a new Sicilian home or returning to an old one from the United States. The effects of such movements on patterns of Sicilian labor militancy during these years need to be considered. This requires, however, a change in focus from the regional to the local level, for only at the local level do existing sources reveal much about these other population movements. Again, Sambuca provides some clues to the linked histories of mobility and militancy in western Sicilian towns.

Internal migration in emigrant-exporting nations like Italy is an almost completely unexplored topic, especially for the years of mass emigration.[22] Systematic sources for its study are not readily available, even at the local level.[23] Sambuca, however, did seem to attract in-migrants after 1900, even though emigration from the town continued to increase at the same time. (See the appendix.) Marriage records and the household registration files used in the twentieth century point to the arrival of in-migrants born elsewhere in Sicily. To some extent, this increase resulted when Sambucesi returned to their hometown from the United States and brought with them a spouse married there but born elsewhere in Italy or Sicily. A sizable group of families also traveled to Sambuca from Favara around 1910. (Favara, a sulfur-mining town to the east, experienced a series of violent strikes from 1901 to 1907; its residents began emigrating in large numbers at about that time. Roughly 2,300 left Favara before 1911; another 6,000 did so over the next twenty years. Like Sambuca, Favara became a red town.)[24] It is difficult to know what attracted the Favaresi to Sambuca; a few families opened craft shops, but many more later ranked among the poorer peasants of the town. Since a small local railroad was under construction in and around Sambuca during the second decade of the century, it may have drawn wage earners from towns like Favara.[25] Obviously Favaresi arriving in Sambuca brought with them some familiarity with workplace organization, a tradition still unknown in Sambuca in the early years of the century.

Much more is known about return migration to Italy as a whole.[26] Betty Boyd

Caroli has estimated that at least 20 percent of all South Italian emigrants returned to their homeland.[27] Dino Cinel has argued more recently that return migration developed logically from Italian patterns of emigration: the desire to purchase land encouraged poorer or younger men in areas of widespread land ownership to leave, accumulate cash resources through wage earning, and return to purchase land. Returners, in his view, represented "new men": while they had lost their respect and fear of local elites, and while they showed a "superficial interest" in cooperation and mutual aid or fraternal societies, the "new man" remained primarily interested in consolidating the social status of his family through land purchase. Released from older communal expectations, these competitive individualists were often "unwilling to associate with people who had never migrated."[28] Cinel's interpretation of return migration resembles many earlier studies in suggesting that return migration had negative consequences for Sicilian labor militants seeking collective and/or political solutions to peasant problems. The presence of returners fragmented the complex class hierarchies of towns with already fluid social boundaries, encouraging peasant familism and conservative politics, not class-based activism in the workplace or political arena.

Developments in Sambuca reveal return migration and its impact on local labor initiatives in a somewhat different light. It is impossible to know whether proportionately fewer Sambucesi returned to their hometown than returned to towns with no history of support for labor militancy. Overall, almost 25 percent of the migrants identified in Sambuca's archive returned to their hometown; this proportion is only somewhat higher than Caroli's estimate for Sicily as a whole.[29] Sambuca's turn to the left continued, and even picked up speed, as emigrants resettled in their hometown. In part this was because return migration reinforced social changes that emigration had begun to introduce in the 1880s.

Table 8.1 summarizes data on return migration to Sambuca. Although early migrants returned in higher proportions than later migrants, the volume of returners became sizable only after 1905, especially as a consequence of the depression of 1907 and the threat of impending European war. The numbers of Sambucesi returning home never came close to matching the numbers leaving, but in the years after 1905 they did become a noticeable and important factor in local population movements. Overall, most who returned were peasants who had worked for a time in Louisiana. Before 1895, bird-of-passage married men in their hometown were 10 to 30 percent of the returners. After 1905, the numbers of families returning from Louisiana increased markedly, as did the arrivals in Sambuca of children born in the United States. Fewer families returned after World War I, but those who did return after 1910 came from a broader range of American locations.

While the number of returners to Sambuca was significant—and probably even larger than local documents could reveal—returners did not always remain permanently in Sicily. Almost half of the Sambucesi who returned to their hometown emigrated again to the United States after living five or six years in Sambuca.

Table 8.1

Migrants Returning to Sambuca, 1885–1939

	Born in U.S.	Years in U.S. (average)	Remain in Sambuca	Returning from			N
				Louisiana	Chicago	New York	
1885–1889	—	5.5	74%	89%	—	11%	19
1890–1894	6%	5.6	62	64	—	34	52
1895–1899	1	5.6	44	73	1%	24	70
1900–1904	21	5.2	39	51	3	29	90
1905–1909	24	8.0	47	44	17	28	161
1910–1919	34	9.6	43	26	32	30	283
1920–1929	29	14.0	45	9	34	21	156
1930–1939	43	21.1	56	1	13	48	86

Figure 8.1

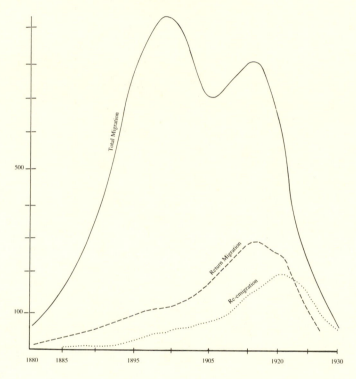

*Return Migration and Re-emigration as Portion of Total Migration
from Sambuca, 1885–1930*

Those who returned to Sambuca to marry were especially likely to re-emigrate, usually within a year of their marriages. Children born in the United States re-emigrated from Sambuca in large numbers during the 1920s. Figure 8.1 compares patterns of emigration, return migration, and re-emigration for the years 1880–1939. The figure reveals a still sizable emigration out of Sambuca during the 1920s despite the fact that the United States closed its doors during the decade. Intercensal population balances corrected for fertility and mortality confirmed that Sambuca lost considerable numbers of its residents between 1921 and 1930.[30] While many may have gone to live elsewhere in Sicily or Italy, others obviously were returned migrants who—by reason of birth, marriage, or kinship—could enter the United States despite the restrictive quota system.

The Sambucesi who returned to live and work permanently in their hometown were neither as upwardly mobile, as socially exclusive, nor as politically conserva-tive as might be expected. Most of the men who returned to Sambuca to stay followed in their parents' footsteps occupationally, while the women married men of the same occupation as their fathers (see Table 8.2). Most migrants also returned to the neighborhoods where they or their parents had been born and raised. Many improved their houses with savings from the United States—mainly by adding a residential second floor—but returned migrants did not erect a new and distinctive section of town (as did some migrants who returned to Sambuca from northern Europe in the 1970s).[31] Since almost half of all returners resettled in the lower town, their improved houses blended easily with the substantial homes of artisans and middle peasants living in the quarter. Finally, there is no evidence that returned migrants or their children intermarried excusively or even extensively. Perhaps this is why Sambucesi today—unlike South Italians in some other towns—identify no distinctive group called "Americani" in the town.

The lower middle classes of Sambuca expanded, but quite modestly and temporarily, as a result of return migration to the town. The number of artisans working in the town remained stable, while the number of middle peasants increased slightly. The expansion of the artisan and middle-peasant populations of Sambuca was not the simple result of upward mobility accompanying emigration and return migration. In part it resulted because the children of middle peasants (and civili as well) were more likely than other migrants to return to Sambuca permanently. Some of the civili who returned to Sambuca found they could not live as rentiers or professionals; their downward mobility into peasant and artisan ranks helped swell the lower middle classes of the town. Fully 15 percent of the children of artisans worked, after their return, as landowning peasants. Upward mobility did occur, of course. Of 202 returned children of poor peasants and shepherds, 56 succeeded in becoming middle peasants (although more frequently peasant lessees than landowners), while another 20 worked as craftsmen and small shopkeepers. The impact of return migration on Sambuca's class hierarchy thus seems limited. The lower middle class grew only modestly in real and proportional size.

Instead, what is striking was the proliferation of closer social ties between artisans, middle peasants, and poor peasants as a result of return migration. Artisans

Table 8.2

Occupational Mobility of Migrants Returning to Sambuca

Occupation of migrant's father	N	No mobility	Upward mobility	Downward mobility
Civile	19	79%	—	21%
Artisan	78	69	3%	28
Middle peasant	66	74	6	20
Poor peasant/shepherd	202	63	37	—

and poor peasants had developed new working relationships during emigration to Louisiana, as chapter 5 showed. Intermarriage and the social mobility that accompanied movement out of and back into Sambuca built additional bridges between the two groups. Beginning in the 1880s, artisans' daughters (who migrated less frequently than their brothers and potential spouses) began to marry the sons of middle peasants and even some poorer peasants.[32] One or more of the sons of such unions then typically became apprentices in the workshops of their artisan grandfathers. The result was that many artisans in Sambuca by 1920 had peasant fathers and cousins. When the emigrated children of artisans returned to Sambuca, they found men of peasant background in artisan workshops; when they themselves found it necessary to cultivate the land, they found themselves working in other ways with peasant neighbors.

The boundaries between artisans and all agriculturists, on the one hand, and those demarcating the once-clear hierarchy of artisan/middle peasant/poor peasant, on the other hand, blurred still further after 1910. Both the children of returned migrants and the general population of those reaching maturity around the time of the first World War matched or exceeded returned migrants' rates of mobility— both up and down. While small numbers (4 percent) of the children of returned artisans became professionals and clerks, many more (18 percent) worked in the fields, either on land they owned or as wage earners for others. Downward mobility into the ranks of poor peasant wage earners was especially noticeable among the children of returned middle peasants, 41 percent of whom worked during the 1930s as day laborers.

Whereas a typical atisan family in 1880 had little social or workplace contact with poor peasants, the typical artisan family forty years later had either a peasant forebear, a peasant son or son-in-law, or at least some peasants among the close kin. While kin ties remained closest among artisans and middle peasants, growing numbers of both groups counted poor wage earners among their close kin, too. Sambuca in 1920 still did not have a working class in a strict sense, although dependence on wage earning had grown, and would increase much more, during the next two decades, under Mussolini's disastrous agricultural policies. Nevertheless, Sambuca's laborers in 1920 formed an increasingly homogeneous and socially interconnected group.

An example of how such changes might have looked to the ordinary returned peasant family comes from Sambuca's household registration files. Crocifissa R., the Louisiana-born daughter of two poor peasants, returned to Sambuca with her parents shortly after her birth in 1905. She lived with her mother, who was widowed during World War I, in the upper town long after her American-born brother and sister returned to the United States. As the only child remaining permanently in Sambuca, Crocifissa R. would inherit her parents' tiny house in 1951, when her mother died. In 1933, at the rather late age of 28, Crocifissa R.

married the widower Calogero G., ten years her senior and the father of two children. Calogero G. was a middle peasant (he leased land long-term), but he lived in the poorest section of Sambuca. One of Crocifissa R.'s stepsons trained as a shoemaker, probably with the brother of his deceased mother. A son born to Crocifissa remained a day laborer into the 1950s. Among her in-laws and cousins, Crocifissa R. thus counted many day laborers, a few middle peasants, and a few artisans. The only significant group to which she had no kinship ties was the civile landowning elite.

The proliferation of social ties among these three groups sheds light on Sambuca's development into a red town. Sambucesi today note that in 1913 new peasant voters easily accepted reform artisan leadership and helped vote the first Socialists into municipal government.[33] While the social foundation for this cooperation is obvious, it seems likely also that artisan Socialists and poor peasants shared some important ideas about public policy. Both remained strongly anti-militaristic and antiwar. In 1916, Socialists in Sambuca organized one of the earliest Sicilian protests against the war: 150 people participated. This was not a spontaneous women's action like the ones in many Sicilian towns.[34] The anti-militarism of local artisans undoubtedly seemed attractive to Sambuca's peasants since they had "voted with their feet" by migrating in astounding proportions just before the war. In the case of the young men migrants, their decisions almost certainly reflected a distaste for military adventure.

Equally interesting was the sudden development of workplace activism among Sambuca's peasants at roughly this time. Unfortunately, local records do not reveal much about the peasant occupation of three large wheat estates that occurred in Sambuca in 1919.[35] An emerging maximalist faction of local Socialists seems to have been involved in the action, and in the formation two years later of Sambuca's Communist Party circle.

For three previous decades, the peasants of Sambuca had remained oblivious to the spread of organization and workplace action in many nearby towns. Is it possible to explain the sudden and belated changes in Sambuca? Obviousy, the effects of proletarianization—the spread of wage earning in agriculture—provide part of an answer. A number of other possibilities might also be considered. Had time in the United States sensitized some reform Socialists to the problems of the wage earner, as it had Giovanni Vaccaro in Tampa? Had kinship and increasing personal experience with wage earning forced town artisans to change course themselves? Or had returned migrant wage earners or Favara in-migrants simply formed an opposition group, differentiating themselves from the reformer artisans of the town?

The composition of Sambuca's new Communist Party in the early 1920s hints at some of the ways in which migration and local changes worked their influence on Sicilian politics at the local level. In-migrants and proletarianized wage earners, whether from Favara or Sambuca, played no obvious roles in the foundation of Sambuca's Communist Party. But in other ways, the early Communists reflected the social changes transforming Sambuca's population.

Of the founders, two had been among those who started the Socialist Party circle, but had rejected reform at some point. (Surprisingly, those founders of the Socialist circle who had emigrated temporarily to Brooklyn remained reformers after their return. Similarly, sons of the founders of the Socialist circle did not usually become Communists; daughters, as we will see, had a different future.) The Socialists who became maximalists and then Communists included the one middle peasant among the early Socialist artisans. And the twelve early Communists, in sharp contrast to the first Socialists, also counted six peasants among their numbers. In addition, several of the young artisan Communists had peasant fathers. They were the children of some of the first mixed marriages of artisans and peasants in the 1880s. Peasants who assumed positions of leadership in the Communist Party in Sambuca tended to be from marginal families of the middle peasantry—young men who could look forward to inheriting only small amounts of land, and who thus must have anticipated a future that included considerable wage earning. Four early Communists were returned migrants or the children of returned migrants who had worked in Louisiana or Chicago. Among these returners was an artisan who probably had functioned as a padrone during the migration to Louisiana in the early 1890s; he worked as a carter.

Whereas a distinctive group of artisans had formed Sambuca's Socialist Party, Sambuca's Communists by 1921 reflected the increased linkages between formerly divided occupational groups in Sambuca. By blurring and eliminating familial, status, and experiential boundaries that had separated artisans from peasants, emigration and return emigration helped produce the social basis for political change in Sambuca.

The Socialist traditions of Sambuca's lower middle class, especially its artisans, were also essential to this development. Where no artisans represented such traditions locally, the expansion of the lower middle class during migration and return migration could have had the apolitical or even conservative consequences described by Cinel and others. In Sambuca, however, upwardly mobile "new men" politically joined lower-middle-class artisans and middle peasants. All remained prominent in the leadership of the Communist Party. They differed from the earlier Socialists mainly in having acquired a closer understanding of wage earning and the economic dependence and workplace conflicts it produced. Migration, upward or downward mobility, and family relationships contributed to their new understanding of workplace problems. All guaranteed as well that the poorer peasants of the town enjoyed ample opportunities to become familiar with the thinking and political strategies of the lower-middle-class ideologues. As clandestine Communists, Sambuca's artisans and middle peasants sought—and obtained—the support of the majority of poor peasants of their town. Sambuca's Communists became the major political group in Sambuca during Mussolini's reign.

Fascism and Postwar Reform

On the surface, Fascist repression worked, in Sambuca and elsewhere. Far from the geographical center of armed opposition, Sicily was quiet throughout the 1930s.[36] Sicilian Socialists and Communists did suffer imprisonment, of course; reduced to a secretive existence, their public influence diminished. But they did not necessarily suffer political isolation as a result, for in the immediate postwar years they enjoyed enormous and widespread popular support—in part because of their resistance to Mussolini. The postwar strength of the Sicilian Communist Party took leaders of the national party by surprise. By the time they responded to Communist initiatives in Sicily, Christian Democrats had taken power in the nation and were in a position to use agrarian reform to undermine peasant support for the left parties. Only where traditions of labor militancy reached back to the pre-Fascist years did Communists or Socialists retain their influence in the 1950s.

Mussolini succeeded in ending open rebellion, but his regime could not eliminate the causes of rural Sicilian discontent. In fact, his rule aggravated rural problems. Italy's "battle for grain" in the 1930s allowed estate owners and civili to reintensify exploitative work discipline and take more of the crop harvested, especially once migration no longer artificially lowered local supplies of laborers.[37] The real wages of agricultural wage earners dropped by as much as 50 percent, one critic of Fascism maintained.[38] The populations of wheat towns throughout Sicily declined. In Sambuca, some peasants found no work at all; the children of poor peasants in the 1930s were far more likely to become servants or dependents in civile households than in the past.[39]

All over Sicily, elite factions formed, came to terms with Mussolini (despite his antimafia campaigns), and again took over local governments. In Sambuca, the Fascist local leaders of the 1930s included descendants of the same wealthy landowners who had welcomed Garibaldi's supporters seventy years before.[40] (By contrast, civili in professional occupations often left Sambuca during the 1930s, to find work either in Palermo or in one of the mainland Italian cities.) Little wonder that peasants in towns like Sambuca remember the arrogance of local elites under Fascism. Whatever short-term comforts migration had introduced, Mussolini's rule wiped away. If migration and political changes prior to World War I had raised peasants' expectations in many wheat-raising towns, then Mussolini's reign dashed them. In Sambuca, the Communist Party benefited.

Public defiance of Fascist rule continued in Sicily, often in highly symbolic form. One young Sambuca carpenter nicknamed "Sessa" (after the well-known

Sicilian Communist), attracted the attention of his peers by chalking "Long live the economic crises!" on the sidewalk of the main street in the lower town. A Socialist shoemaker in Sambuca in 1934 ostentatiously refused to vote for the national ticket, proclaiming that he could not violate his principles by doing so. Local police reported that on May 1, 1936, a young mason and his friend, a carpenter, marched up and down the main street of Sambuca "dressed in their festival clothes." Although they said nothing, both the police and their neighbors understood the significance of this labor-day parade.[41]

Public authorities in Sambuca seemed willing to tolerate symbolic acts like these. What they would not tolerate were clandestine meetings, readings, or organizing among the poorer peasants of town. At least six Socialists and Communists from Sambuca spent long years in Fascist jails for such agitation.[42] Nevertheless, it seems apparent that those who protested publicly, if symbolically, in the 1930s also succeeded in continuing their clandestine organizing. Police informants spoke repeatedly of "friendships forming" between suspected Communists and local peasants. The town's Communists also continued an older town tradition by running a clandestine school which introduced new recruits to the alphabet and to the classics of Marxism.[43]

In July of 1943 (when the Allies landed in Sicily), the archpriest of Sambuca called together the leading Communists of the town, asking them to join with him in forming a citizens' committee. Their responsibility would be to supervise "public health" until order was restored. The priest was politically astute—and the Communists were ready. In a first local election held 1946, Sambuca's citizenry elected as mayor Nino P., the landowning peasant who had helped found first the Socialist and later the Communist parties of Sambuca, a man who had spent almost ten years in Fascist jails. P. apparently proved unacceptable to the occupying forces; he was replaced by a storekeeper Socialist, locally regarded as both a great intellectual and a democrat. This man, too, had been imprisoned in the 1930s.

In Sambuca and in scores of other Sicilian towns in 1943–1949, peasants again occupied lands; organized cooperatives, unions, and peasant leagues; and suffered mafia reprisals. Socialist mayors were murdered, peasant demonstrations attacked, and party and union headquarters bombed.[44] Peasant revolts in this second postwar period occurred in roughly the same towns as in 1919–1922, although in somewhat smaller numbers. Some of these revolts have been called spontaneous, but this is unlikely; what *is* true is that local Communists actively participated without much initial support or guidance from the national party. Only after 1946 did the Communist Party begin to send funds and organizational support.[45]

Peasant protests did not translate immediately into Communist or Socialist strength at the polls. In 1946, Communists received 8 percent and Socialists 12 percent of the popular vote. These figures contrasted poorly with comparable levels of support for the left, especially the Socialists, in 1924. In 1947, however, a coalition of left Socialists and Communists (the *Blocco del Popolo*) gained 30 percent of the popular vote for the regional assembly.[46] As in the past, western Sicilians showed vast local variation in supporting this coalition. Towns with peasant agitations often gave the Blocco clear majorities.[47] Continuity between pre- and post-Fascist patterns of militancy was striking. Militant towns of the pre-Fascist era were much more likely to support the Blocco del Popolo than were towns where labor militancy had never emerged or where it had declined after the 1890s.[48] Three-quarters of Sambuca's voters chose the Blocco del Popolo. Apparently, Sambuca's activists had been quite successful in maintaining their local popularity under Fascism.

In his careful analysis of peasant communism in the Italian South, Sidney Tarrow argues that the Communist Party foundered on a fundamental contradiction in the years after World War II. Committed to the nonrevolutionary course it believed appropriate for a developed nation, the Party was unable and unwilling to harness the revolutionary potential of peasants in the undeveloped southern countryside. By directing its own energies, and peasants' struggles, toward agrarian reform, it undermined its ideological appeal and threatened its base of support.[49] Tarrow assumes that the promise of revolution retained a powerful ideological appeal to peasants occupying Sicilian lands. He also assumes that when the Christian Democrats, responding to pressure, began agrarian reforms, they secured the political support of the newly landed peasants such reforms created. The result was a decline in support for the Communist Party among southern peasants throughout the 1950s. While the Blocco del Popolo received 30 percent of Sicilian votes in 1951, Communist Party votes in Sicily throughout the 1950s varied between 21 and 22 percent.[50]

In towns like Sambuca, however, support for the Communist Party remained strong; it began to decline, and then only slowly, in the late 1950s. Sambuca's voters seemed undisturbed by the nonrevolutionary strategy of the Party. Neither did land reform have the expected results. Sambuca's local historian notes that some of the newest landed peasants benefiting from reform did vote for the Christian Democrats; he emphasizes, however, the influence of the town's older middle peasants, who continued their traditions of supporting parties of the left. In fact, according to a discreet agreement, municipal positions within the Party alternated between those of artisanal and those of agricultural background.[51]

Use of the word tradition in this context is important: it points to an aspect of Communist Party successes unnoted by Tarrow and many other students of peasant politics in the Italian South. Patterns of labor militancy persisted from earlier to later twentieth century because so many Sicilian families made their political convictions part of their familial traditions. The absorption of politics by the family realm explains much about the spread of Communism in Sambuca during the 1920s and 1930s and the continued predominance of the Party in the town into the 1960s and 1970s.

In very clear contrast to Sicilians in the United States, Socialist and Communist fathers in Sambuca raised Socialist and Communist children. Over a third of the leftists elected to municipal offices in the 1950s and 1960s were sons or nephews of the town's early Socialists and Communists. While police in the 1930s had at least some chance to interfere with clandestine organizing efforts, it was almost impossible for them to interfere with the socialization of children within such families. By the 1950s, many of the most politically active men of the town were linked by kin and marriage ties as well. These had developed in one of two ways. Several of the young Communists had married each other's sisters; several more married the daughters or granddaughters of the early Socialists. For example, the daughter of Michele B. (the man who purportedly "brought socialism" to Sambuca) arranged for her own daughter to marry a young Communist in the 1930s. While the relatively cordial relations betweeen Sambuca's Communists and Socialists had many sources in the postwar years, marriage ties among them were at least one.

The fact that some Sambuca families made political ideology part of the tradition they passed on to their children raises questions about the role women played in this development.[52] Sambuca's women had all but disappeared from local protests after the peasant revolt of 1848. Excluded from politics, they, like Sicilian women in general in the 1890s, may have preserved the old communally based tradition. Local sources in Sambuca rarely mention women's protests, and the town's local historian did not mention women's protests in his detailed recounting of the labor movement and its activists in Sambuca. Nevertheless, such protests still occur in Sambuca today.[53]

It seems unlikely, too, that women in Sambuca knew nothing of the male labor movement and its goals or of male political parties and their needs. For it was women who arranged the marriages that created political family alliances.[54] Furthermore, women in Sambuca differ from women in some other southern Italian towns in one important respect: they show no marked political preference for Christian Democracy. Although they rarely joined the Communist Party, and never sought political office in the postwar years, they nevertheless voted Communist almost as often as their brothers, sons, husbands, and fathers.[55] Few older women today claim total ignorance of or indifference to the political world. If Sambuca's children, especially the boys, learned political ideology mainly from their fathers and in their workplaces, the lessons they learned at home from their mothers did not undermine or contradict those teachings. Few people in Sambuca mention intense conflicts betweeen Catholic mothers and Communist fathers for the loyalties of children. One controversial point seems to be whether marriage in the Church should follow the civil ceremony required by law. Some mothers continue to insist on the religious ceremony, too, even when they and their children otherwise ignore religious practice. Other women, however, consciously wish to be exemplary Communists and omit the religious ceremony proudly. In

Sambuca, as in other parts of Italy, most Communists have reached a general if uneasy truce with their religious, but anticlerical, heritage.[56]

Thus, when Sambucesi today worry, as they do, about declining support for the Communist Party since the 1950s, they offer a unique perspective on this development. Many are quite aware of how Party success in achieving reform at the local level has undermined its base of support, especially by allowing some of the poorer peasants of the town to acquire a bit of property. In general, however, what Sambuca's Communists fear most is the loss of the young. For reasons they themselves cannot fully explain, parents no longer routinely succeed in passing on their political beliefs to their children. To their distress, their children sometimes perceive the Party as outdated and irrelevant. The generational conflicts common in Sicilian immigrant families since 1900 have parallels in Sicily in the last third of the twentieth century. The implications for a red town like Sambuca are still not clear.

Conclusion

Return migration to Sicily offers a final complex example of the varied historical linkages between population movement and labor movement. Both in what it changed and in what it left unchanged, migration seems to have accentuated the patterns of the past, whatever they were. In towns without a strong local labor movement, returned migrants looked out for themselves and their families as "new men" under Fascism. In towns like Sambuca, where a local tradition of labor activism had taken root, returned migrants accommodated themselves to and often joined that movement. Neither massive emigration, two world wars, nor Mussolini broke the legacy of the 1890s in the militant towns of western Sicily.

The key to labor militants' successes at the local level changed over time. In the prewar years, artisan antimilitarists, especially those who supported peasant initiatives in the workplace, easily attracted peasant supporters, both among returned migrants and among the newly enfranchised. Throughout the period, increased intermarriage, and the use of informal and kinship ties to consolidate political alliances, grew in importance. Under Fascism, in particular, these alliances of the private world, combined with the socialization of children, helped consolidate and even extend Communist influence during a period of considerable public repression. The involvement of local leftists in the second postwar occupations of lands proved essential to Communist Party growth in the late 1940s and early 1950s.

Migration had no one single effect on the development of labor militancy among Sicilians. In the United States, Sicilians rarely remained militants with ties to the movements of the homeland; in Sicily, labor movements often grew despite the mobility of the peasant and artisan populations. These differing outcomes represented one important way in which immigrant workers and Sicilians in Europe had diverged from their common origins.

Conclusion

Militants and Migrants focused on Sicilian migration and militancy primarily through the lens of a labor historian. Themes like the transformation of rural traditions of protest, the transplantation of European militancy to the United States, and the workplace and community conditions under which mobile peasants and workers organized labor movements received systematic attention

Without a doubt, J. S. MacDonald pointed scholars interested in militancy and migration in the right direction. The western Sicilian case provided ample documentation that both were characteristic responses of rural Europeans to the decline of subsistence production and subsequent challenges of the market in the nineteenth century. The two did not always conflict, however. Rural revolt had long been endemic in the European countryside, while migration seemed motivated by the search for cash that accompanied economic and political change during a distinctive moment in the formation of world markets. The migration process itself significantly shaped subsequent militancy in Sicily and the United States by transforming relations between artisan militants and proletarianized workers. Immigrant communities of wage earners and small businessmen linked by family solidarities proved the most militant in the United States, especially where American or other labor activists were already influential in the workplace when Italians began taking jobs.

These are important themes, but there are other equally important points raised by *Militants and Migrants* that have been subordinated in previous chapters to the questions of the labor historian. The purpose of this conclusion is to delineate some of the other implications of the linked histories of militants and migrants from Sambuca and western Sicily. Discussions of Italian-American kinship, American ethnic groups, the "big questions" of social history, and the lower middle class suggest other perspectives on the material presented in this book.

Kinship and Migration

The family has been a central focus of most research on Italian immigrants in the United States. In part this reflects the real importance of family and kinship in the everyday life of South Italians and immigrants; in part it probably also reflects the ideological importance that family sentiments assumed as immigrant parents

sought to hold their children's loyalties, countering cultural agents of Americanization who sought to change women's roles, childrearing practices, and home life.
Italian-Americans today often believe proudly (and inaccurately, it seems to me)
that their loyalty to family differentiates them fundamentally from Americans of
other backgrounds.[1]

While previous chapters did not ignore the role of the family in supporting or
undermining Sicilian militancy, it nevertheless might be helpful to summarize
the significance of family in the migration process itself. Overall, *Militants and
Migrants* emphasizes that it was occupation that shaped chain migration from
Sambuca.[2] This interpretation conflicts with the usual view of kinship as the
primary link in migration chains. How real is this conflict?

First, and most obviously, kin and occupational groups overlapped considerably
in the towns of western Sicily. In Sambuca, shoemakers counted many shoemakers among their kin, while shepherds had many kin who herded animals, too.
(Such groupings were the result of Sicilians' preference for marriage partners of
the same *condizione*.)[3] Undoubtedly, ties of kinship facilitated occupational solidarity among artisan groups in Sambuca; it did not, however, hind the considerably larger populations of sharecroppers, peasant landowners, and day laborers.
Also, kinship was never the only basis for artisanal solidarities: artisans moved
around enough in the nineteenth century that a significant proportion of the practi-
tioners of any one trade lived, worked, and cooperated with nonkin.

Similarly, there can be no doubt that kinship ties within some occupational
groups encouraged a preference for one destination or another among Sambuca's
migrants. While all but a few of Sambuca's many migrating carpenters and tailors
left for New York City, only 80 percent of Sambuca's mobile shoemakers found
new homes there. All the emigrated plasterers from Sambuca went to New
Orleans, and all were kin.

Despite this important overlap of kinship and occupation, it is wrong to
conclude that kinship therefore determined the occupational patterns of chain
migration examined in chapter 5. If South Italians could identify kin "to the fourth
degree," as Leonard Covello insisted, then an average Sicilian might easily count
up to 1,000 persons as kin.[4] Many, but never all, would have shared his occupation; among Sambucesi, about a third of migrants with migrated kin counted both
artisans and peasants among them after 1900.

In instances like these the interaction of kinship and occupation in the migration
process can be viewed in better detail. Of sixty artisans born into peasant families
in Sambuca, two-thirds migrated not to peasant kin in Chicago or Louisiana, but to
fellow shoemakers and barbers in New York. The reverse was true among a small
group of artisans' sons who had worked the land in Sambuca.

For all these reasons, one should be wary of drawing broad conclusions from
oral historians' reports that elderly immigrants "always" tell of migrating to join
kin.[5] Historians have succeeded in interviewing mainly those who arrived in the

United States after the transition from bird-of-passage to kinship migration. Had we interviewed earlier arrivals, especially those fathers and working-age men who ultimately returned to Sicily, we might have received different descriptions of chain migration. We have viewed chain migration as it appeared to people arriving in the United States as young children in the years after 1900. Children naturally see all significant decisions as made by relatives (their parents), and their world usually is limited to the intimate one of the family. Few children like these had an occupational identity when they arrrived in the United States, and this, too, shapes their understanding of the past. The perspective of elderly immigrants on chain migration is an important one, but it is not the only one; as this book has attempted to establish, other sources reveal occupation as equally or more important in the social organization of migration. In chapters 6 and 7, the occupational links in migration chains were shown to have shaped the histories of Sambuca's settlements in the United States as much as did the more extensively studied ties of family and community.

Ethnicity and Uprooting

At one time scholars viewed immigrants as uprooted and as participants in culturally coherent and socially identifiable ethnic groups. Twenty years of studies in immigration history seem to have convincingly refuted Oscar Handlin's image of uprooted European immigrants, while evidence of ethnic diversity suggests that ethnicity may be primarily an aspect of individual identity in the United States.[6] The experience of western Sicilians departs somewhat from prevailing interpretations, by showing that uprooting sometimes did occcur, but it confirms the diversity of social behavior and values among people who consider themselves members of one ethnic group.

Studies replacing images of uprooted immigrants with those of transplanted ones have typically focused on family, work, and community life. It is in precisely these arenas of life where relatively easy transplantation seems to have been the rule. *Militants and Migrants* reminds us, however, that rural political traditions did not so easily take root in American soil. Perhaps historians ought not to abandon completely the concept of uprooting, for some immigrants from western Sicily do seem to have been rudely uprooted from familiar political practices—and depoliticized in the process. The clearest example of this was probably the ideologically committed but largely apolitical group of Brooklyn artisans described in chapter 7.

Why was uprooting characteristic of immigrants' political experiences? In chapter 1, we saw that Europeans and Americans disagreed about possible explanations for immigrant workers' political passivity. It seems likely that Europeans' structural explanations best explain artisanal passivity, while the cultural explanations preferred by U.S. scholars in recent years apply more easily to peasants who had

not yet entered the polity in Europe. The United States in the years of mass migration was already a liberal and democratic republic, and one with a rather minimal
state structure; this may or may not have been part of what attracted Italian artisans
to the country, but it certainly shaped their political behavior once there. The
United States differed significantly from the political worlds familiar to rural Europeans just coming to terms with life in their own nation-states. Migration probably
allowed some immigrants the important illusion that they had successfully escaped
the state: gone were the taxes, the draft, and the overbearing elite officeholders of
Sicilian towns. Perhaps this is why so few alien workers, even those intending to
remain permanently in the United States, became citizens. Only when immigrants
had personal, economic, or communal motivations, as in Chicago, did they think
about becoming voters. This case study confirms what has been a general point in
studies of contemporary labor migrations: immigrant workers are attractive laborers
not simply because they are cheap and easily transplanted but also because they
remain politically uninvolved in the nations where they work.

Politically, as in every other respect, migrants from Sambuca were nevertheless
an astonishingly diverse group. If historians of ethnicity were to read their many
stories without knowing their national identities, some wildly inaccurate guesses
about their origins could easily be made. Sambucesi appeared in various locations
as peasant leftists, migrant harvesters, padrone slaves, immigrant familists, militant
factory workers, and factionalized small businessmen. Who would guess that all
were also fellow villagers?

Despite increasing evidence to the contrary, we still expect more uniformity of
people who share common roots than we find in the pages of this book, which
should remind the reader just how particularistic ethnic and class groupings actually were.[7] While most of the people described in this book undoubtedly thought
of themselves as Italians or Italian-Americans by the twentieth century, they shared
surprisingly few experiences. In some respects, they lacked even a common core
of values, especially when it came to understanding power.

The western Sicilian case demonstrated further that immigrant diversity did not
originate solely in regional variation, although such variation was real enough.
Even within one small region in western Sicily or within one immigrant settlement
in the United States, class produced deep divisions among Sicilians in experience,
tradition, culture, and social life. This is an aspect of ethnic identity that still needs
scholarly attention.[8]

The "Big" Changes

Responding to charges that their method encourages an excessive antiquarianism
and a liberal disinterest in power, social historians have struggled to redefine their
territory. Charles Tilly recently suggested that social history take as its agenda an

analysis of how ordinary people "lived the big changes," connecting ". . . every-day experience to the large structures of historical analyses and major changes of the past."[9] This book has attempted to do precisely that. It shows both the possibilities and problems of utilizing a social-historical method to examine major structures like the world market for labor, or major changes like those sometimes termed modernization.

In a general way, the Sicilian examples suggest that historians stand to learn much from social scientists' analysis of the evolution of the world system. Work by Wallerstein, Sasken-Koob, and others provides American scholars of immigration with one way of understanding the timing and volume of migration from a variety of ever-changing rural areas. In particular, the world-systems paradigm helps immigration historians escape an exclusive concentration on migrations from individual nation-states—something many scholars have acknowledged as an important goal for the years ahead.[10] Much of this book has described how an international market for labor developed, drawing Sicilians of quite specific backgrounds to equally specific workplaces in the United States. While Sicilian migrants probably never used the term "world system," many had a detailed understanding of its operation.

Militants and Migrants also demonstrates that attention to ordinary people and their experiences can highlight flaws in our descriptions of big structures and large changes. How production for the market was organized—not the existence of the market itself—was of critical importance in determining rates of migration. Whether capitalist or not, new forms of workplace organization (which Mac-Donald called "agricultural organization") fundamentally shaped Sicilians' decisions about migration in the nineteenth century. More important, no obvious market crisis pushed artisans to venture abroad. Market relations can explain much, but certainly not everything, about migration patterns.

Similarly, while Eric Wolf's path-breaking work showed how expansion of world markets shaped patterns of rural militancy, the Sicilian case study revealed the limits of the market's influence. By the nineteenth century, many Sicilian revolts emerged from workplace and political conflicts. Although cash problems cannot be detached from either, Sicilians increasingly protested in their workplaces and in the municipal hall, not in the market square and the grain storehouses as they had in previous centuries (and as women would continue to do on occasion into the twentieth century). This reminds us, among other things, that political disenchantment, not merely agricultural crises, may also have spurred migrations in the late nineteenth century—something rarely considered in studies of labor migrations.

In general, a focus on the formation of world markets does not explain much about changes in the workplace, yet it was there that one important form of rural unrest originated in 1880–1920. (Critics have often noted that the world-system approach can limit our understanding of class struggle or politics, both of which until very recently have been national phenomena.) The large wheat estates of western Sicily were not capitalist workplaces in the strictest sense, yet they also resembled capitalist workplaces in Europe and the United States. In fact, the workplace experiences of wheat cultivators in western Sicily, cane harvesters in Louisiana, and railroad laborers in Chicago can be considered remarkably similar. All such jobs were seasonal, organized as gangs, controlled by middlemen, poorly paid, and abusively supervised. A visible enemy, usually a foreman, dominated each of these workplaces. This meant that a wheat cultivator could probably more easily grasp the principle of class struggle than could an immigrant industrial wage earner in Rockford or Brooklyn, where the use of machinery in large-scale factories often rendered the middleman and the abusive supervision unnecessary. Little wonder, then, that Socialist revolutions often began in the countryside, or that class-conscious theorists—focusing, as they had to, on structural relations among states, economies, classes, or nations—long found this development puzzling. Like many world-systems theoreticians, they did not understand the organization of work in precapitalist, rural, or nonfactory settings. Social historians can correct some of these blind spots.

Finally, this book provides ample examples of how individuals perceived and responded to large structures and changes not of their own making. It also, fortunately, shows that causation sometimes flowed in the other direction. It is precisely this aspect of their method that should encourage social historians to persist in their attention to the individual and local levels: they can remind readers of human agency in history. Inquisitive and sharp rural middlemen, carters and millers turned *padroni*, did not so much respond to the existence of an international market for labor as they helped create that market. In the descriptions of a world system, regional and international markets sometimes seem to develop from an internal logic of their own; social history reminds us that human hands and desires poked and prodded them into the forms they assumed.

So, too, the Sicilians described in this work participated actively in transforming themselves into "modern" Italians or Americans. Social historians have long insisted that rural people in the nineteenth and into the twentieth centuries experimented constantly with varying amalgams of tradition and new ideas; Sicilians were no exception to this rule.

Still, the social and cultural transformation presented in this book is a different one from that outlined by Eugen Weber in his study of the modernization of peasants into Frenchmen.[11] Among Sicilians, there was no homogenization of rural diversity into either Italian or American modernity. In their political ideologies and in their behavior as workers and voters, the Sicilian populations in this book became, to all appearances, *more* diverse in the years between 1800 and 1930. That was true both of those who remained in Sicily and of those who migrated to the United States. From a fairly simple and broadly shared understanding of a world divided between "the rich and the poor," Sicilians became

Communists, Fascists, apolitical familists, pragmatic trade unionists, Democratic Socialists, Catholic activists, and loyal liberal supporters of the Democratic and Republican parties of the United States. While all might be declared politically "modern" at the end of this transformation—Sicilian women, of course, remaining an important exception to this generalization—it would be hard to portray their modernization as destructive of diversity. In fact, it was the opposite.

The Lower Middle Class

Artisans and small businessmen were prominent actors in the linked histories of Sicilian migration and militancy. Most discussions of the lower middle classes of Europe wrestle with the class position and political alliances of such men and women. Were they "penny capitalists" within the working classes, leaders because they bore older traditions of workers' independence and dignity?[12] Sambuca's artisans sometimes fit this description in the twentieth century. Certainly they were not the petty bourgeoisie of older Marxist analyses, politically attracted to Fascist leaders like Mussolini and Hitler. More recent studies have portrayed artisans and small businessmen as something else entirely—a "radical middle."[13] This last characterization seems to fit Sambuca's artisans most aptly, for it captures their willingness to experiment with new ideas and strategies, while always maintaining their position in their communities as mediators. The exact form of their mediations also varied, of course, in politically significant ways from location to location.

Trying to arrive at simple statements about immigrants of the lower middle class proves even more complex. The importance of small businessmen in the creation of ethnic community institutions—and in Americanization—has long been recognized.[14] In fact, some scholars tend to see small businesses as themselves "community" institutions.[15] Yet immigrant shopkeepers and artisans were no more inherently conservative or radical than were their Sicilian peers, a point that confirms John Cumbler's argument that the character of ethnic communities was thus "affected strongly by the room for maneuverability possessed by its middle-class leadership.[16] Depending on which group of Sambucesi is in focus, artisans can be seen both leading peasants into leftist politics or corrupt unions and suppressing wage-earners' aspirations as padroni or master barbers. It seems true that immigrant small businessmen tried always to lead, and that sometimes they attempted to create a community in order to do so. But *where* they led, and whether they actually succeeded in attracting followers, varied from community to community. Peasants and wage earners had few options in both Sicily and the United States, yet they were never passive followers.

Examples like these serve as a reminder that the lower middle class cannot be viewed as a fixed entity, defined in the workplace or the market; rather, it can be viewed only in its relations to other groups, and then only historically. The presence or absence of alliances or conflicts with civili or wage earners repeatedly shaped the ideology and political behavior of artisans and small businessmen in Sambuca, Louisiana, Illinois, and New York. While *Militants and Migrants* focuses mainly on such developments among a single imporant generation, a similar analysis could probably be done of the children of that generation. It is striking, for example, that artisans and small businessmen both in Sicily and in some immigrant settlements in the United States raised children who moved into clerical, administrative, and professional occupations, thus forging familial connections between old and new middle classes. Teacher, pharmacist, doctor, lawyer, and clerk sons were fairly common in Sicily, even given the tremendous difficulties in educating children there; they were very common, indeed, among Brooklyn's small-business families. In Sicily, of course, many of these sons could only find employment in state positions. Politics continued to be important in their lives, in a way it would not be for their New World counterparts. As yet, however, we know too little of the lives of the doctors and lawyers of the second generation—except for their affinity for the Democratic Party in parts of Brooklyn—to speculate about their position in either ethnic or nonethnic worlds.

The political behavior of artisans and small businessmen was also more than a simple reflection of their historically evolving alliances, however. Chapter 8 in particular shows the importance of tradition, reproduction, and socialization in the creation of a politically radical middle class. The fact that a handful of shoemakers became Socialists in the 1890s did not make the transformation of Sambuca into a red town inevitable. Similar Socialists had little luck in creating class-conscious ethnic communities in many American cities. Still, it is important to remember that had those individuals not become Socialists in Sambuca, the transformation of their hometown might never have occurred at all. When we know more about socialization and family life in the immigrant middle classes, we will be in a better position to judge the failure of the immigrant radicals and the meaning of American exceptionalism.

Appendix
A Critical Look at the Sources

Most studies of chain migration from the Italian south have relied on oral interviews with small groups of elderly immigrant men, or on parish records from urban neighborhoods in the United States.[1] Both methods have obvious attractions, but equally clear problems. Parish records usually describe provincial origins, if that, while oral histories with even the oldest immigrant survivors cannot reveal much about the years before 1900, when migration from much of southern Italy began. Furthermore, both methods fail to say much about the sizable group of migrants that returned to Italy, a group estimated at up to 40 percent of all Italian migrants.

Chapters 5, 6, 7, and 8 drew on other sources to describe chain migration from Sambuca. These sources, too, have their limitations, which this appendix describes. Still, they represent a rarely used alternative to the parish or oral document from the United States. It is worthwhile comparing the picture of migration that European sources reveal. This is especially so because we still know relatively little about how migration chains were linked together socially.

The major sources used in this book were public records in Sicily, complemented by transatlantic record linkage to selected American sources. Information about Sambuca's migrants came from draft, marriage, birth, and death records, as well as from local population registers stored in Sambuca's municipal offices and community archive. Draft records (described in chapter 3) identified young men living in the United States at the time of their draft call. Birth records noted newborns with fathers living in the United States. Series of birth, death, and marriage records also included transcriptions of vital events sent back to the homeland by emigrated Sambucesi. Population registers arranged by family group were begun in Sambuca during Mussolini's first decade in power: in 1931, at the time of the national census, Sambuca's clerks noted residents of Sambuca who were living in the United States.[2] In addition, local population registers provided strong circumstantial evidence of migration, especially when linked with other local sources: "disappearing individuals" (those with no vital records subsequent to their births) and "irregular childbearers" (women who bore children over long periods but at irregular intervals, presumably because husbands emigrated temporarily).

Sambuca's record keepers commonly noted the American city or state that became the new residence for emigrants from their town. Sometimes they gave more precise information—a church name or even a street address. Sicilian sources also provided scattered information about the subsequent moves of migrants living in the United States. No destination was available for about 330 migrants, who were noted only as "in America." Thus, it seemed safe to assume that the sources used provided relatively accurate information about the main destinations chosen and about the Sambucesi who migrated to each American city or state.[3]

Since several American destinations appeared regularly in Sambuca's records, an effort was made to trace Sambucesi in some American sources as well. I did not try to trace all migrants, but instead focused on only three chains. Searches in Brooklyn city directories, Louisiana manuscript census listings for 1900, and in the 1910 manuscript census listings for Brooklyn and Rockford, Illinois, proved time-consuming but not without results. About 10 percent of migrants originally identified in Sambuca's archive were eventually relocated in American sources. If this figure strikes the reader as dismally small, it is worth repeating that not all chains were checked in the American sources. A significant problem was that manuscript census listings for Louisiana in 1900 did not include temporary migrant laborers. The sources were most complete for Brooklyn, and the linkage rate was also highest for this chain: there, I found almost one-third of the emigrants first identified in Sicilian sources.

Both the American and the Sicilian sources raised questions about definitions of migrants. I decided to call migrants those who had applied for permission to migrate, even if no positive evidence of migration existed. I included among Sambuca's migrants those outside Sambuca if they had either married or had children in Sambuca prior to migration. I included "disappearing individuals" and the husbands of "irregular childbearers" only when they met certain other conditions.[4] I also included in my analysis the children born abroad to Sambuca parents if they susequently returned, even temporarily, to their parents' hometown. (Most then subsequently re-emigrated to the United States.) However, I did not include children born abroad and remaining permanently in the United States.[5]

Of the more than 3,600 migrants analyzed, 80 percent were positively identified first in Sicilian sources. Strong circumstantial evidence in Sambuca's archive identified an additional 13 percent. About 8 percent of my file of migrants were first found in the American sources. (Weaker circumstantial evidence of migration existed for about 500 Sambucesi. Although I gathered data about these people, I did not include them in my analysis.)

I have no illusions that my file of 3,600 migrants represents all the individuals who left Sambuca between 1879 and 1935, but I do estimate that it represents somewhere between one-half and two-thirds. The completeness of the file is difficult to estimate mainly because no completely satisfactory measure of total emigration from Sambuca can be made from other types of sources. Statistics published by the state suggest that over 7,000 Sambucesi applied to leave the town before 1915, while analyses of net population changes (corrected for fertility and mortality) suggests a loss of about 6,000 residents for 1881 to 1930.[6] My file represents slightly more than 50 percent of the first figure and somewhat more than 60 percent of the second.

One last method of assessing the completeness of the migrant file was attempted. I did not (and could not, given restrictions on the use of census manuscripts after 1910) search all American sources systematically. Nevertheless, my partial search did reveal immigrants unidentified in the Sicilian sources; typically, these persons were siblings and parents of the migrants identified in Sambuca's archive. For every fourteen migrants linked to an American source, I found ten additional migrants not listed in any Sicilian source. Thus, had I been able to link all the migrants found in Sambuca to American sources, I would have found an additional 2,377 migrants. This would have raised the total size of the migrant file to over 6,000 migrants—or about Sambuca's estimated population losses from 1881 to 1930.

The 280 migrants discovered only in the American sources provided one way to check for possible biases in the Sicilian sources. There were differences between the migrants identified in Sicilian and American sources: Sicilian records definitely underrecorded the migration of women, and both the parents and the younger female siblings of men who migrated as members of family groups. The Sicilian sources identified women as only 28 percent of all migrants, whereas women made up almost 40 percent of the migrants identified first in the American sources.[7] Biases like these were taken into account in interpreting migration patterns in chapter 5.

Table A.1 contrasts the data from the migrant file with published statistics on applications for *nulla osta* and passports from Sambuca after 1880. With one exception, the migrant file identified 40 to 50 percent of the migrants applying to leave Sicily during any five-year period. It is difficult to assess the significance of this proportion. Published sources exaggerated the actual numbers of emigrants by describing only intention to migrate, and by failing to differentiate among those applying for the first time and those applying repeatedly. (Local records revealed many men applied two or three times for the *nulla osta* in the years between 1895 and 1900.) The same problem results from the fact that more than 10 percent of the migrants in the file went to the United States more than once.

In general, however, the pattern of migration revealed in the file roughly resembles that which emerges in nationally collected statistics, at least until World War I. The only troubling discrepancy is for the five-year period between 1905 and 1909, when published sources and migrant file offer conflicting evidence on the volume of migration. There is no way to know whether migration from Sambuca increased rapidly during these years—as national statistics suggest—or whether it leveled off—as the migrant file shows—after 1905. Net population balances for Sambuca do suggest a decline in population loss during the first

Table A.1

Migration from Sambuca in National Statistics and in the Migrant File

	1880–1884	1885–1889	1890–1894	1895–1899	1900–1904	1905–1909	1910–1919	1920–1929	1930–1939
Applications for *nulla osta* and passports	88	407	761	1,457	1,655	1,819	1,208	—	—
Positive identification or strong circumstantial evidence, date of migration known	62	158	320	668	789	554	557	187	37
Positive identification or strong circumstantial evidence, date of migration unknown*	6	16	32	67	80	56	56	19	4

Persons migrating a second or third time (Re-emigrants)	—	3	5	19	34	54	120	166	63
Total	68	177	357	754	903	664	733	372	104
Weak circumstantial evidence of migration	28	66	96	119	76	78	61	—	
Total	96	243	453	873	979	742	794	372	104
Migrants returning	—	19	49	70	90	161	283	156	86

*Estimates, assuming that migrants who departed at unknown times followed the same general patterns of those with known departure dates.

Figure A.1

Peasant and Artisan Migration from Sambuca, 1880–1919

decade of the century.[8] Lower rates of net out-migration could have reflected return migration, which picked up at that time. It may also have reflected the fact that Sambuca attracted in-migrants, like those from Favara, during this decade; many of these recent arrivals may have had a child or two before applying for passports and subsequently migrating from the town. This would explain both the decline in net population losses and the failure of local records to "catch" the in-migrants, since neither draft records nor later household registration files would have been available for those not born in the town or permanently settling there.

It may also be that the American depression of 1907 caused some of the discrepancies between passport applications, net population change, and my migrant file during this period. The depression caused immediate increases in return migration to Sambuca, as well as a sudden, if temporary, drop in passport applications. A considerable proportion of those who applied in record numbers for passports in 1906 and 1907 may never have left their hometown, or may have reapplied later and thus appear in the migrant file as having left after 1909.

Finally, it seems probable that the "missing migrants" during this period were mainly peasants heading for the Chicago area. Brooklyn's manuscript census listings for 1910 revealed relatively few artisanal Sambucesi unidentified in Sicilian sources. A search of Rockford's primarily peasant population in 1910 identified many more. Figure A.1 suggests much the same thing. While the number of artisans migrating declined slowly after 1895, peasant migration continued to increase into the twentieth century. The real problem in interpreting the migrant file, then, is determining how seriously it underrecorded peasant migration—and thus distorted my analysis of peasant destinations—during this period. That problem would require further and far more systematic research in the American sources.

Notes

Works cited in the Bibliography are given without publication information in the Notes.

Introduction

1. J. D. McCarthy and M. Zald, "Resource Mobilization and Social Movements," *American Journal of Sociology* 82 (May 1977):1212–1241.

2. In the United States, labor historians and immigration historians have shown new interest in immigrant workers. See Dirk Hoerder, ed., *Struggle a Hard Battle—Working-Class Immigrants* (DeKalb, Ill.: Northern Illinois University Press, 1986) and Charles Stephenson and Robert Asher, eds., *Life and Labor: Dimensions of Working-Class History* (Albany: State University of New York Press, 1987). Interest in the history of migration and labor among students of European movements is also increasing. See Dirk Hoerder, ed., *Labor Migration in the Atlantic Economies* (Westport, Conn.: Greenwood Press, 1985). Two excellent examples of the social scientific study of rural conflict are Henry A. Landsberger, ed., *Rural Protest: Peasant Movements and Social Change* (London and New York: MacMillan, 1974) and Eric Wolf, *Peasant Wars of the Twentieth Century* (New York: Harper & Row, 1968).

3. Stephan Thernstrom, "Socialism and Social Mobility," in John H. M. Laslett and Seymour Martin Lipset, eds., *Failure of a Dream? Essays in the History of American Socialism,* revised ed. (Berkeley, Los Angeles, and London: University of California Press, 1974), 408–24, here 411–12; Stephan Thernstrom and Peter Knights, "Men in Motion: Some Data and Speculations on Urban Population Mobility in Nineteenth-Century America," *Journal of Interdisciplinary History* 1 (1970):7–35; MacDonald, "Argricultural Organization, Migration and Labor Militancy in Rural Italy"; MacDonald, "Some Socio-Economic Emigration Differentials in Rural Italy." For an important critique of the assumption that mobility undermines or serves as an alternative to labor organization, see Charles Stephenson, "A Gathering of Strangers? Mobility, Social Structure and Political Participation in the Formation of Nineteenth-Century American Workingclass Culture," in Milton Cantor, ed., *American Workingclass Culture* (Westport, Conn.: Greenwood Press, 1979), 31–66.

4. For example, Briggs, *An Italian Passage,* ch. 2; Virginia Yans-McLaughlin, *Family and Community; Italian Immigrants in Buffalo, 1880–1930,* 109–10; Barton, *Peasants and Strangers: Italians, Rumanians and Slovaks in an American City, 1890–1930,* 28–34; John Bodnar, "Immigration, Kinship and the Rise of Working-Class Realism in Industrial America," *Journal of Social History* 14 (1980):45–65.

5. Di Giovanna, *Inchiostro e Trazzere,* 55; A. di Terravecchia, "Da Allora Sambuca fu Battezzata Piccola Mosca," *La Voce di Sambuca* (April/March 1978). Although I used

Sambuca in my first book to illustrate typical Sicilian social and settlement patterns in the nineteenth century, the book was not, as some of its reviewers seemed to think, a study of Sambucesi settlements in the United States: Donna Gabaccia, *From Sicily to Elizabeth Street: Housing and Social Change among Italian Immigrants, 1880–1930.*

6. Thomas Archdeacon, "Problems and Possibilities in the Study of American Immigration and Ethnic History," *International Migration Review* 19 (Spring 1985):112–34; Samuel Baily, "The Future of Italian-American Studies: An Historian's Approach to Research in the Coming Decade," in Tomasi, *Italian-Americans: New Perspectives in Italian Immigration and Ethnicity,* 193–201.

7. Biographies of industrial red cities exist for France. See Jean Paul Brunet, *Saint Denis, la Ville Rouge* (Paris: Hachette, 1980); John M. Merriman, *The Red City, Limoges and the French Nineteenth Century* (New York: Oxford University Press, 1985). Village-outward studies in the history of emigration have already been undertaken, see Douglass, *Emigration in a South Italian Town: An Anthropological History.*

8. Lopreato, "Social Stratification and Mobility"; Cerase, "A Study of Italian Migrants Returning from the U.S.A."; Caroli, *Italian Repatriation from the United States, 1900–1914,* 61.

Chapter 1: Of Militants and Migrants

1. For comparative discussions of migration to the United States, see Thomas J. Archdeacon, *Becoming American: An Ethnic History* (New York and London: The Free Press and Collier MacMillan, 1983). For comparative studies of one group, see Klein, "The Integration of Italian Immigrants into the United States and Argentina: A Comparative Analysis," and Baily, "The Adjustment of Italian Immigrants in Buenos Aires and New York, 1870–1914." Historical studies of migration and the formation of Europe's working classes are in Hoerder, *Labor Migration;* Gary S. Cross, *Immigrant Workers in Industrial France, The Making of a New Laboring Class* (Philadelphia: Temple University Press, 1983); Klaus J. Bade, ed., *Auswanderer, Wanderarbeiter, Gastarbeiter,* 2 vols. (Ostfildern: Scripta Mercaturae Verlag, 1984); Shula Marks and Peter Richardson, eds., *International Labour Migration: Historical Perspectives* (Hounslow, U.K.: Institute of Commonwealth Studies, University of London, 1984).

2. Mark J. Miller, *Foreign Workers in Western Europe: An Emerging Political Force* (New York: Praeger, 1981); Gary P. Freeman, *Immigrant Labor and Racial Conflict in Industrial Societies, The French and British Experience, 1945–1975* (Princeton, N.J.: Princeton University Press, 1978); George Tapinos, *l'Immigration Etrangère en France* (Paris: Presses Universitaires de France, 1975); Otto Uhlig, *Die Ungeliebten Gäste, Ausländische Arbeitnehmer in Deutschland* (Munich: Praeger, 1974).

3. Isaac Hourwich, *Immigration and Economics* (New York: G. P. Putnam's Sons, 1912), 329; John Higham, *Strangers in the Land: Patterns of American Nativism, 1860–1925* (New York: Atheneum, 1973), 45–57; Donald Avery, *'Dangerous Foreigners': European Immigrant Workers and Labour Radicalism in Canada, 1896–1932* (Toronto: McClelland and Stewart, 1979).

4. Higham, *Strangers in the Land,* 219–33. See also Stanley Cobin, "A Study in Nativism: The American Red Scare of 1919–1920," *Political Science Quarterly* 79 (1964):

52–75; William Preston, Jr., *Aliens and Dissenters, Federal Suppression of Radicals, 1903–1933* (Cambridge, Mass.: Harvard University Press, 1963).

5. The classic antiradical report with a focus on immigrant troublemakers is New York State, *Revolutionary Radicalism*.

6. Carrol D. Wright, "The Influence of Trade Unions on Immigrants," *U.S. Bureau of Labor Bulletin* 56 (1905):1–6; Robert D. Parmet, *Labor and Immigration in Industrial America* (Boston: Twayne, 1981); Robert Asher, "Union Nativism and the Immigrant Response," *Labor History* 23 (1982):325–48; Gwendolyn Mink, *Old Labor and New Immigrants in American Political Development* (Ithaca: Cornell University Press, 1986).

7. Reinhard Lohrmann and Klaus Manfrass, eds., *Ausländerbeschäftigung und Internationale Politik* (Munich-Vienna: Oldenbourg, 1974); Stephen Castles and Godula Kosack, "The Function of Labour Immigration in Western European Capitalism," *New Left Review* 73 (1972):3–21; Craig J. Jenkins, "The Demand for Immigrant Workers: Labor Scarcity or Social Control?" *International Migration Review* 12 (Winter 1978):514–35. For the influence on lands of origin, see Reynieri, "Emigration and Sending Areas as a Subsidized System in Italy"; Claus Leggiewie and Marios Nikolinakis, "Europäische Peripherie. Zur Frage der Abhängigkeit des Mittelmeerraums von Westeuropa. Tendenzen und Entwicklungsperspektiven," *Die Dritte Welt,* Special Issue (1975); Peter Kammerer, "Probleme von Entsendeländern im Internationalen Vergleich; das Beispiel der Mittelmeerländer," in Bade, *Auswanderer,* 531–57.

8. Stephen Castles and Godula Kosack, *Immigrant Workers and Class Structure in Western Europe* (London: Oxford University Press, 1973); Alejandro Portes and John Walton, *Labor, Class and the International System* (New York: Academic Press, 1981); Marios Nikolinakos, *Politische Ökonomie der Gastarbeiterfrage. Migration und Kapitalismus* (Reinbeck: Rowohlt, 1973). American scholars have explored similar themes, if somewhat differently: Michael Piore, *Birds of Passage, Migrant Labor and Industrial Societies* (Cambridge: Cambridge University Press, 1979); David M. Gordon, Richard Edwards, and Michael Reich, *Segmented Work, Divided Workers* (Cambridge: Cambridge University Press, 1982), esp. ch. 3; Michael Hechter, "The Position of Eastern European Immigrants to the United States in the Capitalist Division of Labor: Some Trends and Prospects," in Walter Goldfrank, ed., *The World System of Capitalism: Past and Present* (Beverly Hills: Sage Publications, 1979), 111–30.

9. Edna Bonacich, "A Theory of Ethnic Antagonism: The Split-Labor Market," *American Sociological Review* 37 (October 1972):547–59; Godula Kosack and Stephen Castles, *Ausländische Arbeiter und Klassenkampf* (Offenbach: Verlag 2000, 1972); Manuel Castells, "Immigrant Workers and Class Struggle," *Politics and Society* 5 (1975):33–66; Paolo Cinanni, *Emigrazione ed Unità Operaia* (Milan: Feltrinelli, 1972).

10. Charles F. Sabel, *Work and Politics, The Division of Labor in Industry* (Cambridge: Cambridge University Press, 1982), 132–36.

11. On the period of free migration, see Aristide Zolberg, "International Migration Policies in a Changing World System," in William H. McNeill and Ruth S. Adams, eds., *Human Migration: Patterns and Policies* (Bloomington: Indiana University Press, 1978), 241–86. Charlotte Erickson also dismisses any view of this migration as employer-initiated, *American Industry and the European Immigrant* (New York: Russel and Russel, 1957).

12. Gerald Rosenblum, *Immigrant Workers: Their Impact on American Labor Radicalism* (New York: Basic Books, 1973), ch. 5

13. John Bodnar, *Workers' World; Kinship, Community and Protest in Industrial Society* (Baltimore and London: The Johns Hopkins University Press, 1982), 166–68.

14. Herbert G. Gutman, "Work, Culture and Society in Industrializing America, 1815–1919," in Gutman, *Work, Culture and Society in Industrializing America, Essays in American Working-Class and Social History* (New York: Alfred A. Knopf, 1976), 3–78. It is impossible and unnecessary to cite all the recent monographs influenced by Gutman's formulation. See, for example, Michael H. Frisch and Daniel J. Walkowitz, eds., *Working-Class America: Essays on Labor, Community and American Society* (Urbana: University of Illinois Press, 1983).

15. David Brody, "Labor," in Stephan Thernstrom et al., eds., *Harvard Encyclopedia of American Ethnic Groups* (Cambridge, Mass.: Harvard University Press, 1980), 612–13.

16. Ira Katznelson, *City Trenches: Urban Politics and the Patterning of Class in the United States* (Chicago and London: The University of Chicago Press, 1981). On the Jewish exception, see Gerald Sorin, *The Prophetic Minority: American Jewish Immigrant Radicals, 1880–1920* (Bloomington: Indiana University Press, 1985); Arthur Liebman, *Jews and the Left* (New York: John Wiley, 1979).

17. John Bodnar, *The Transplanted* (Bloomington: Indiana University Press, 1985), ch. 3.

18. Clifton K. Yearly, *Britons in American Labor, 1820–1914* (Baltimore: Johns Hopkins Press, 1957); Nora Levin, *While Messiah Tarried: Jewish Socialist Movements, 1871–1917* (New York: Schocken Books, 1977); John H. M. Laslett, *Labor and the Left, A Study of Socialist and Radical Influences in the American Labor Movement, 1881–1924* (New York-London: Basic Books, 1970); Amy Zahl Gottlieb, "The Influence of British Trade Unionists on the Regulation of the Mining Industry in Illinois, 1872," *Labor History* 19 (Summer 1978):397–415.

19. Banfield, *The Moral Basis of a Backward Society;* Theodor Shanin, "The Peasantry as a Political Factor," *Sociological Review* 24 (1966):5–27; Karl Marx, *The Eighteenth Brumaire of Louis Bonaparte* (New York: International Publishers, 1957), 109.

20. Barrington Moore, Jr., *Social Origins of Dictatorship and Democracy* (Boston: Beacon Press, 1967), 453.

21. Hamza Alavi, "Peasantry and Revolution," in Ralph Miliband and John Saville, eds., *The Socialist Register* (New York: Monthly Review Press, 1965), 241–77; Wolf, *Peasant Wars;* Eric R. Wolf, "Peasant Revolution," in Norman Miller and Roderick Aya, eds., *National Liberation, Revolution in the Third World* (New York: The Free Press, 1971), 48–67.

22. Not surprisingly, we also know most about rural discontents there. Maurice Agulhon, *The Republic in the Village,* transl. Janet Lloyd (Cambridge: Cambridge University Press, 1982); Suzanne Berger, *Peasants Against Politics, Rural Organization in Brittany, 1911–1967* (Cambridge, Mass.: Harvard University Press, 1972); Laura Levine Frader, "Grapes of Wrath: Vineyard Workers, Labor Unions and Strike Activity in the Aude, 1903–1913," in Louise A. Tilly and Charles Tilly, eds., *Class Conflict and Collective Action* (Beverly Hills: Sage Publications, 1981), 185–206; Peter Jones, *Politics and Rural Society, the Southern Massif Central, c. 1750–1880* (New York: Cambridge University Press, 1979); Ted W. Margadant, *French Peasants in Revolt: The Insurrection of 1851* (Princeton, N.J.: Princeton University Press, 1979); Peter McPhee, "Popular Culture,

Symbolism and Rural Radicalism in Nineteenth-Century France," *Journal of Peasant Studies* 5 (January 1978):238–53.

23. Giuseppe Galasso, *Le Rivolte Contadine nell'Europa del Secolo XVII* (Naples: Libreria Scientifica, 1970); Frank M. Snowden, *Violence and Great Estates in the South of Italy: Apulia, 1900–1922* (New York: Cambridge University Press, 1986); Aya, *The Missed Revolution;* David Gilmore, "Land Reform and Rural Revolt in Nineteenth-Century Andalusia," *Peasant Studies* 6 (October 1977):142–47; Edward Malefakis, *Agrarian Reform and Peasant Revolution* (New Haven: Yale University Press, 1970); Samuel Clark and James S. Connelly, Jr., eds., *Irish Peasants: Violence and Political Unrest, 1780–1914* (Madison: The University of Wisconsin Press, 1983); Michael Bearnes, *Peasants and Power, The Whiteboy Movements and their Control in Pre-Famine Ireland* (New York: St. Martin's Press, 1983); John Bohstedt, *Riots and Community Politics in England and Wales, 1790–1810* (Cambridge, Mass.: Harvard University Press, 1983); Daniel Chirot and Charles Ragin, "The Market, Tradition and Peasant Rebellion: The Case of Rumania in 1907," *American Sociological Review* 40 (1975):428–44; Daniel Chirot, *Social Change in a Peripheral Society, The Creation of a Balkan Colony* (New York: Academic Press, 1976); David Mitrany, *Marx Against the Peasant* (New York: Collier, 1961); R. Wirtz, *Widersetzlichkeiten, Excese, Crawalle, Tumulte und Skandale: Sozialbewegung und Sozialer Protest in Baden, 1815–1848* (Frankfurt: Ullstein, 1981). I have omitted the sizable literature on the Russian revolution.

24. Early studies of these forms of protest include George Rudé, *The Crowd in History. A Study of Popular Disturbances in France and England, 1730–1848* (New York: Wiley, 1964); E. P. Thompson, "The Moral Economy of the English Crowd in the Eighteenth Century," *Past and Present* 50 (1971):76–136; Louise Tilly, "The Food Riot as a Form of Political Conflict in France," *Journal of Interdisciplinary History* 2 (1971):23–57.

25. Helen I. Safa and Brian M. DuToit, *Migration and Development: Implications for Ethnic Identity and Political Conflict* (The Hague: Mouton, 1975); Allan Rodgers, "Migration and Industrial Development: the Southern Italian Experience," *Economic Geography* 42 (April 1970):111–35; R. Rhoades, "European Cyclical Migration and Economic Development: the Case of Southern Spain," in George Gmelch and Walter P. Zenner, eds., *Urban Life: Readings in Urban Anthropology* (New York: St. Martin's Press, 1980), 110–19; Alejandro Portes, "Migration and Underdevelopment," *Politics and Society* 8 (1978):1–48.

26. Moore, *Social Origins,* xvii.

27. MacDonald and MacDonald, "A Simple Institutional Framework for the Analysis of Agricultural Development Potential"; MacDonald and MacDonald, "Institutional Economics and Rural Development: Two Italian Types"; MacDonald, "Italy's Rural Social Structure and Emigration."

28. Bodnar, *The Transplanted,* 1.

29. Immanuel Wallerstein, *The Modern World System: Capitalist Agriculture and the Origins of the European World-Economy in the Sixteenth Century* (New York: Academic Press, 1976) and Wallerstein, *The Modern World-System II: Mercantilism and the Consolidation of the European World Economy, 1600–1750* (New York: Academic Press, 1980).

30. While most focus on contemporary migration, some also offer an historical perspective. Besides many of the works cited in n. 7 and n. 8 above, see Zolberg, "International Migration"; Saskia Sassen-Koob, "Towards a Conceptualization of Immigrant Labor,"

Social Problems 29 (October 1981):65–85; Sassen-Koob, "The International Circulation of Resources and Development: The Case of Migrant Labour," *Development and Change* 9 (October 1978):509–45; Marios Nikolinakis, "Notes Towards a General Theory of Migration in Late Capitalism," *Race and Class* 17 (1975):5–17; R. Rhoades, "Foreign Labor and German Industrial Capitalism, 1871–1978; the Evolution of a Migratory System," *American Ethnologist* 5 (August 1978):553–75; Michael Hechter, *Internal Colonialism: The Celtic Fringe in British National Development, 1536–1966* (London: Routledge and Kegan Paul, 1975); "Immigration and the Changes in the International Division of Labor," *Contemporary Marxism,* Special Issue 5 (1982).

31. Besides Wallerstein, see the work of the dependency theorists, especially Samir Amin, *Unequal Development: An Essay on the Social Formations of Peripheral Capitalism,* transl. Brian Pearce (New York: Monthly Review Press, 1976); Amin, *Accumulation on a World Scale, a Critique of the Theory of Underdevelopment,* transl. Brian Pearce (New York: Monthly Review Press, 1974).

32. Two good discussions are Alain de Janvry, *The Agrarian Question and Reformism in Latin America* (Baltimore: The Johns Hopkins University Press, 1981), chs. 2–3; Eric R. Wolf, *Europe and the People Without History* (Berkeley, Los Angeles, London: University of California Press, 1982), esp. ch. 3 and 296–98.

33. For eastern Europe, see Wallerstein, *Modern World System,* ch. 6; for the Mediterranean, see Fernand Braudel, *The Mediterranean and the Mediterranean World in the Age of Philip II,* 2 vols. (New York: Harper & Row, 1976), here 1:75–78 and 570–604.

34. Peter Kriedte, *Peasants, Landlords and Merchant Capitalists, Europe and the World Economy, 1500–1800,* transl. V. R. Berghahn (Leamington Spa: Berk Publishers, 1983); Moore, *Social Origins,* 433–38.

35. Wolf, *Europe and People without History,* 79–88. By choosing a new name for it, Wolf hopes to establish that feudalism in the peripheries was not the economic or social equivalent of the feudalism described by Marc Bloch.

36. See, for example, Braudel, *Mediterranean,* 1:427–44.

37. Peter Kriedte, Hans Medick, and Jürgen Schlumbohm, *Industrialization before Industrialization: Rural Industry in the Genesis of Capitalism* (Cambridge and Paris: Cambridge University Press and Editions de la Maison des Sciences de l'Homme, 1981), orig. publ. 1977; Rudolf Braun, *Industrialisierung und Volksleben: Die Veränderung der Lebensformen in einem ländlichen Industriegebiet vor 1800* (Erlenback-Zurich: E. Rentsch, 1960); Maxine Berg, Pat Hudson, and Michael Sonenscher, eds., *Manufacture in Town and Country before the Factory* (Cambridge: Cambridge University Press, 1983).

38. Kriedte links the spread of wage earning in agriculture to the low productivity of large estates, *Peasants, Landlords,* 2. See also Charles Tilly and Richard Tilly, "Agenda for European Economic History in the 1970s," *Journal of Economic History* 31 (1971):184–98.

39. Bodnar, *The Transplanted,* 1; Sassen-Koob, "Toward a Conceptualization," 65.

40. The best theoretical discussion of this transition is Joel S. Migdal, *Peasants, Politics and Revolution: Pressures Toward Political and Social Change in the Third World* (Princeton, N.J.: Princeton University Press, 1974), 106–7 and ch. 9. For an historical discussion, see Charles, Louise, and Richard Tilly, *The Rebellious Century* (Cambridge, Mass.: Harvard University Press, 1975), 47–49.

41. Arlacchi, *Mafia, Peasants and Great Estates, Society in Traditional Calabria.* On

the persistence of small-scale household production for subsistence and market, see Peter McPhee, "A Reconsideration of the 'Peasantry' of Nineteenth Century France," *Peasant Studies* 9 (Fall 1981):4–23; Kostas Vergopolous, "Capitalism and Peasant Productivity," *Journal of Peasant Studies* 5 (1978):446–65; Harriet Friedman, "World Market, State and Family Farm: Social Bases of Household Production in the Era of Wage Labor," *Comparative Studies in Society and History* 20 (October 1978):545–86; Friedman, "Household Production and National Economy: Concepts for the Analysis of Agrarian Formations," *Journal of Peasant Studies* 7 (January 1980):158–84.

42. Kriedte, Medick, Schlumbohm, *Industrialization Before Industrialization*, 292–321; Yda Saueressig-Schreuder, "Emigration and the Decline of Traditional Industries in Mid-Nineteenth Century Europe," *The Immigration History Newsletter* 17 (May 1985); Harald Runblom and Hans Norman, eds., *From Sweden to America: A History of the Migration* (Minneapolis: University of Minnesota Press, 1976), 156–59, 163–64; Walter D. Kamphoefner, *Westfalen in der Neuen Welt, Eine Sozialgeschichte der Auswanderung im 19. Jahrhundert* (Münster: F. Coppenrath Verlag, 1982), ch. 2.

43. Bodnar, *The Transplanted*, 23–44; MacDonald, "Agricultural Organization," 74.

44. Brinley Thomas, *Migrations and Economic Growth: A Case Study of Great Britain and the Atlantic Economy*, 2nd. ed. (Cambridge: Cambridge University Press, 1973); Brinley Thomas and William Petersen, "Migrations," in David Sills, *Encyclopedia of the Social Sciences* (New York: MacMillan and The Free Press, 1968), 286–300.

45. Michael Burawoy, "The Functions and Reproduction of Migrant Labor: Comparative Material from Southern Africa and the United States," *American Journal of Sociology* 81 (March 1976):1076–87; see also Joan Smith, Immanuel Wallerstein, and Hans-Dieter Evers, eds., *Households and the World-Economy* (Beverly Hills: Sage Publications, 1984).

46. Carol A. Smith, "Labor and International Capital in the Making of a Peripheral Social Formation: Economic Transformations in Guatemala, 1850–1950," in Charles Bergquist, ed., *Labor in the Capitalist World-Economy* (Beverly Hills: Sage Publications, 1984), 135–56.

47. C., L., and R. Tilly, *Rebellious Century*, 299.

48. For an example, see Agulhon, *Republic in the Village*, 17.

49. Andre Gunder Frank, *Lumpen-Bourgeoisie: Lumpen-Development*, transl. Marion Davis Berdecio (New York: Monthly Review Press, 1972).

50. Good discussions are in de Janvry, *Agrarian Question*, 106–9, and Frank, *Lumpen-bourgeoisie*. See also Frank W. Young, *Interdisciplinary Theories of Rural Development* (Greenwich, Conn., and London: JAI Press, 1983).

51. Schneider, Schneider, and Hansen, "Modernization and Development: The Role of Regional Elites and Noncorporate Groups in the European Mediterranean."

52. Moore especially emphasizes the importance of rural elites' differential responses to economic change for the development of commercial agriculture and modern politics, *Social Origins*, xvii, 466–67. For their responses to crises in agriculture, see Arlacchi, *Mafia, Peasants*, 170–74; Chirot, *Social Change*, 147–48.

53. On the material basis of communalism, see David E. Vassberg, *Land and Society in Golden Age Castile* (Cambridge: Cambridge University Press, 1984).

54. Wallerstein, *The Modern World System*, 21; Braudel, *Mediterranean*, 2:735–55; Kriedte, *Peasants, Landlords*, 16–17.

55. C., L., and R. Tilly, *Rebellious Century*, 53–54.

56. Hobsbawm, *Primitive Rebels: Studies in Archaic Forms of Social Movement in the 19th and 20th Centuries;* Hobsbawm, *Bandits* (New York: Dell, 1969).

57. Hobsbawm, *Primitive Rebels*, 93.

58. Barton, "Eastern and Southern Europeans," in Higham, *Ethnic Leadership in America*, 151–54.

59. Thomas Bender, *Community and Social Change in America* (Baltimore and London: The Johns Hopkins University Press, 1978), 8.

60. Basile Kerblay, "Chayanov and the Theory of Peasantry as a Specific Type of Economy," in Theodor Shanin, eds., *Peasants and Peasant Societies, Selected Readings* (Harmondsworth: Penguin Books, 1971), 150–60.

61. James Scott, *The Moral Economy of the Peasant, Rebellion and Subsistence in Southeast Asia* (New Haven and London: Yale University Press, 1976).

62. For an early statement, see Michael Lipton, "The Theory of the Optimising Peasant," *Journal of Development Studies* 4 (April 1968):327–51. More recent is Samuel L. Popkin, *The Rational Peasant, The Political Economy of Rural Society in Vietnam* (Berkeley: University of California Press, 1979).

63. Scott, *The Moral Economy of the Peasant*, vii.

64. A good starting place is Arthur L. Stinchcombe, "Agricultural Enterprise and Rural Class Relations," *American Journal of Sociology* 67 (September 1961):165–76. There is a sizable anthropological literature on the assumptions and political strategies of peasants. Besides works cited in notes 74 and 79 below, see, as examples, George Foster, "Peasant Society and the Image of Limited Good," *American Anthropologist* 67 (April 1965): 293–312; Cancian, "The South Italian Peasant: World View and Political Behavior." See also Gerrit Huizer, *The Revolutionary Potential of Peasants in Latin America* (Lexington, Mass.: D. C. Heath, 1972).

65. An excellent summary of most recent case studies is Bodnar, *The Transplanted*.

66. Bodnar, *The Transplanted*, 3–4 and ch. 1, passim.

67. Torsten Hägerstrand, "Migration and Area, Survey of a Sample of Swedish Migration Fields and Hypothetical Considerations on their Genesis," in David Hannerberg, Torsten Hägerstrand, and Bruno Odering, *Migration in Sweden: A Symposium* (Lund: C. W. K. Gleerup, 1957); Hägerstrand, "Aspects of the Spatial Structure of Social Communications and the Diffusion of Information," in Paul Ward English and Robert C. Mayfield, eds., *Man, Space and Environment* (New York and Toronto: Oxford University Press, 1972), 328–39; Richard L. Morrill and Forest R. Pitts, "Marriage, Migration and the Mean Information Field: A Study in Uniqueness and Generality," in ibid., 359–84.

68. Bodnar, *The Transplanted*, 23–30; MacDonald, "Agricultural Organization," 69–70.

69. Mack Walker, *Germany and the Emigration, 1816–1885* (Cambridge, Mass.: Harvard University Press, 1964), 70–71; Moses Rischin, *The Promised City, New York's Jews, 1870–1914* (New York: Harper & Row, 1962), 25–27. See also n. 42 above.

70. Bodnar, *The Transplanted*, 10; MacDonald, "Agricultural Organization," 65; Arlacchi, *Mafia, Peasants*, 183.

71. This aspect of local economies has not received as much systematic attention, at least from historians of emigration. See H. J. Habakkuk, "Family Structure and Economic Change in Nineteenth Century Europe," in Norman W. Bell and Ezra F. Vogel, *A Modern Introduction to the Family* (Glencoe, Ill.: The Free Press, 1960), ch. 13, esp. 167–68;

Leonard Kasdan, "Family Structure, Migration and the Entrepreneur," *Comparative Studies in Society and History* 7 (July 1965):345–54; Jack Goody, Joan Thirsk, and E. P. Thompson, *Family and Inheritance, Rural Society in Western Europe, 1200–1800* (Cambridge: Cambridge University Press, 1976).

72. "Peasants and Political Mobilization in Latin America and in the Balkans," *Comparative Studies in Society and History,* Special Issues 17 (1975) and 18 (1976); Jeffery M. Paige, *Agrarian Revolution: Social Movements and Export Agriculture in the Underdeveloped World* (New York: The Free Press, 1975); Migdal, *Peasants;* Henry A. Landsberger, *Latin American Peasant Movements* (Ithaca and London: Cornell University Press, 1969); Robert P. Weller and Scott E. Guggenheim, eds., *Power and Protest in the Countryside, Studies of Rural Unrest in Asia, Europe and Latin America* (Durham, N.C.: Duke University Press, 1982); Huizer, *Revolutionary Potential;* Claude E. Welch, Jr., *Anatomy of Rebellion* (Albany: State University of New York Press, 1980); Bert Useem, "Peasant Involvement in the Cuban Revolution," *Journal of Peasant Studies* 5 (October 1977): 99–111. More theoretical work in this area includes Elbaki Hermassi, "Towards a Comparative Study of Revolutions," *Comparative Studies in Society and History* 18 (April 1976):- 211–35; Mark N. Hagopian, *The Phenomenon of Revolution* (New York: Dodd, Mead, 1974); Ted R. Gurr, *Why Men Rebel* (Princeton, N.J.: Princeton University Press, 1970), Rod Aya, "Theories of Revolution Reconsidered: Contrasting Models of Collective Violence," *Theory and Society* 8 (July 1979):39–99; Walter L. Goldfrank, "Theories of Revolution and Revolution Without Theory: The Case of Mexico," *Theory and Society* 7 (January/March 1979):135–65; John Dunn, *Modern Revolutions: An Introduction to the Analysis of a Political Phenomenon* (Cambridge: Cambridge University Press, 1972).

73. Theda Skocpol, "France, Russia, China: A Structural Analysis of Social Revolutions," *Comparative Studies in Society and History* 18 (April 1976): 175–210; Skocpol, *States and Social Revolutions: A Comparative Analysis of France, Russia and China* (Cambridge: Cambridge University Press, 1979); Skocpol, "Explaining Revolutions: In Quest of a Social-Structural Approach," in Lewis A. Coser and Otto N. Larsen, eds., *The Uses of Controversy in Sociology* (New York: The Free Press, 1976); David Snyder and Charles Tilly, "Hardship and Collective Violence in France, 1830 to 1860," *American Sociological Review* 37 (October 1972):520–32; Charles Tilly, *From Mobilization to Revolution* (Reading, Mass.: Addison-Wesley, 1978), ch. 7.

74. James C. Davies, "Toward a Theory of Revolution," *American Sociological Review* 27 (February 1962):5–19; Crane Brinton, *The Anatomy of Revolution* (Englewood Cliffs, N.J.: Prentice-Hall, 1965), 250–64.

75. Skocpol, "France, Russia, China."

76. Wolf, *Peasant Wars;* Alavi, "Peasantry and Revolution."

77. Besides the case studies in Wolf, *Peasant Wars,* see, for example, Ronald Waterbury, "Non-Revolutionary Peasants: Oaxaca Compared to Morelos in the Mexican Revolution," *Comparative Studies in Society and History* 17 (October 1975):410–42.

78. Wolf, *Peasant Wars,* 291.

79. MacDonald, "Agricultural Organization," 67.

80. Paige, *Agrarian Revolution,* ch. 1.

81. Skocpol, "What Makes Peasants Revolutionary?" in Weller and Guggenheim, *Power and Protest,* 157–79.

82. Yans-McLaughlin, *Family and Community,* 34–35.

83. Wolf, *Peasant Wars*, 293–94.

84. Paige, *Agrarian Revolution*, 115.

85. Skocpol, "France, Russia, China"; Angus W. McDonald, Jr., *The Urban Origins of Rural Revolutions* (Berkeley: University of California Press, 1978); John Walton, *Reluctant Rebels: Comparative Studies of Revolution and Underdevelopment* (New York: Columbia University Press, 1984); Charles Tilly, "Town and Country in Revolution," in John Wilson Lewis, ed., *Peasant Rebellion and Communist Revolution in Asia* (Stanford: Stanford University Press, 1974).

86. Bodnar emphasizes that the middle and lower-middle levels of local social hierarchies were most likely to emigrate, *The Transplanted*, 13–22, passim.

87. Bodnar, *The Transplanted*, 30–33 and 86–87.

Chapter 2: A Mobile and Unruly Countryside

1. An especially clear example is Sladen and Lorimer, *Queer Things About Sicily*. See also Sladen, *In Sicily;* Sladen, *Sicily, the New Winter Resort;* Douglas, *Old Calabria*. For a scholarly example, see Mack Smith, *Italy, A Modern History*, 40.

2. Neufeld, *Italy: School for Awakening Countries;* Carlyle, *The Awakening of Southern Italy;* Lutz, *Italy: A Study in Economic Development*.

3. Early studies of the problem are numerous. More recently, see Clough and Livi, "Economic Growth in Italy: An Analysis of the Uneven Development of North and South"; Eckaus, "The North-South Differential in Italian Economic Development"; Chapman, "Theories of Development and Underdevelopment in Southern Italy"; Lepre, *Il Mezzogiorno dal Feudalismo al Capitalismo;* Berger and Piore, *Dualism and Discontinuity in Industrial Societies*, ch. 4.

4. Jane and Peter Schneider, *Culture and Political Economy in Western Sicily*, chs. 2 and 3.

5. Maurice Aymard, "La Sicile, Terre d'Immigration," in M. Aymard et al., *Les Migrations dans les Pays Méditerranéennes*, 134–57. See also Aymard, "Sicilia: Sviluppo Demografico," 194–215. For a description of Sicily's early sources for the study of population, see Titone, *Origini della Questione Meridionale*, vol. 1.

6. Lepre, *Il Mezzogiorno*.

7. Schneider, "Trousseau as Treasure: Some Contradictions of Late Nineteenth-Century Change in Sicily," 328–29.

8. Besides Lepre, *Il Mezzogiorno*, 39–45, see Cancila, *Gabellotti e Contadini in un Comune Rurale;* J. and P. Schneider, *Culture and Political Economy*, chs. 6 and 8; Renda, *La Sicilia nel 1812*.

9. On agricultural change in Italy, see Sereni, *Il Capitalismo nelle Campagne, 1860–1900;* Sereni, *Storia del Paesaggio Agrario Italiano*. Works which focus on Sicily and economic change during this period include Romano, *La Sicilia nell'Ultimo Ventennio del Secolo XIX;* de Stefano and Oddo, *Storia della Sicilia dal 1860 al 1910;* F. Brancato, *La Sicilia nel Primo Ventennio del Regno d'Italia* (Bologna: Dott. Cesare Zuffi, 1956); Siegenthaler, "Sicilian Economic Change since 1860"; Hilowitz, *Economic Development and Social Change in Sicily;* Squarzina, *Produzione e Commercio dello Zolfo in Sicilia nel Secolo XIX*.

10. Giuseppe Giarrizzo, "La Sicilia e la Crisi Agraria," in Giuseppe Giarrizzo et al., *I Fasci Siciliani* (Bari: De Donato, 1975), 7–63.

11. Izzo, "Free Trade and the Southern Question in Early Post-Unification Italy."

12. J. and P. Schneider, *Culture and Political Ecomony,* 121–22.

13. Orazio Cancila, "Variazioni e Tendenze dell'Agricoltura Siciliana a Cavallo della Crisi Agraria," in Dollo et al., *I Fasci Siciliani,* 297–336.

14. Nigrelli, "La Crisi della Industria Zolfifera Siciliana in Relazione al Movimento dei Fasci"; G. Giarrizzo, "La Sicilia e la Crisi," 53–54.

15. Giuseppe Barone, "Ristrutturazione e Crisi del Blocco Agrario dai Fasci Siciliani al Primo Dopoguerra," in Barone et al., *Potere e Società in Sicilia nella Crisi dello Stato Liberale,* 1–71.

16. Italian localism is, of course, well documented. On the impact of the physical environment on diversity, see J. and P. Schneider, *Culture and Political Economy,* 36–40; Sonnino, *I Contadini in Sicilia,* 10.

17. On the adoption of the French administrative system, see Neufeld, *School for Awakening Countries,* 76.

18. Town-by-town information about agriculture is in Giunta per l'Inchiesta Agraria, *Atti della Giunta per l'Inchiesta Agraria e sulle Condizioni della Classe Agricola,* 13:parts 1 and 2, cited hereafter as *Inchiesta Agraria;* Giunta Parlamentare, *Inchiesta sulle Condizioni dei Contadini nelle Provincie Meridionali e nella Sicilia,* vol. 6, hereafter cited as *Inchiesta sulle Condizioni dei Contadini.* On local industry see "Notizie sulle Condizioni Industriali della Provincia di Palermo," *Annali di Statistica,* serie 4, no. 69, part 48 (1893); "Notizie sulle Condizioni Industriali della Provincia di Trapani," *Annali di Statistica,* serie 4, no. 69, part 61 (1896); "Notizie sulle Condizioni Industriali della Provincia di Girgenti," *Annali di Statistica,* serie 4, no. 69, part 60 (1896), cited hereafter as "Notizie sulle Condizioni Industriali."

19. Communal data on population growth are given in *Comuni e loro Popolazione.* Local intercensal population balances, adjusted for fertility and mortality, are in Somogyi, *Bilanci Demografici dei Comuni Siciliani dal 1861 al 1961.* Applications for *nulla osta* and passports are summarized in *Statistica della Emigrazione.*

20. Information on workers' societies is in *Statistica delle Società di Mutuo Soccorso; Le Società di Mutuo Soccorso;* Ministero di Agricoltura, Industria e Commercio, "Statistica delle Organizzazioni di Lavoratori al 1 Gennaio, 1913," *Bollettino dell'Ufficio del Lavoro* 20 (1914):184–200. On strikes, see *Statistica degli Scioperi, I Conflitti del Lavoro.* Regional voting behavior is summarized in *Statistica Elettorale Politica.*

21. Besides J. and P. Schneider, *Culture and Political Economy,* 27, see Barton, *Peasants and Strangers,* 28–30, and MacDonald, "Agricultural Organization," 72–73; Renda, *l'Emigrazione in Sicilia,* 44.

22. Communal-level data are in *Inchiesta Agraria.* For types of peasantries associated with various forms of agricultural organization see Eric R. Wolf, *Peasants* (Englewood Cliffs, N.J.: Prentice-Hall, 1966), pt. 2.

23. On food imports by town, see *Inchiesta Agraria.* For local manufacturing see "Notizie sulle Condizioni Industriali."

24. More than 50 percent of Sicily's work force was engaged in nonagricultural pursuits, Siegenthaler, "Sicilian Economic Change," 368–70. For a regional example, see Renda, *Il Movimento Contadino nella Società Siciliana,* 23.

25. Pitrè, *Proverbi Siciliani*, 8:ch. 24, "Contrattazioni, Mercatura." See, for example, "Don't make a contract with a friend and don't buy grain from a merchant," 8:322.

26. Pitrè, *La Famiglia, la Casa, la Vita del Popolo Siciliano*, 34, 89; J. Schneider, "Trousseau as Treasure," 323; Pitrè, *Usi e Costumi, Credenze e Pregiudizi del Popolo Siciliano*, vol. 15.

27. Communal data are in "Notizie sulle Condizioni Industriali."

28. Gabaccia, *From Sicily to Elizabeth Street*, 22–23.

29. Sonnino, *I Contadini*, 18–28; *Inchiesta Agraria*, 2:116; J. and P. Schneider, *Culture and Political Economy*, 57–60.

30. *Inchiesta Agraria*, 2:263; Sonnino, *I Contadini*, 133–35; *Inchiesta sulle Condizioni dei Contadini*, 231–32.

31. Communal data are in "Notizie sulle Condizioni Industriali."

32. *Censimento, 1901*.

33. Communal data are in "Notizie sulle Condizioni Industriali."

34. Communal data are in *Inchiesta Agraria*. For the organization of the large wheat estates, see MacDonald, "Agricultural Organization," 72–73; Sereni, *Capitalismo nelle Campagne*, 146–52 and more generally the chapter "Il Capitalismo nelle Campagne e la Formazione di un Proletariato Agricola di Massa." See also Mack Smith, "The Latifundia in Modern Sicilian History."

35. Communal data are in *Inchiesta Agraria* and "Notizie sulle Condizioni Industriali." See also Rossi-Doria, "Land Tenure System and Class in South Italy."

36. Barton, *Peasants and Strangers*, 34; Briggs, *An Italian Passage*, 5–8. On the middle classes, see Loncao, *Considerazioni sulla Genesi ed Evoluzione della Borghesia in Sicilia*.

37. Renda, *Emigrazione*, 45–46; see also n. 5 above.

38. Figured from communal data in S. Somogyi, *Bilanci Demografici*. More generally, see Cinel, "The Seasonal Emigration of Italians in the Nineteenth Century: From Internal to International Destinations."

39. Compared to other western European nations, Italy's internal migrations have attracted little attention. For an early attempt, see Sitta, *Le Migrazioni Interne, Saggio di Statistica Applicata*. A recent study is Kertzer and Hogan, "On the Move: Migration in an Italian Community, 1865–1921." It seems likely that Sicily's concentrated settlement pattern of large agrotowns made mobility connected with marriage less necessary, and that overall rates of mobility were lower than in northern Italy.

40. Braudel, *Mediterranean*, 2:734–55. Daniel Horowitz extended the analysis, calling Italy, "a good country for revolutionaries, but a poor one for revolutions," *The Italian Labor Movement*, 1.

41. Mack Smith, *A History of Sicily*, parts 10, 12–14, and 15, passim.

42. Tilly, *From Mobilization to Revolution*, chs. 5–6; C., L., and R. Tilly, *Rebellious Century*, 49–52, 191–93. See also n. 26 above.

43. Braudel, *Mediterranean*, 2:734–56; Galasso, *Rivolte Contadine*, 216–17; Mack Smith, *History of Sicily*, 1:chs. 14, 21, 23 and 2:chs. 31, 33, 38, 49.

44. Mack Smith, *History of Sicily*, 1:149.

45. Tilly, *From Mobilization to Revolution*, 145–49.

46. Mack Smith, *History of Sicily*, 1:ch. 6.

47. On this period, see Renda, *Risorgimento e Classe Popolari in Sicilia, 1820–1821*;

Cortese, *Il Governo Napoletano e la Rivoluzione Siciliana del MDCCCXX–XXI;* Labate, *Un Decennio di Carboneria in Sicilia, 1821–1831;* Falci, *Scienzati e Patriotti Siciliani negli Albori del Risorgimento.*

48. Nicastro, *Dal Quarantotto al Sessanta.*

49. While only 15 percent of Sicilian peasants and shepherds could read by 1871, literacy among various artisanal groups varied from 30 to 50 percent, Bonetta, *Istruzione e Società nella Sicilia dell'Ottocento,* 71.

50. The expression is from Francesco Crispi, Prime Minister at the time of the fasci revolts (see chapter 4); see Colajanni, *Gli Avvenimenti di Sicilia e le loro Cause.*

51. Romano, *Momenti del Risorgimento in Sicilia;* la Pena, *La Rivoluzione Siciliana del 1848 in Alcune Lettere Inedite di Michele Amari.*

52. Del Carria, *Proletari senza Rivoluzione,* chs. 1–2

53. C., L., and R. Tilly, *Rebellious Century,* 260–62; Galasso, *Rivolte Contadine,* 211.

54. Banfield, *Moral Basis.* Banfield's critics include Cancian, "The South Italian Peasant"; Silverman, "Agricultural Organization, Social Structure and Values in Italy, Amoral Familism Reconsidered"; Tarrow, *Peasant Communism in Southern Italy,* 56–58. Besides Nelli's essay in the *Harvard Encyclopedia of American Ethnic Groups,* see Nelli, *From Immigrants to Ethnics: the Italian Americans,* ch. 7.

55. Pitrè, *Proverbi Siciliani,* passim. For a discussion, see Gabaccia, *From Sicily to Elizabeth Street,* 3–5.

56. This point is made by most of Banfield's critics. There is an extensive literature on the social and cultural alternatives to familism and voluntary association in southern Italy. See, for example, J. and P. Schneider, *Culture and Political Economy,* ch. 5; Moss and Cappannari, "Patterns of Kinship, Comparaggio and Community in a South Italian Village"; Graziani, "Patron-Client Relations in Southern Italy."

57. Giordano, *Handwerker- und Bauernverbände in der Sizilianischen Gesellschaft,* 17–18; see also Mack Smith, *History of Sicily,* 2:308–11.

58. Giordano, *Handwerker,* 22.

59. See, for example, Pitrè, *Proverbi Siciliani,* 9:ch. 54.

60. My main sources for this and the paragraphs that follow are the communal-level data (available mainly in Sicilian provincial archives), summarized in detail by Giordano, *Handwerker,* app. 2.

61. For evidence on early organization in individual towns, see Cerrito, *Radicalismo e Socialismo in Sicilia (1860–1882).* See also Cerrito, "Saverio Friscia nel Primo Periodo di Attività dell'Internazionale in Sicilia"; Alatri, *Lotte Politiche.*

62. *Statistica Elettorale Politica* (1883). See also Raphael Zariski, *Italy, the Politics of Uneven Development* (Hinsdale, Ill.: The Dryden Press, 1972), 29.

63. Smith, *Family Connections, A History of Italian and Jewish Immigrant Lives in Providence Rhode Island, 1900–1940,* ch. 4.

64. Giordano, *Handwerker,* 119–29.

65. For conflicting views, contrast Villari, *La Sicilia e il Socialismo,* 96, and Briggs, *An Italian Passage,* ch. 2.

66. On the role of gender in modern fraternalism, see Mary Ann Clawson, "Early Modern Fraternalism and the Patriarchal Family," *Feminist Studies* 6 (Summer 1980): 368–91.

67. In his work on Catholic activism, Francesco Renda ignores early efforts, which date

from the 1860s, *Socialisti e Cattolici in Sicilia, 1900–1904, le Lotte Agrarie.* But see instead, Renda, *Movimento Contadino,* 12.

68. Blok, "Mafia and Peasant Rebellion as Contrasting Factors in Sicilian Latifundism"; Blok, *The Mafia of a Sicilian Village,* ch. 5. The rise of mafia seems more closely linked to the decline of brigandage than to the decline of peasant jacquerie, see Falzone, *Storia della Mafia,* ch. 12.

69. "The mafia phenomenon," writes Pino Arlacchi, "had little or nothing to do with . . . the latifondo," *Mafia, Peasants,* 120. Arlacchi explicitly compares developments in coastal Calabria to similar market areas in western Sicily, 117.

Chapter 3: The Genesis of a Red Town

1. On the representativeness of the town, see J. and P. Schneider, *Culture and Political Economy,* 14–15; Gabaccia, *From Sicily to Elizabeth Street,* 15–21. I made research trips to Sambuca in 1977, 1980, and 1982. While archival research was my main purpose, I did observe and talk with people there; my account reflects both kinds of sources, with emphasis on the former.

2. For some contrasts to Sambuca, see Danilo Dolci, *Waste,* transl. R. Munroe (New York: Monthly Review Press, 1964).

3. J. and P. Schneider, *Culture and Political Economy,* 15; di Giovanna, *Inchiostro,* 343.

4. Tarrow, *Peasant Communism.*

5. My interview with B. G., September 1980.

6. Sources in Sambuca's archives, discussed in the appendix, revealed most of this number.

7. See, for example, Kertzer and Hogan, "On the Move," and, for rural France, Leslie Moch, *Paths to the City* (Beverly Hills: Sage Publications, 1983). Somewhat similar sources were exploited by Kristian Hvidt, *The Social Background of 300,000 Danish Emigrants* (New York: Academic Press, 1975).

8. Di Giovanna, *Inchiostro,* 36–39.

9. Unless otherwise noted, my account of Sambuca's early history follows Scaturro, *Storia della Città di Sciacca e dei Comuni della Contrade Saccanese fra il Belice e il Platani.*

10. *Comuni e loro Popolazione.*

11. J. and P. Schneider, *Culture and Political Economy,* ch. 8.

12. Scaturro, *Storia della Città di Sciacca,* 2:70–71.

13. Ibid., 2:373; *Inchiesta Agraria,* 2:112, 141.

14. A rough estimate, based on my analysis of "Atti di Matrimonio," Office of the Stato Civile, Sambuca, and a "Catasto dei Fabbricati," 1877, Municipal Archive, Sambuca. The Catasto identified civile houses as such. The number of families in Sambuca in 1881 is from *Censimento, 1881,* vol. 1.

15. *Inchiesta Agraria,* 2:570; Sonnino, *I Contadini,* 37–38; *Inchiesta sulle Condizioni dei Contadini,* 113.

16. My estimate, from "Atti di Matrimonio."

17. For descriptions of this type of contract, see *Inchiesta Agraria,* 1:235; *Inchiesta sulle Condizioni dei Contadini,* 178–79.

18. Gabaccia, *From Sicily to Elizabeth Street,* 22–23.

19. "Catasto dei Fabbricati."

20. "Electoral List, 1896," Municipal Archive, Sambuca; the list identified merchants by the kinds of materials they sold.

21. See entries for Sambuca in "Notizie sulle Condizioni Industriali della Provincia di Girgenti."

22. Birth, marriage, and death record series, in Sambuca's office of the Stato Civile, all used the same term. "Industrioso" also sometimes applied to men who, while not peasants, did manufacturing work not recognized as a skilled trade.

23. On the centrality of cloth work, see J. Schneider, "Trousseau as Treasure"; Pitrè, *La Famiglia*, chs. 9–10; Pitrè, *Usi e Costumi*, 15:19–22, 27–32.

24. *Inchiesta Agraria,* 2:117.

25. One view of South Italy's elite is Villari, *Italian Life in Town and Country,* 27; see also MacDonald, "Agricultural Organization," 70.

26. J. and P. Schneider, *Culture and Political Economy,* 151–52.

27. Di Giovanna, *Inchiostro,* 52.

28. Jane and Peter Schneider, "The Reproduction of the Ruling Class in Latifundist Sicily, 1860–1920," 141–69.

29. Alatri, *Lotte Politiche,* 310.

30. Scaturro, *Storia della Città di Sciacca,* 2:503–04.

31. J. and P. Schneider, *Culture and Political Economy,* 156–57.

32. Alatri, *Lotte Politiche,* 310.

33. Jane and Peter Schneider, "Demographic Transitions in a Sicilian Rural Town," 253, table 3.

34. Again, birth, marriage, and death record series revealed the same change.

35. "Notizie sulle Condizioni Industriali della Provincia di Girgenti."

36. J. and P. Schneider, "Demographic Transitions," 256, table 4.

37. *Censimento, 1881;* see also Giarrizzo, "La Sicilia e la Crisi," 22–24.

38. Ibid., 23.

39. J. and P. Schneider, *Culture and Political Economy,* 123.

40. Romano, *La Sicilia,* 100–7; Marino, *Socialismo nel Latifondo,* 216.

41. Pitrè, *Proverbi,* 8:ch. 20.

42. Zariski, *Politics of Unequal Development,* 16.

43. Giordano, *Handwerker,* 19.

44. No local register (such as the one used by Kertzer in northern Italy) existed in Sambuca for the period. Population registers from the early twentieth century did list earlier marriages, births, and deaths occurring outside the town. Marriage records also noted the birthplaces of people arriving in Sambuca to marry.

45. Jane and Peter Schneider kindly shared their data on these early marriage cohorts. The proportion of artisan couples bearing no children in Sambuca far exceeded proportions among peasants. It is unlikely that such large numbers of these couples were controlling fertility at this date, see J. and P. Schneider, "Demographic Transitions," 258–59.

46. J. and P. Schneider, *Culture and Political Economy,* 71; Peter Schneider, "Rural Artisans and Peasant Mobilization in Late Nineteenth Century Sicily," 74.

47. Cerrito, *Radicalismo e Socialismo,* 325.

48. Navarro della Miraglia, *La Nana; Storielle Siciliane.*

49. Alatri, *Lotte Politiche,* 523.

50. Cerrito, *Radicalismo e Socialismo,* 319.

51. Giordano, *Handwerker,* 163.

52. Briggs, *An Italian Passage,* 22–28.

53. "Electoral List," 1896.

54. Blok, *Mafia of a Sicilian Village,* 47–49.

55. Peasant/artisan matches represented less than 10 percent of all artisan marriages before 1880.

56. Renda, *I Fasci Siciliani, 1892–94,* 342.

57. Ibid.

58. Di Giovanna, *Inchiostro,* 27.

59. J. and P. Schneider, *Culture and Political Economy,* 158.

60. For another example, see Blok, *Mafia of a Sicilian Village,* 122–23.

61. Di Giovanna, *Inchiostro,* 27.

62. One very different example of social networks acquiring political content is Patricia Zavella, "'Abnormal Intimacy': The Varying Work Networks of Chicana Cannery Workers," *Feminist Studies* 11 (1985):554.

63. Di Giovanna, *Inchiostro,* 27.

64. Ibid., 36–40.

65. "Lista della Leva, 1880–1930," Municipal Archive, Sambuca.

66. A decline in migration during the early 1890s was general; see *Annuario Statistico.* Nor was the decline limited to Italy, see Walter F. Willcox, ed., *International Migrations* (New York: National Bureau of Economic Research, 1929).

67. J. and P. Schneider, *Culture and Political Economy,* 158.

68. MacDonald, "Agricultural Organization," table 1.

69. To cite just one example, see Bernard H. Moss, *The Origins of the French Labor Movement: The Socialism of the Skilled Worker, 1830–1914* (Berkeley: University of California Press, 1976).

70. See Judt, *Socialism in Provence,* ch. 4; Jean-Claude Farcy, "Rural Artisans in the Beauce during the Nineteenth Century," in Geoffrey Crossick and Heinz-Gerhard Haupt, eds., *Shopkeepers and Master Artisans in Nineteenth-Century Europe* (London: Methuen, 1984), 219–38.

71. Sicilian Marxists themselves could not understand the appeal. One writer reminded his fellows of the contempt Marx expressed for the small producer and his politics of "bottegocrazia," Loncao, *Considerazioni sulla Genesi,* 214.

72. That areas of out-migration can simultaneously attract migrants is well documented; see Klaus Bade, "Vom Auswanderungsland zum 'Arbeitseinfuhrland," in Bade, *Auswanderer,* 433–85, here 436–47.

73. Navarro della Miraglia, *La Nana,* 34.

74. J. and P. Schneider, "Reproduction of the Ruling Class," 162.

75. P. Schneider, "Rural Artisans."

76. Renda, *I Fasci Siciliani,* 34–35.

Chapter 4: From Fasci to Emigration

1. Renda, *I Fasci Siciliani,* app. 1.

2. The best chronology is Renda, *I Fasci Siciliani.*

3. For three conflicting views, see Hobsbawm, *Primitive Rebels,* ch. 6; Aya, *Missed Revolution,* 120; Blok, *Mafia of a Sicilian Village,* 122.

4. Contemporary accounts include Colajanni, *Avvenimenti di Sicilia;* di San Giuliano, *Le Condizioni Presenti della Sicilia, Studi e Proposti;* Rossi, *Die Bewegung in Sizilien;* Cammareri-Scurti, *La Lotta di Classe in Sicilia;* Cavalieri, "I Fasci dei Lavoratori e le Condizioni della Sicilia"; di Rudini, "Terre Incolte e Latifondi."

5. Among more recent studies, see Carbone, *Le Origini del Socialismo in Sicilia;* Marsilio, *I Fasci Siciliani; Movimento Operaio* 6 (1954); Francesco Renda, "Origine e Caratteristiche del Movimento Contadino della Sicilia Occidentale," *Movimento Operaio* 7 (1955):659–61; Salvatore Francesco Romano, *Storia dei Fasci Siciliani;* Giarrizzo et al., *Fasci* Siciliani; Gestri, "I Fasci Siciliani"; Casarrubea, *I Fasci Siciliani e le Origine delle Sezioni Socialiste.*

6. Marino, *Costumi e Usanze dei Contadini di Sicilia,* 27.

7. Contemporaries emphasized different aspects of the fasci revolts. Colajanni, *Avvenimenti di Sicilia* almost completely ignored workplace actions, while Rossi, *Bewegung in Sizilien* emphasized their importance. The most balanced interpretation remains Romano, *Storia dei Fasci.*

8. Renda, *I Fasci Siciliani,* ch. 15.

9. For one example, see Romano, *Storia dei Fasci,* 168; alternatively, Colajanni, *Avvenimenti di Sicilia,* 115.

10. On women's revolts, see Hohsbawm, *Primitive Rebels,* 183; Renda, *I Fasci Siciliani,* 352; Rossi, *Bewegung in Sizilien,* 1, 3–4, 8–9, ch. 5; Romano, *Storia dei Fasci,* 228–30. The most complete recent account is Calapso, *Donne Ribelli,* ch. 5. See also Birnbaum, *Liberazione della Donna, Feminism in Italy,* 13.

11. Rossi, *Bewegung in Sizilien,* 62–64.

12. Renda, *I Fasci Siciliani,* apps. 1 and 2.

13. On the varied activities of the fasci, see Colajanni, *Avvenimenti di Sicilia,* 13–14. On the early cooperatives, see Sorbi, *Le Cooperative Agricole per la Conduzione dei Terreni in Italia.*

14. For an elaboration of the different work experiences of wheat and grape or citrus cultivators, see Gabaccia, "Migration and Peasant Militance, Western Sicily, 1880–1910."

15. Renda, *I Fasci Siciliani,* 84; Blok, *Mafia of a Sicilian Village,* 124.

16. Renda, *I Fasci Siciliani,* ch. 8, esp. 84–85. See also P. Schneider, "Rural Artisans."

17. Andreucci and Detti, *Il Movimento Operaio Italiano, Dizionario Biografica, 1853–1943.*

18. Renda, *I Fasci Siciliani,* app. 1.

19. The towns were Piana dei Greci, Corleone, Alcamo, S. Giuseppe Jato, Prizzi, Partinico, and San Cipirello. See Colajanni, *Avvenimenti di Sicilia.*

20. Ibid., 219; Romano, *Storia dei Fasci,* 467.

21. Romano, *Storia dei Fasci,* 228.

22. Some of the best sources are contemporary photographs and drawings. See Rossi, *Bewegung in Sizilien;* Marsilio, *Fasci Siciliani;* Villari, *Il Sud nella Storia d'Italia.*

23. Colajanni, *Avvenimenti di Sicilia,* 211–14.

24. Renda, *I Fasci Siciliani,* 264–265; Romano, *Storia dei Fasci,* 463, 467; Colajanni, *Avvenimenti di Sicilia,* 13–14, 181–84.

25. Renda, *I Fasci Siciliani,* 354; Colajanni, *Avvenimenti di Sicilia,* 175–77.

26. Renda, *I Fasci Siciliani,* chs. 3, 17, 18.

27. Procacci, "Movimenti Sociali e Partiti Politici in Sicilia dal 1900 al 1904."

28. Aya, *Missed Revolution,* 122.

29. Rossi, *Bewegung in Sizilien,* 113; Romano, *Storia dei Fasci,* 1–5. Romano notes that the "specter of socialism and communism" was raised constantly in contemporary debates about the significance of the fasci revolts. Many recent studies remain fascinated with the problem, see Dollo et al., *Fasci Siciliani,* 7.

30. Hobsbawm, *Primitive Rebels,* ch. 6.

31. Popkin, *Rational Peasant,* 4. On the Sicilian peasantry's views of property ownership and communal rights, see Romano, *Storia dei Fasci,* 241; Blok, *Mafia of a Sicilian Village,* 118–19.

32. Blok, *Mafia of a Sicilian Village,* 122–23; Aya, *Missed Revolution,* ch. 3; Romano, *Storia dei Fasci,* 367–68. For a contemporary's account, see Rossi, *Bewegung in Sizilien,* ch. 8.

33. Aya, *Missed Revolution,* 120.

34. Mitrany, *Marx Against the Peasant,* 76–81.

35. J. and P. Schneider, *Culture and Political Economy,* 124.

36. According to Moore, democracy could develop only where the peasantry was transformed into "some other kind of social formation," *Social Origins,* 422.

37. Hobsbawm, *Primitive Rebels,* 105.

38. The best statement of this interpretation remains MacDonald, "Agricultural Organization," 73.

39. The best recent study of Sicilian emigration is Renda, *l'Emigrazione.* See also Martellone, *I Siciliani fuori dalla Sicilia, l'Emigrazione Transoceanica fino al 1925.* Early accounts include Bruccoleri, *l'Emigrazione Siciliana;* Raia, *Il Fenomeno Emigratorio Siciliano con Speciale Riguardo al Quinquennio, 1902–1906.* For general studies of Italian emigration, see Coletti, *dell'Emigrazione Italiana;* Foerster, *The Italian Emigration of Our Times;* Rosoli, *Un Secolo di Emigrazione Italiana, 1876–1976.*

40. *Inchiesta Agraria,* 2:97; more generally on changes on the wheat estates, see G. Barone, "Ristrutturazione e Crisi," 20–35.

41. Renda, *l'Emigrazione,* 42.

42. Besides Procacci, see for the early twentieth century, Renda, *Socialisti e Cattolici;* Calapso, *Donne Ribelli;* Marino, *Movimento Contadino e Blocco Agrario nella Sicilia Giolittiana;* Scoppola, "Cattolici e Moti Sociali in Italia Intorno al 1900." For government sources on this period, see n. 20 above. Systematic studies of the postwar years are few. Helpful are Accati, "Lotta Rivoluzionaria"; Marino, *Partiti e Lotta di Classe in Sicilia da Orlando a Mussolini;* Chiurco, *Storia della Rivoluzione Fascista;* Micciché, *Dopoguerra e Fascismo in Sicilia, 1919–1927.*

43. The nature of the unrest varied, of course, across time. I counted as unrest such events as attracted police action or resulted in violence.

44. Bruno, "La Diffusione Territoriale delle Migrazioni."

45. See, for example, *Statistica della Emigrazione* for the 1890s. For summaries of Sicilians' occupations, see *Annuario Statistico della Emigrazione.*

46. *Statistica della Emigrazione* (1889).

Chapter 5: Links in the Migration Chain

1. American scholars have borrowed the chain metaphor from Australians studying migration to the Pacific. R. A. Lochore, *From Europe to New Zealand* (Wellington: A. H.

and A. W. Reed in conjunction with the New Zealand Institute for International Affairs, 1951); W. E. Borrie, *Italians and Germans in Australia* (Melbourne: Australian National University by F. W. Cheshire, 1954); Price, *Southern Europeans in Australia;* MacDonald and MacDonald, "Chain Migration, Ethnic Neighborhood Formation and Social Networks."

2. Juliani, *The Social Organization of Immigration: The Italians in Philadelphia.*

3. All names have been changed.

4. Bodnar, *The Transplanted,* 57–60; Baily, "Chain Migration of Italians to Argentina, Case Studies of the Agnonesi and the Sirolesi"; John S. MacDonald and Leatrice D. MacDonald, "Italian Migration to Australia: Manifest Function of Bureaucracy versus Latent Functions of Informal Networks"; June Granatir Alexander, "Staying Together: Chain Migration and Patterns of Slovak Settlement in Pittsburgh Prior to World War I," *Journal of American Ethnic History* 1 (1981):56–83.

5. Bodnar, *The Transplanted,* 3, 13.

6. Arlacchi, *Mafia, Peasants,* 183.

7. I estimated migration rates for each group as follows. First, I used occupational distributions among male and female migrants of known occupational backgrounds to estimate the total numbers of migrants from each background. To estimate the population of each group in Sambuca in 1881, I used occupation distributions for the 1870s (estimated from birth and marriage records, see ch. 3) to determine the number of households of each background in 1881. (The Italian census gives the total number of households for Sambuca in that year.) In the case of the elite, artisans, and shepherds, I estimated five persons per household; for peasants, I estimated four persons per household.

8. For general ratios of men to women among Sicilians, see *Annuario Statistico della Emigrazione Italiana.*

9. See J. and P. Schneider, "The Demographic Transition," p. 257. For a rather different view of the relationship of migration and illegitimacy, see Piselli, *Parentela ed Emigrazione,* 53–56.

10. It is common in southern Italy today for women to inherit houses, although prior to the 1880s female owners of real property were rare. See J. Schneider, "Trousseau as Treasure," and John Davis, "An Account of Changes in the Rules of Transmission of Property," in J. G. Peristiany, ed., *Mediterranean Family Structures* (Cambridge: Cambridge University Press, 1976), 287–304.

11. This pattern is clearly revealed in Sambuca's *fogli di famiglia* (household registration files) from the early twentieth century. The case of Baldassare D.'s daughter was quite common, suggesting that parents struggling to make ends meet in the years after 1880 abandoned older customs of acquiring and assigning property at the time of children's marriages. Parents provided cash or training to older children but guaranteed their own security in old age by keeping the youngest son (or, more frequently, daughter) at home until death was near. This child was then rewarded with parental property. The practice is still common in Sambuca.

12. Pitrè, *Proverbi,* 8:228–29.

13. My thinking on migrants' networks has been much influenced by Jeremy Boissevain and J. C. Mitchell, eds., *Network Analysis: Studies in Human Interaction* (The Hague: Mouton, 1973) and M. Estellie Smith, "Networks and Migration Resettlement: Cherchez la Femme," *Anthropological Quarterly* 49 (1976):20–27. On campanilismo, see Vecoli,

"Contadini in Chicago: A Critique of 'The Uprooted,'" 406, 408, 412–13, 416–17, and J. S. and L. MacDonald, "Chain Migration."

14. On regionalismo, see Dino Cinel, "Between Change and Continuity: Regionalism among Immigrants from the Italian Northwest"; Briggs, *Italian Passage,* 81; Franc Sturino, "Family and Kin Cohesion among South Italian Immigrants in Toronto," in Caroli, Harney, Tomasi, *The Italian Immigrant Woman in North America,* 288–311, here 291.

15. *Statistica della Emigrazione,* 1889.

16. For those emphasizing the importance of the padrone, see LaSorte, *La Merica: Images of Italian Greenhorn Experience,* ch. 3; Nelli, "The Italian Padrone System in the United States"; Luciano Iorizzo, "The Padrone and Immigrant Distribution," in Tomasi and Engel, *The Italian Experience in the United States,* 43–75; Harney, "The Padrone and the Immigrant"; Iorizzo, *Italian Immigration and the Impact of the Padrone System.* By contrast, Bodnar questions the general importance of the middlemen labor agents, *The Transplanted,* 58–60. Significant numbers of studies of Italian migration make almost no mention of the padrone in the settlement of migrants in the United States. Among these are Briggs, *Italian Passage;* Yans-McLaughlin, *Family and Community;* Gabaccia, *From Sicily to Elizabeth Street;* and Judith Smith, *Family Connections.* See also Suzanne Ziegler, "The Family Unit and International Migration: The Perception of Italian Immigrant Children," *International Migration Review* 11 (1977):326–33. There is a sizable general literature that supports the central importance of family and kinship in the migration process. See, for example, Leonard Blumberg and Robert Bell, "Urban Migration and Kinship Ties," *Social Problems* 16 (1959):328–33; James S. Brown et al., "Kentucky Mountain Migration and the Stem Family: An American Variation on a Theme by LePlay," *Rural Sociology* 28 (1963):48–69; Robert E. Bieder, "Kinship as a Factor in Migration," *Journal of Marriage and the Family* 35 (1973):429–39; Harvey M. Choldin, "Kinship Networks in the Migration Process," *International Migration Review* 7 (1973):163–75; Irene Hecht, "Kinship and Migration," *Journal of Interdisciplinary History* 8 (1977):45–68.

17. Nelli, *From Immigrants to Ethnics,* ch. 3.

18. Scarpaci, "Labor for Louisiana's Sugar Fields: An Experiment in Immigrant Recruitment."

19. Scarpaci, *Italian Immigrants in Louisiana's Sugar Parishes: Recruitment, Labor Conditions, and Community Relations, 1880–1910,* 52.

20. W. B. Bailey, "The Bird of Passage," *American Journal of Sociology* 18 (1912): 391–97. Recent works which feature the experiences of birds of passage are LaSorte, *La Merica* and Robert F. Harney, "Men Without Women: Italian Migrants in Canada: 1885–1930," in Caroli, Harney, and Tomasi, *Italian Immigrant Woman,* 79–102, here 86.

21. Scarpaci, *Italian Immigrants,* ch. 4. See also Scarpaci, "Immigrants in the New South: Italians in Louisiana's Sugar Parishes, 1880–1910."

22. In some cases, dependency led to peonage. See Merlino, "Italian Immigrants and their Enslavement," and Daniel, *The Shadow of Slavery: Peonage in the South, 1901–1969,* ch. 5.

23. On the men, see Harney, "Men Without Women."

24. Romano, *Sicilia nell'Ultimo Ventennio,* 154.

25. Piselli finds much higher rates of illegitimacy, but she defines as illegitimate all babies born during the absence of an emigrated father, *Parentela ed Emigrazione,* 55.

26. Jane Schneider, "Of Vigilance and Virgins: Honor, Shame and Access to Resources in Mediterranean Societies"; Gabaccia, *From Sicily to Elizabeth Street,* 49.

27. For a somewhat similar case, see Frances Kraljic, "Round Trip Croatia, 1900–1914," in Hoerder, *Labor Migration,* 399–421, here, 412–13.

28. Besides the work cited in n. 16 above, see Tamara Hareven, *Family Time and Industrial Time: The Relationship Between the Family and Work in a New England Industrial Community* (Cambridge: Cambridge University Press, 1982).

29. Sonnino, *Contadini in Sicilia,* 45, 51.

30. At $20 to $25, the cost of passage was about half that of a small house.

31. *Statistical Review of Immigration,* 360–61.

32. Scarpaci, *Italian Immigrants,* 192–93.

33. Ibid., 109.

34. See, for example, Riis, *How the Other Half Lives,* 38–39.

35. J. S. and L. MacDonald, "Chain Migration."

36. The key works in this change are Oscar Handlin, *The Uprooted* (Boston: Little, Brown, and Company, 1951); Vecoli, "Contadini in Chicago"; and Bodnar, *The Transplanted.*

37. For definitions of collective action, see Tilly, *From Mobilization to Revolution,* 7.

38. MacDonald, "Agricultural Organization," 70; Bodnar, *The Transplanted,* 56.

39. Popkin, *Rational Peasant,* 25; Bodnar, *The Transplanted,* 85.

40. Renda, *l'Emigrazione,* 19. Renda noted the popularity of this idea among earlier Italian writers like Raia, Nitti, and Coletti.

41. J. and P. Schneider, *Culture and Political Economy,* 127.

42. Gramsci, *Selections from the Prison Notebooks,* 59.

43. See, for example, Peter Kammerer, "Probleme von Entsendeländern."

44. Arlacchi, *Mafia, Peasants,* 174.

45. Nelli, *Immigrants to Ethnics,* ch. 2.

46. Hobsbawm, *Primitive Rebels,* ch. 6.

47. Blok, *Mafia of a Sicilian Village,* 121.

48. Yans-McLaughlin, *Family and Community,* 62–63.

49. Gabaccia, *From Sicily to Elizabeth Street,* 58–59.

50. J. and P. Schneider, *Culture and Political Economy,* 73.

51. Ibid., 180–81.

52. Two studies of radicals as migrants are Cerrito, "Sull'Emigrazione Anarchica Italiana negli Stati Uniti d'America"; Emilio Franzina, "l'Emigrazione Schedata: Lavoratori Sovversivi all'Estero e Meccanismi di Controllo Poliziesco in Italia fra Fine Secolo e Fascismo," in Bezza, *Gli Italiani Fuori d'Italia,* 773–829.

Chapter 6: Louisiana and Chicago

1. See, for example, Hartmut Keil, "German Working-Class Radicalism in the United States from the 1870s to World War I," in Hoerder, *Struggle a Hard Battle,* 71–94; Liebman, *Jews and the Left;* Levin, *While Messiah Tarried;* Irving Howe, *The World of Our Fathers* (New York and London: Harcourt Brace Jovanovich, 1976), chs. 9–10.

2. Besides Yans-McLaughlin, *Family and Community,* Gabaccia, *From Sicily to Elizabeth Street;* and Smith, *Family Connections;* see Gambino, *Blood of My Blood;* Tomasi, *The Italian American Family: The Southern Italian Family's Process of Adjustment to an Urban America.*

3. *Statistica della Emigrazione,* 1884–1914.

4. Nelli, "Italians," 547–48.

5. *Immigrants in Cities* provides detailed provincial origins for the residents of selected New York and Chicago neighborhoods.

6. Besides *Immigrants in Cities,* see DeMarco, *Ethnics and Enclaves, Boston's Italian North End.*

7. Mormino and Pozzetta, *The Immigrant World of Ybor City,* 9; Briggs, *Italian Passage,* tables 5.4 and 5.5.

8. Briggs, *Italian Passage,* table 5.4; Mormino, *Immigrants on the Hill, Italian Americans in St. Louis, 1882–1982.*

9. Cinel, *From Italy to San Francisco,* 201.

10. Olivier Zunz, *The Changing Face of Inequality: Urbanization, Industrial Development, and Immigrants in Detroit, 1880–1920* (Chicago: University of Chicago Press, 1982), 401.

11. Nelli, "Italians," 549–52.

12. For a case study of a multiethnic workplace, see James R. Barrett, "Unity and Fragmentation: Class, Race, and Ethnicity on Chicago's South Side, 1900–1922," in Hoerder, *Struggle a Hard Battle,* 229–53.

13. Giordano, "Italian Immigration in the State of Louisiana: its Causes, Effects and Results"; Margavio, "The Reaction of the Press to the Italian-Americans in New Orleans, 1880–1920"; Lunberg, "The Italian Community in New Orleans," in Cooke, *New Orleans Ethnic Cultures;* Margavio and Salomone, "The Passage, Settlement and Occupational Characteristics of Louisiana's Italian Immigrants"; Baiamonte, *Spirit of Vengeance: Nativism and Louisiana Justice, 1921–1924.*

14. Scarpaci, *Italian Immigrants,* 33, 55.

15. Ibid., 270.

16. Magnaghi, "Louisiana's Italian Immigrants Prior to 1870"; Margavio and Salomone, "Passage, Settlement and Occupational Characteristics."

17. Margavio and Molyneaux, "Residential Segregation of Italians in New Orleans and Selected American Cities."

18. My analysis of these early migrants' destinations in the United States is based on civil documents transcribed in Sambuca's birth, marriage, and death registers.

19. Scarpaci, *Italian Immigrants,* ch. 4.

20. Besides ibid., see Lawrence, "European Immigration Trends of Northeast Louisiana, 1880–1900"; *Immigrants in Industries,* part 24, "Recent Immigrants in Agriculture: Italians."

21. Scarpaci, *Italian Immigrants,* 123–30.

22. Ibid., 130–31.

23. Ibid., 148–51.

24. For analysis of St. Mary's Italian population, see Margavio and Salomone, "Passage, Settlement and Occupational Characteristics."

25. Robert E. Park and Herbert A. Miller, *Old World Traits Transplanted* (New York: Harper and Brothers, 1921), map opp. 146.

26. Margavio and Salomone, "Passage, Settlement and Occupational Characteristics"; see also Scarpaci, *Italian Immigrants,* 135.

27. Scarpaci, *Italian Immigrants,* 121.

28. Not one Italian appeared to own land in the sugar parish manuscript census listings I examined for 1900.

29. Nelli, *From Immigrants to Ethnics*, 45.

30. Besides Scarpaci, *Italian Immigrants*, chart 2, see Thomas Lynn Smith, "Depopulation of Louisiana's Sugar Bowl," *Journal of Farm Economics* 20 (1938):503–9.

31. Magnaghi, "Louisiana's Italian Immigrants"; Scarpaci, *Italian Immigrants*, 100–2.

32. Gambino, *Vendetta*, 45. See also Nelli, "The Hennessy Murder and the Mafia in New Orleans"; Reynold, *Machine Politics in New Orleans, 1897–1926*.

33. *Il Proletario*, Dec. 17, 1905 and Dec. 24, 1905.

34. *Il Proletario*, May 7, 1905.

35. *Il Proletario*, November 11, 1905, and January 7, 1906.

36. Scarpaci, *Italian Immigrants*, 254; Sylvers, "Sicilian Socialists in Houston, Texas, 1896–98."

37. Dirk Hoerder, "Immigration and the Working Class: The Remigration Factor," *International Labor and Working-Class History* 21 (1982):28–41, here, 28.

38. Becnel, *Labor, Church and the Sugar Establishment*, 6.

39. Ibid.

40. Scarpaci, *Italian Immigrants*, 140–45.

41. Becnel, *Labor, Church and the Sugar Establishment*,

42. Scarpaci, *Italian Immigrants*, 160–61.

43. Ibid., 162–67.

44. For general treatments of the role of Catholic priests in Italian communities, see Vecoli, "Prelates and Peasants: Italian Immigrants and the Catholic Church"; Silvano M. Tomasi, "The Ethnic Church and the Integration of Italian Immigrants in the United States," in Tomasi and Engel, *Italian Experience in the United States*. For the priest as intermediary, see Rev. Stephen M. DiGiovanni, "Michael Augustine Corrigan and the Italian Immigrants: The Relationship Between the Church and the Italians in the Archdiocese of New York, 1885–1902," in Tomasi, *Italian Americans*, 302–19.

45. Virginia Yans-McLaughlin, "A Flexible Tradition: Immigrant Families Confront New Work Experiences," *Journal of Social History* 7 (1974):429–45.

46. My estimates, based on migrants to Rockford identified in Sambuca's archives, and names in present-day telephone listings for the town.

47. U.S. Works Progress Administration (USWPA), *Rockford*.

48. Interview, P. M., Sambuca, March 1977.

49. USWPA, *Rockford*, 7.

50. *Il Proletario*, November 11, 1905.

51. *Il Proletario*, March 17, 1911.

52. See section on Near North Side's "Little Sicily," Abbott, *The Tenements of Chicago*.

53. Biagi, *The Purple Aster, a History of the Order of the Sons of Italy*, 264. See also Manzardo, "Struggles and Growth of Labor in Illinois: Some Italian Contributions."

54. Faust, "The Rockford Swedes"; USWPA, *Rockford*, 64; Ulf Beijbom, "Swedes," *Harvard Encyclopedia of American Ethnic Groups*, 978.

55. Schwieder, *Black Diamonds, Life and Work in Iowa's Coal Mining Communities, 1895–1925*; Betty Boyd Caroli, "Italians in the Cherry, Illinois, Mine Disaster," in Pozzetta, *Pane e Lavoro: The Italian American Working Class*, 67–70; Stephanie E. Booth, "The Relationship between Radicalism and Ethnicity in Southern Illinois Coal Fields, 1870–1940," Unpublished Ph.D. Dissertation, Illinois State University, 1983; Quartaroli, "La Tragedia Mineraria di Cherry, Ill." For a somewhat comparable case, see

Baily, "The Italians and Organized Labor in the United States and Argentina, 1880–1910," and "The Italians and the Development of Organized Labor in Argentina, Brazil and the United States, 1880–1914."

56. Fiorentini, "La Storia di un Nobile Cavaliere del Lavoro nei Campi Minerari dei Illinois."

57. Schwieder, *Black Diamonds,* 148.

58. Fiorentini, "Storia di un Nobile Cavaliere," 120–21; on Pennsylvania miners, see *Il Proletario,* April 16, 1905.

59. On Chicago's Italians, see Schiavo, *The Italians in Chicago, a Study in Americanization;* Nelli, *The Italians in Chicago, a Study in Ethnic Mobility;* Vecoli, "Contadini in Chicago," and Vecoli, "The Formation of Chicago's Little Italies."

60. Nelli, *Italians in Chicago,* ch. 2.

61. U.S. Senate, *Immigrants in Cities.* By comparison, 71 percent of South Italian immigrants in Cleveland, 66 to 67 percent in Milwaukee and Buffalo, and only to 35 to 39 percent in Boston and Philadelphia worked as common laborers. On the end of the padrone era, see Nelli, *Italians in Chicago,* 66.

62. Abbott, "The Chicago Employment Agency," 293.

63. Vecoli, "Contadini in Chicago," 413.

64. Grace Abbott, *The Immigrant and the Community* (New York: The Century Co., 1917), ch. 2, esp. 26–27, 31–33.

65. Nelli, *Italians in Chicago,* 172–74.

66. Ibid.

67. Ibid., 138.

68. Ibid., 105, 134, 180, 220, 224.

69. U.S. Senate, *Immigrants in Cities,* Table 407.

70. Nelli, *Italians in Chicago,* ch. 4.

71. Vecoli, "Formation of Chicago's Little Italies," 12.

72. Nelli, *Italians in Chicago,* 79–85.

73. Ibid., 105–112, 79–80.

74. On the A.C.W.A., see Charles Zaretz, *The Amalgamated Clothing Workers of America, a Study in Progressive Trades-Unionism* (New York: Ancon Publishing Co., 1934). On the Chicago strike, see Nelli, *Italians in Chicago,* 81–85; N. Sue Weiler, "The Uprising in Chicago: the Men's Garment Workers' Strike, 1910–1911," in Joan M. Jensen and Sue Davidson, eds., *A Needle, A Bobbin, A Strike* (Philadelphia: Temple University Press, 1984), 114–39.

75. "Statando una Vecchia Leggenda," *La Parola del Popolo* 9 (1958–59):166–78; Nelli, *Italians in Chicago,* 85.

76. Three useful accounts of the split among Italian-American radicals are De Ciampis, "Storia del Movimento Socialista Rivoluzionario Italiano"; de Ciampis, "Note sul Movimento Socialista tra gli Emigrati Italiani in U.S.A. (1890–1921)"; Martellone, "Per una Storia della Sinistra Italiana negli Stati Uniti: Riformismo e Sindicalismo, 1890–1911." On Chicago's reformers, see Nelli, *Italians in Chicago,* 84–85; Clemente, "The Story of an Italian Labor Newspaper"; Velona, "Genesi del Movimento Socialista Democratico e della Parola del Popolo."

77. Nelli, *Italians in Chicago,* 161; see also *Il Proletario,* August 27, 1905.

78. Velona, "Genesi del Movimento Socialista"; see also Nelli, *Italians in Chicago,* 85.

79. Schiavo, *Italians in Chicago,* 166.

80. Nelli, *Italians in Chicago,* 209–11.

Chapter 7: Tampa and Brooklyn

1. By contrast, 50 to 75 percent of South Italians in Cleveland, Chicago, and Buffalo claimed such a background; see *Immigrants in Cities.*

2. See, for example, Kessner, *The Golden Door, Italian and Jewish Immigrant Mobility in New York City, 1880–1915.*

3. For an early work, see Long, "La Resistencia: Tampa's Immigrant Labor Union." More recent work includes Anthony P. Pizzo, "The Italian Heritage In Tampa," in Harney and Scarpaci, *Little Italies in North America,* 123–40. The most complete study is Mormino and Pozzetta, *Immigrant World.*

4. Mormino and Pozzetta, *Immigrant World,* 81–83.

5. Ibid., ch. 4.

6. Ibid., 9.

7. Renda, *Fasci Siciliani,* app. 2.

8. *Inchiesta Agraria:* "Notizie sulle Condizioni Industriali della Provincia di Girgenti."

9. Mormino and Pozzetta, *Immigrant World,* 82–83.

10. Ibid., 261–64.

11. Mormino, "We Worked Hard and Took Care of Our Own: Oral History and Italians in Tampa."

12. Mormino and Pozzetta, *Immigrant World,* 261.

13. My estimates from numbers cited in Mormino and Pozzetta, *Immigrant World,* table 5.

14. Pozzetta and Mormino, "Immigrant Women in Tampa, the Italian Experience"; Hewitt: "Women in Ybor City: An Interview with a Woman Cigar Worker."

15. Mormino and Pozzetta, *Immigrant World,* 262–63, 273–80.

16. My estimates, from numbers cited in Mormino and Pozzetta, *Immigrant World,* table 6.

17. Mormino and Pozzetta, "Concord and Discord: Italians and Ethnic Interactions in Tampa, Florida, 1886–1930," Tomasi, *Italian Americans,* 341–57. See also Gerald E. Poyo, "The Impact of Cuban and Spanish Workers on Labor Organizing in Florida, 1870–1900," *Journal of American Ethnic History* 5 (Spring 1986):46–63; Mormino and Pozzetta, "Spanish Anarchism in Tampa, Florida, 1886–1931," in Hoerder, *Struggle a Hard Battle,* 170–98.

18. Pozzetta, "Immigrants and Radicals in Tampa, Florida"; Pozzetta, "Italians and the Tampa General Strike of 1910," in Pozzetta, *Pane e Lavoro,* 29–46; Pozzetta, "Italian Radicals in Tampa, Florida: A Research Note"; Mormino, "Tampa and the New Urban South: the Weight Strike of 1899."

19. Uncovering Vaccaro's story was the result of a productive exchange with George Pozzetta. I had explored the Sicilian sources; Pozzetta had interviewed Vaccaro's son. Surprisingly few discrepancies emerged in our comparison of the two kinds of sources.

20. Diggins, *Mussolini and Fascism: The View from America,* 114.

21. Mormino and Pozzetta, "The Cradle of Mutual Aid: Immigrant Cooperative Societies in Ybor City."

22. Mormino and Pozzetta, *Immigrant World,* ch. 9.

23. George E. Pozzetta, "The Mulberry District of New York City: The Years before World War One," in Harney and Scarpaci, *Little Italies,* 7–40, here, 18.

24. Fenton, *Immigrants and Unions, a Case Study: Italians and American Labor, 1870–1920;* see also Fenton, "Italians in the Labor Movement"; Fenton, "Italian Immigrants in the Stoneworkers' Union." More recent works include Vecoli, "Pane e Giustizia: a Brief History of the Italian American Labor Movement"; Pozzetta, *Pane e Lavoro.*

25. Buhle, "Italian-American Radicals and the Labor Movement, 1905–1930."

26. I consulted Brooklyn City Directories for 1884/1885, 1894/1895, 1909, 1913, and 1933/1934, as well as Manhattan directories for the same dates. For Queens, I traced Sambucesi only in the directory for 1933/1934.

27. William Toll, *The Making of an Ethnic Middle-Class: Portland Jewry Over Four Generations* (Albany: State University of New York Press, 1983), 193.

28. My source for this society is a poster announcing its festival; it is in the possession of Alfonso di Giovanna in Sambuca.

29. Fenton, *Immigrants and Unions,* 160.

30. Ibid., 141.

31. "Map of the Borough of Brooklyn, Showing Location and Extent of Racial Colonies" (New York: The Ohman Map Company, 1920).

32. Brooklyn Chamber of Commerce, *Brooklyn, New York City, Why it is the Fourth Industrial City of the United States* (Brooklyn: Industrial Department of the Brooklyn Chamber of Commerce, 1923).

33. See E. Belcher Hyde Map Company, *Atlas of the Borough of Brooklyn, City of New York* (Brooklyn: E. Belcher Hyde, 1911).

34. Gabaccia, *From Sicily to Elizabeth Street,* 75–76 and 80–81.

35. This table, and the paragraphs below, summarize occupational data available in city directories for 1909 and 1913, as well as from a systematic search of Brooklyn manuscript listings for the federal census of 1910.

36. Kessner, *The Golden Door,* 79; Gabaccia, *From Sicily to Elizabeth Street,* 63.

37. Gabaccia, *From Sicily to Elizabeth Street,* 63.

38. Kessner and Caroli, "New Immigrant Women at Work: Italians and Jews in New York City, 1880–1905"; Miriam Cohen, "From Workshop to Office: Italian Women and Family Strategies in New York City, 1900–1950," Unpublished Ph.D. Dissertation, University of Michigan, 1978.

39. Gabaccia, *From Sicily to Elizabeth Street,* 63.

40. Kessner, *The Golden Door,* 183.

41. Cohen, "Changing Educational Strategies Among Immigrant Generations: New York Italians in Comparative Perspective."

42. Fenton, *Immigrants and Unions,* 269.

43. Hall, *The Journeyman Barbers' International Union of America.*

44. Speranza, "Many Societies of Italian Colony: Their Uses and Abuses Discussed by an American Citizen"; Mangano, "The Associated Life of Italians in New York," *Charities* 12 (1904):476–82. The histories of many of these societies can be traced in *Il Corriere Siciliano,* a newspaper that began appearing in 1931.

45. *Corriere Siciliano,* March 14, 1931.

46. Ibid.

47. Fenton, *Immigrants and Unions,* 29. Compare to Michael R. Weisser, *A Brotherhood of Memory: Jewish Landsmanshaftn in the New World* (New York: Basic Books, 1985).

48. See, for example, *Il Proletario,* September 28, 1913.

49. This is my conclusion, based on the 100 mutual aid societies from western Sicilian towns noted in *Corriere Siciliano,* 1931–1935.

50. *Il Proletario,* December 2, 9, and 16, 1906.

51. *Il Proletario,* September 6, 1906.

52. For general surveys of Italians in the Socialist Party, see Dore, "Socialismo Italiano negli Stati Uniti"; Charles Leinenweber, "The American Socialist Party and the /'New' Immigrants," *Science and Society* 32 (1968):2–25; Fenton, *Immigrants and Unions,* ch. 5.

53. *Il Proletario,* February 17, 1911.

54. Ibid.

55. For example, *Il Proletario,* March 24, 1911.

56. *Il Proletario* regularly ran a column called "In the Socialist Family," which reported marriages undertaken without benefit of clergy, and the birth of babies with names like Vera Ribelle. It is probably significant that about half of the vital records sent by Brooklyn artisans to Sambuca's archive were civil, not chruch, records.

57. *Il Proletario,* November 8, 1911.

58. Fenton, *Immigrants and Unions,* 308–10.

59. *Il Proletario,* July 14, 1911.

60. *Corriere Siciliano,* November 12, 1932.

61. *Il Proletario,* August 3, 1912.

62. *Il Proletario,* June 30, 1911.

63. Martellone, "Storia della Sinistra Italiana."

64. Fenton, *Immigrants and Unions,* 274–81.

65. For the subsequent history of the barbers, see "Rosario Drami e il Sindicato dei Barbieri," *La Parola del Popolo* 9 (1958–59):233–37.

66. *Il Proletario,* August 9, 1913.

67. *Il Proletario,* March 19, 1905.

68. Elisabetta Vezzosi, "La Federazione Socialista Italiana del Nord America tra Autonomia e Scioglimento nel Sindicato Industriale, 1911–1921," *Studi Emigrazione* 11 (1984):81–109.

69. Fenton, *Immigrants and Unions,* 311.

70. *Il Proletario,* January–June 1913. The newspaper expanded in size during this period; its list of new contributors included many benefit societies. The number of agents selling the paper also increased, as did the number of correspondents reporting on mutual benefit quarrels over workers' issues.

71. See, for example, *Il Proletario,* January 5, 1912.

72. *Il Proletario,* April 5, 1913.

73. Biagi, *Purple Aster,* 214.

74. See, for example, *Revolutionary Radicalism,* which focuses on immigrant activists.

75. Di Giovanna, *Inchiostro,* 17.

76. For this transition, see Cohen, "From Workshop to Office."

77. There is an extensive literature on the influence of Fascists in Italian-American communities. See Saudino, "Il Fascismo alla Conquista dell'Ordine Figli d'Italia"; Ferrari,

Days Pleasant and Unpleasant in the Order of the Sons of Italy in America; Charles Ferguson, "Embattled Haberdashery: The Fascist Shirts," in *Fifty Million Brothers: A Panorama of American Lodges and Clubs* (New York: Farrar and Rinehard, 1937); "The Italian-American Press on the Mussolini Regime," *Literary Digest* 88 (1926):14–16; Cannistraro, "Fascism and Italian Americans in Detroit"; Cannistraro, "Fascism and Italian Americans," in Tomasi, *Perspectives in Italian Immigration and Ethnicity*, 51–66.

78. Salvadori, "Anti-Fascisti Italiani negli Stati Uniti"; Diggins, "The Italo-American Anti-Fascist Opposition"; Cannistraro, "Luigi Antonini and the Italian Anti-Fascist Movement in the United States, 1940–1943."

79. Diggins, *Mussolini and Fascism*, ch. 6; the story of one such transformation is Montalbo, *Diciannove Anni di Vita e di Lotta*.

80. Salvemini, *Italian Fascist Activities in the United States*, 204.

81. *Corriere Siciliano*, December 24, 1932.

82. *Corriere Siciliano*, December 19, 1932.

83. Jonathan Rieder, *Canarsie: the Jews and Italians of Brooklyn against Liberalism* (Cambridge, Mass.: Harvard University Press, 1985), 39–40.

84. Peel, *The Political Clubs of New York City*.

85. *Corriere Siciliano*, November 12, 1922.

86. *Corriere Siciliano*, April 30, 1932.

87. *Corriere Siciliano*, May 1, 1932.

88. *Corriere Siciliano*, September 17, 1932.

89. *Corriere Siciliano*, December 24, 1932.

90. *Corriere Siciliano*, April 30, 1932. See Mariano, *The Italian Contribution to American Democracy*, pt. 4.

91. *Corriere Siciliano*, March 2, 1931.

92. Tomasi, *Piety and Power*, 56; see also Antonio Mangano, *Sons of Italy: A Social and Religious Study of the Italians in America* (New York: Missionary Education Movement, 1917).

93. Nelli, *From Immigrants to Ethnics*, ch. 5.

94. Rudolph J. Vecoli, "Italian American Workers, 1880–1920: Padrone Slaves or Primitive Rebels?" in Tomasi, *Perspectives in Italian Immigration*, 25–49; Vecoli, "The Italian Immigrants in the U.S. Labor Movement from 1880 to 1920," in Bezza, *Italiani Fuori d'Italia*, 257–306; Vecoli, *Italian American Radicalism, Old World Origins and New World Developments*.

95. It may, of course, be that women rioters simply do not appear in the Italian-language press. Recent research suggests that similar communal protest traditions did travel to the United States with Jewish women from Eastern Europe; see Paula Hyman, "Immigrant Women and Consumer Protest: the New York City Kosher Meat Boycott of 1902," *American Jewish History* 70 (1980):91–105.

96. Victor Greene, *The Slavic Community on Strike: Immigrant Labor in Pennsylvania Anthracite* (South Bend, Indiana: Notre Dame University Press, 1968).

97. For example, *Il Proletario*, January 21, 1906.

98. *Il Proletario*, July 13, 1912.

99. Gary Mormino notes the fact that few informants shared memories of Tampa's considerable radical heritage, "We Worked Hard."

100. *Il Proletario*, August 16, 1913, and September 6, 1913.

Chapter 8: Rural Conflict after 1900

1. Biagi, *Purple Aster,* 71.

2. *Statistica della Emigrazione.*

3. Marino, *Movimento Contadino,* ch. 6; see also the works cited in ch. 2, n. 42.

4. Procacci, *La Lotte di Classe in Italia agli Inizi del Secolo XX,* esp. 148–59; *Statistica degli Scioperi;* Procacci, "Movimenti Sociali"; Marino, *Movimento Contadino.*

5. Renda, *Socialisti e Cattolici;* Scoppola, "Cattolici e Moti Sociali."

6. Sorbi, *Cooperative Agricole.* See also Arnone, "Il Latifondo e le Cooperative in Sicilia"; Cacace, *Il Crollo delle Cooperative Agricole Siciliane;* J. and P. Schneider, "Economic Dependency and the Failure of Cooperatives in Western Sicily." Also helpful is Schifani, "Sulla Cooperazione Agricola in Sicilia nel Periodo fra le Due Guerre e Dopo la Seconda Guerra."

7. There were twenty-eight agricultural and ten nonagricultural strikes in Sicily, 1892–1893. Between 1901 and 1905, there were thirty-seven agricultural and eighteen nonagricultural strikes.

8. *Statistica della Emigrazione.*

9. *Statistica Elettorale, 1877–1925.* See Giusti, *Le Correnti Politiche Italiane Attraverso due Riforme Elettorali dal 1909 al 1921,* and Schepis, *Le Consultazioni Popolari in Italia dal 1848 al 1957, Profilo Storico-Statistico.*

10. For general studies of the postwar period, see Lyttelton, "Revolution and Counter-Revolution in Italy, 1919–1922"; Maione, *Il Biennio Rosso;* Zaninelli, *Le Lotte nelle Campagne dalla Grande Crisi Agricola al Primo Dopoguerra, 1880–1921.* See also Papa, "Guerra e Terra, 1915–1918." For Sicily, see Accati, "Lotta Rivoluzionaria," Marino, *Partiti e Lotta di Classe,* and Chiurco, *Storia della Rivoluzione Fascista.*

11. Marino, *Partito e Lotta di Classe,* 158.

12. *Conflitti del Lavoro.*

13. Marino, *Partito e Lotta di Classe,* 158.

14. Calapso, *Donne Ribelli,* ch. 7.

15. Ibid., ch. 8.

16. Tilly, *Mobilization to Revolution,* 185–87.

17. Salvemini, *The Origins of Fascism in Italy;* Tasca, *The Rise of Italian Fascism, 1918–1922;* Vivarelli, "Italy, 1919–21: The Current State of Research"; Amendola, *Fascismo e Mezzogiorno;* Vivarelli, "Revolution and Reaction in Italy, 1918–1922."

18. Besides Chiurco, *Storia della Rivoluzione Fascista,* and Tasca, *Rise of Italian Fascism,* see Vetri, "Le Origini del Fascismo in Sicilia."

19. For early regionalist sentiments, see Vaina, *Popolarismo e Nasismo in Sicilia.* See also Reece, "Fascism, the Mafia and the Emergence of Sicilian Separatism."

20. Diggins, *Mussolini and Fascism,* 79.

21. For a completely different case, see William H. Chafe, *The American Woman, her Changing Social, Economic and Political Roles, 1920–1970* (New York: Oxford University Press, 1972), 30.

22. For an important beginning, see Kertzer and Hogan, "On the Move."

23. Some Italian towns, like the one studied by Kertzer and Hogan, maintained proper immigration and emigration registers as part of the household registration system. I have yet to visit a Sicilian municipal archive that kept such registers before 1948 or so.

24. For population changes in Favara, see Somogyi, *Bilanci Demografici*.

25. Di Giovanna, *Inchiostro*, 81.

26. Studies of return migration to Italy include Cerase, "A Study of Italian Migrants"; Gilkey, "The United States and Italy: Migration and Repatriation"; Cerase, "Migration and Social Change: Expectations and Reality: A Case Study of Return Migration from United States to Southern Italy"; Cerase, "Nostalgia or Disenchantment: Considerations on Return Migration," in Tomasi and Engel, *Italian Experience in the United States*, 217–38. For a study of return migration today, see Kammerer, *Arbeit Gibt's Immer*. Useful general studies of return migration are Frank Bovenkirk, *The Sociology of Return Migration* (The Hague: Nijhoff, 1974) and George Gmelch, "Return Migration," *Annual Review of Anthropology* 9 (1980):135–59.

27. Caroli, *Italian Repatriation*, 42.

28. Cinel, "Land Tenure Systems, Return Migration and Militancy in Italy."

29. Caroli, *Italian Repatriation*, 42.

30. See Somogyi, *Bilanci Demografici*.

31. J. and P. Schneider, *Culture and Political Economy*, 224.

32. Seven percent of Sambuca women born in the 1860s migrated; in subsequent birth cohorts until the 1890s, the migration rate was about 25 percent.

33. J. and P. Schneider, *Culture and Political Economy*, 158.

34. Calapso, *Donne Ribelle*, 141–42.

35. J. and P. Schneider, *Culture and Political Economy*, 128.

36. For a recent treatment of the period, see DeGrand, *Italian Fascism*.

37. Studies of Italian agriculture under Mussolini include Schmidt, *The Plough and the Sword: Labor, Land and Property in Fascist Italy;* Preti, "La Politica Agraria del Fascismo"; "Fascism and Rural Life," *Quaderni Storici*, Special Issue 10 (1975); Cohen, "Fascism and Agriculture in Italy: Politics and Consequences." See also Arlacchi, *Peasants, Mafia*, 192–95.

38. Salvemini, *Origins of Fascism*, 418.

39. J. and P. Schneider, "Demographic Transition," 261. See also Trèves, *Le Migrazioni Interne nell'Italia Fascista; Politica e Realtà Demografica*.

40. *Corriere Siciliano*, July 1, 1933.

41. Di Giovanna, *Inchiostro*, 39. Similar forms of cultural opposition in Italy's industrial north are explored in Luisa Passerini, *Fascism in Popular Memory: The Cultural Experience of the Turin Working Class*, transl. Robert Lumley and Jude Bloomfield (Cambridge: Cambridge University Press, 1987).

42. Di Giovanna, 35–40.

43. Ibid., 36.

44. Cinanni, *Lotte per la Terra nel Mezzogiorno, 1943–1953;* Kammerer, "Bauernkämpfe und Landreform 1943–1953 in Süditalien"; Talamo, *Lotte Agrarie nel Mezzogiorno, 1943–44;* Amelia and Mario Alcaro-Paparazzo, *Lotte Contadine in Calabria (1943–50);* Restifo, *Sottosviluppo e Lotte Popolari in Sicilia, 1943–1974;* Scaturro, "l'Esperienza Siciliana nella Lotta per la Terra"; Cipolla, "La Lotta per la Terra dei Contadini Siciliani"; "Il Grano Rosso, Vita e Morte di Salvatore Carnevale," *l'Attualità*, May 8, 1956.

45. Ginsborg, "The Communist Party and the Agrarian Question in Southern Italy,

1943–1948"; La Torre, *Comunisti e Movimento Contadino in Sicilia;* Serio, "Il PCI in Sicilia"; Calandrone, *Comunista in Sicilia, 1946–1951;* Macaluso, *I Comunisti e la Sicilia.*

46. For voting results, see Macaluso, *Comunisti e Sicilia,* or Schepis, *Consultazioni Popolari.*

47. Town-by-town results are in Schepis, *Consultazioni Popolari.*

48. Gabaccia, "Neither Padrone Slaves nor Primitive Rebels: Sicilians on Two Continents," in Hoerder, *Struggle a Hard Battle,* 95–117.

49. Tarrow, *Peasant Communism,* 298–99; Rossi-Doria, *Riforma Agraria e Azione Meridionalista;* Landi, "La Riforma Agraria in Sicilia"; Diem, "Land Reform and Reclamation in Sicily"; Blok, "Land Reform in a Western Sicilian Latifondo Village."

50. Macaluso, *Comunisti e Sicilia.*

51. Di Giovanna, *Inchiostro,* 77, 83, 343.

52. Birnbaum, *Liberazione della Donna,* ch. 4.

53. To give one example, I experienced a minor such demonstration in July 1982. Running water—supplied during the dry months only every other morning for several hours—did not appear on schedule one hot sunny day. Within half an hour, every woman in the neighborhood was in the street; in another half-hour all had disappeared. They had gone to the city hall to demand water. City officials apparently made the necessary phone calls; within an hour the water arrived.

54. Pitrè, *la Famiglia,* 34.

55. Birnbaum, *Liberazione della Donna,* 34–37 and 94–95.

56. Kertzer, *Comrades and Christians: Religion and Political Struggle in Communist Italy.*

Conclusion

1. Gambino, *Blood of My Blood.*

2. For a somewhat similar case, see Patrizia Audenino, "The Paths of the Trade: Italian Stone Masons in the United States," *International Migration Review* 20 (1986):779–95.

3. Pitrè, *La Famiglia, la Casa,* 33–36.

4. Covello, *The Social Background of the Italo-American School Child,* 149.

5. See, for example, Juliani, *Social Organization of Migration,* or, more recently, Mormino, *Immigrants on the Hill,* 45.

6. Olivier Zunz, "American History and the Changing Meaning of Assimilation," *Journal of American Ethnic History* 4 (Spring 1985): 53–72, here, 56.

7. See Mormino and Pozzetta, *The Immigrant World of Ybor City,* 6–7.

8. For a good start on another immigrant group, see John Bukowczyk, *And My Children Did Not Know Me; A History of the Polish-Americans* (Bloomington: Indiana University Press, 1987). An important and more general statement is in John Cumbler, "Migration, Class Formation, and Class Consciousness: The American Experience," in Michael Hanagan and Charles Stephenson, eds., *Confrontation, Class Consciousness, and the Labor Process, Studies in Proletarian Class Formation* (New York, Westport, and London: Greenwood Press, 1986), 39–64.

9. Olivier Zunz, *Reliving the Past; The Worlds of Social History* (Chapel Hill and London: The University of North Carolina Press, 1985), 5, 11.

10. Archdeacon, "Problems and Possibilities in the Study of American Immigration and Ethnic History"; Bodnar, *The Transplanted,* pp. xvi–xvii.

11. Eugen Weber, *Peasants into Frenchmen* (Stanford: Stanford University Press, 1976).

12. John Benson, *The Penny Capitalists, A Study of Nineteenth-Century Working-Class Entrepreneurs* (New Brunswick: Rutgers University Press, 1983).

13. Crossick and Haupt, *Shopkeepers and Master Artisans.*

14. Most recently, see Victor R. Greene, *American Immigrant Leaders, 1800–1910* (Baltimore: Johns Hopkins University Press, 1987). For a discussion of class and assimilation, see Zunz, "American History and the Changing Meaning of Assimilation," 66.

15. Harney and Scarpaci, *Little Italys in North America.* See also Bukowcyzk, *And My Children Did Not Know Me,* 35.

16. Michael Hanagan and Charles Stephenson, "Introduction," in Hanagan and Stephenson, *Confrontation, Class Consciousness and the Labor Process,* 5.

Appendix

1. See, for example, Juliani, *Social Organization of Migration;* Sturino, "Family and Kin Cohesion," Briggs, *Italian Passage,* ch. 5; Mormino, *Immigrants on the Hill.*

2. For the types of sources used here, consult Bellini, *Guida Pratica ai Municipi.*

3. I found only one blatant case of lying once I began linking Sicilian and American sources: one family of peasants, headed by a man who had been in jail for several years before leaving Sicily, consistently reported its new home as Chicago, although the family actually lived in Brooklyn.

4. I called a woman an irregular childbearer with a migrant husband if a gap of more than five years separated the birth of any two children except the last two.

5. This seemed a sensible decision since these births were not systematically recorded in the Sicilian sources.

6. For applications, see *Statistica della Emigrazione,* 1881–1915. Net population balances are in Somogyi, *Bilanci Demografici.*

7. This was about comparable to the percentage of women migrating from Sicily as a whole before World War I; see *Annuario Statistico della Emigrazione.* In general, female migration from Sicily was higher than from some other South Italian provinces.

8. Somogyi, *Bilanci Demografici.*

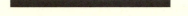

South Italians on Two Continents:
A Selective Bibliography of Published Sources

Government Publications

Italy. Commissariato dell'Emigrazione. *Annuario Statistico della Emigrazione*. Rome: l'Universale, 1926.

————. Direzione Generale della Statistica. *Censimento della Popolazione del Regno d'Italia al 31 Dicembre, 1881*. 4 vols. Rome: 1882–1884.

————. *Censimento della Popolazione del Regno d'Italia al 10 Febbraio, 1901*. 5 vols. Rome: Tipografia Nazionale G. Bertero, 1902–1904.

————. Ministero di Agricoltura, Industria, e Commercio. *Annali di Statistica*. Rome: Tipografia Nazionale G. Bertero, 1893, 1896.

————. *Statistica della Emigrazione Italiana per l'Estero*. Rome: 1881–1915.

————. *Statistica Elettorale Politica*. Rome: 1877–1925.

————. *Statistica degli Scioperi Avvenuti in Italia*. Rome: 1884–1911.

————. *Statistica delle Società di Mutuo Soccorso*. Rome: 1873, 1878, 1885.

————. *Le Società di Mutuo Soccorso in Italia al 31 Dicembre 1904*. Rome: Tipografia G. Bertero, 1906.

————. Ministero dell'Economia Nazionale. *I Conflitti del Lavoro in Italia nel Decennio 1914–1923*. Rome: Industria "Grafica," 1924.

————. *Comuni e Loro Popolazione ai Censimenti dal 1861 al 1951*. Rome: ISTAT, 1960.

————. Giunta per l'Inchiesta Agraria. *Atti della Giunta per l'Inchiesta Agraria e sulle Condizioni della Classe Agricola*. Rome: 1884–1885.

————. Giunta Parlamentare. *Inchiesta sulle Condizioni dei Contadini nelle Provincie Meridionale e nella Sicilia*. Rome: 1909–1910.

New York State. Joint Committee for the Investigation of Seditious Activities. *Revolutionary Radicalism*. 4 vols. Albany: J. B. Lyon Company, 1920.

United States. 61st Congress. Reports of the Immigration Commission. *Immigrants in Cities*. 2 vols. Washington, D.C.: Government Printing Office, 1911.

————. *Immigrants in Industries*. Washington, D.C.: Government Printing Office, 1911.

————. *Statistical Review of Immigration, 1819–1910; Distribution of Immigrants, 1850–1900*. Washington, D.C.: Government Printing Office, 1911.

————. Works Progress Administration. *Rockford*. Rockford: Graphic Arts Corporation, 1941.

Books and Articles

Abbott, Grace. "The Chicago Employment Agency and the Immigrant Worker." *American Journal of Sociology* 14 (1908):289–305.

Abbott, Edith. *The Tenements of Chicago*. 1936. Reprint, New York: Arno Press, 1980.

Accati, L. "Lotta Rivoluzionaria dei Contadini Siciliani e Pugliese nel 1919–1920." *Il Ponte* 26 (1971):1263–93.

Alatri, Paolo. *Lotte Politiche in Sicilia sotto il Governo della Destra (1866–1874)*. Turin: Giulio Einaudi, 1954.

Alcaro-Paparazzo, Amelia and Mario. *Lotte Contadine in Calabria (1943–50)*. Cosenza: Lerici, 1977.

Amendola, Giorgio. *Fascismo e Mezzogiorno*. Rome: Ed. Riuniti, 1973.

Andreucci, Franco and Tommaso Detti, eds. *Il Movimento Operaio, Dizionario Biografico, 1853–1943*. 5 vols. Rome: Ed. Riuniti, 1975.

Arlacchi, Pino. *Mafia, Peasants and Great Estates. Society in Traditional Calabria*. Trans. Jonathan Steinberg. 1980. Reprint, Cambridge: Cambridge University Press, 1983.

Arnone, Salvatore. "Il Latifondo e le Cooperative in Sicilia." *Rivista Internazionale di Scienze Sociali e Discipline Ansiliarie* 18 (1910):20–49 and 544–56.

Aye, Roderick. *The Missed Revolution: The Fate of Rural Rebels in Sicily and Southern Spain, 1840–1950*. Amsterdam: Anthropologisch-Sociologisch Centrum, University of Amsterdam, 1975.

Aymard, Maurice et al. *Les Migrations dans les Pays Méditerranéans au XVIIIe et au début du XIXème*. Nice: Centre de la Méditerranée Moderne et Contemporaine, 1974.

————. "Sicilia: Sviluppo Demografico e sue Differenziazioni Geografiche, 1500–1800." In Ercole Sori, ed., *Demografia Storica*, pp. 194–215. Bologna: Il Mulino, 1975.

Baily, Samuel. "The Adjustment of Italian Immigrants in Buenos Aires and New York, 1870–1914." *American Historical Review* 88 (April 1983):281–305.

————. "Chain Migration of Italians to Argentina, Case Studies of the Agnonesi and the Sirolesi." *Studi Emigrazione* 19 (1982):73–91.

————. "The Italians and the Development of Organized Labor in Argentina, Brazil, and the United States, 1880–1914." *Journal of Social History* 3 (1969):123–34.

————. "The Italians and Organized Labor in the United States and Argentina." *International Migration Review* 1 (1967):56–66.

Baiamonte, John V. *Spirit of Vengeance: Nativism and Louisiana Justice, 1921–1924*. Baton Rouge: Louisiana State University Press, 1986.

Banfield, Edward. *The Moral Basis of a Backward Society*. Glencoe, Ill.: The Free Press, 1958.

Barone, Giuseppe et al. *Potere e Società in Sicilia nella Crisi dello Stato Liberale: Per una Analisi del Blocco Agraria*. Catania: Pellicano Libri, 1977.

Barton, Josef J. *Peasants and Strangers: Italians, Rumanians and Slovaks in an American City, 1890–1950*. Cambridge, Mass.: Harvard University Press, 1975.

————. "Eastern and Southern Europeans." In John Higham, ed., *Ethnic Leadership in America*, pp. 151–54. Baltimore: Johns Hopkins University Press, 1978.

Becnel, Thomas. *Labor, Church and the Sugar Establishment: Louisiana, 1887–1976*. Baton Rouge and London: Louisiana State University Press, 1980.

Bellini, Lorenzo. *Guida Pratica ai Municipi per il Rilascio di Atti e Documenti in Uso Pubblico e Privato*. Suzzara: Tipografia della Suzzarese, 1901.

Berger, Suzanne and Michael E. Piore. *Dualism and Discontinuity in Industrial Societies*. Cambridge: Cambridge University Press, 1980.

Bezza, B., ed. *Gli Italiani Fuori d'Italia*. Milan: Franco Angeli, 1983.

Biagi, Ernest L. *The Purple Aster: A History of the Order Sons of Italy*. New York: Veritas Press, 1961.

Birnbaum, Lucia Chiavola. *Liberazione della Donna, Feminism in Italy*. Middletown, Conn.: Wesleyan University Press, 1986.

Blok, Anton. "Land Reform in a Western Sicilian Latifondo Village: Persistence of a Feudal Structure." *Anthropological Quarterly* 39 (1966):1–16.

————. "Mafia and Peasant Rebellion as Contrasting Factors in Sicilian Latifundism." *European Journal of Sociology* 10(1969):95–116.

————. *The Mafia of a Sicilian Village*. New York: Harper & Row, 1974.

Bonetta, Gaetano. *Istruzione e Società nella Sicilia dell' Ottocento*. Palermo: Sellerio Ed., 1981.

Briggs, John. *An Italian Passage: Immigrants to Three American Cities, 1890–1930*. New Haven: Yale University Press, 1978.

Bruccoleri, Giuseppe. *l'Emigrazione Siciliana: Caratteri ed Effetti Secondo le Piu Recenti Inchieste*. Rome: Cooperativa Tipografica A. Manuzzi, 1911.

Bruno, Vincenzo. "La Diffusione Territoriale delle Migrazioni." *Rivista Italiana di Economia, Demografia e Statistica* 1–2 (1960):122–233.

Buhle, Paul. "Italian-American Radicals and the Labor Movement, 1905–1930." *Radical History Review* 17 (1978):121–51.

Cacace, Eugenio. *Il Crollo delle Cooperative Agricole Siciliane—Storia di una Lotta*. Palermo: Tipografia Corselli, 1925.

Calandrone, Giacomo. *Comunista in Sicilia, 1946–1951*. Rome: Ed. Riuniti, 1972.

Calapso, Jole. *Donne Ribelli: Un Secolo di Lotte Femminili in Sicilia*. Palermo: S. F. Flaccovio, 1980.

Cammareri-Scurti, Sebastiano. *La Lotta di Classe in Sicilia*. Milan: Ufficio della Critica Sociale, 1896.

Cancian, Frank. "The South Italian Peasant: World View and Political Behavior." *Anthropological Quarterly* 31 (1961):1–18.

Cancila, Orazio. *Gabellotti e Contadini in un Comune Rurale (Secoli XVIII–XIX)*. Caltanissetta-Rome: Salvatore Sciascia, 1974.

Cannistraro, Phillip. "Fascism and Italian Americans in Detroit." *International Migration Review* 9 (1975):29–40.

————. "Luigi Antonini and the Italian Anti-Fascist Movement in the United States, 1940–1943." *Journal of American Ethnic History* 5 (1985):21–40.

Carbone, Salvatore. *Le Origini del Socialismo in Sicilia*. Rome: Ed. Italiane, 1947.

Carlyle, Margaret. *The Awakening of Southern Italy*. London: Oxford University Press, 1962.

Caroli, Betty Boyd. *Italian Repatriation from the U.S., 1900–1914*. Staten Island: Center for Migration Studies, 1973.

————, Robert F. Harney, and Lydio F. Tomasi. *The Italian Immigrant Woman in North America*. Toronto: The Multicultural History Society of Ontario, 1978.

Casarrubea, Giuseppe. *I Fasci Contadini e le Origine delle Sezioni Socialiste della Provincia di Palermo*. 2 vols. Palermo: S. F. Flaccovio, 1978.

Cavalieri, Enea. "I Fasci dei Lavoratori a le Condizioni della Sicilia." *Nuova Antologia* 49 (1894):122–55.

Cerase, Franceso P. "Migration and Social Change: Expectations and Reality: A Case Study of Return Migration from the United States to Southern Italy." *International Migration Review* 8 (1974):245–62.

Cerrito, Gino. "Sull'Emigrazione Anarchica Italiana negli Stati Uniti d'America." *Volontà* 22 (1969):269–76.

———. *Radicalismo e Socialismo in Sicilia (1860–1882)*. Messina and Florence: G. D'Anna, 1958.

———. "Saverio Friscia nel Primo Periodo di Attività dell'Internazionale in Sicilia." *Movimento Operaio* 5 (1953):464–75.

Chapman, Graham. "Theories of Development and Underdevelopment in Southern Italy." *Development and Change* 9 (1978):365–95.

Chiurco, Giorgio Alberto. *Storia della Rivoluzione Fascista*. 5 vols. Florence: Vallecchi, 1929.

Cinanni, Paolo. *Lotte per la Terra nel Mezzogiorno, 1943–1953*. Venice: Marsilio Ed., 1979.

Cinel, Dino. "Between Change and Continuity: Regionalism Among Immigrants from the Italian Northwest." *Journal of Ethnic Studies* 9 (1981):19–36.

———. *From Italy to San Francisco*. Stanford: Stanford University Press, 1982.

———. "Land Tenure Systems, Return Migration and Militancy in Italy." *Journal of Ethnic Studies* 12 (1984):55–76.

———. "The Seasonal Emigrations of Italians in the Nineteenth Century: From Internal to International Destinations." *Journal of Ethnic Studies* 10 (1982):43–68.

Cipolla, Nicola. "La Lotta per la Terra dei Contadini Siciliani." *Riforma Agraria* 2 (1954):10–12.

Clemente, Egidio. "The Story of an Italian Labor Newspaper." *Parola del Popolo* 26 (1976):231–34.

Clough, Shepard B. and Carlo Livi. "Economic Growth in Italy: an Analysis of the Uneven Development of North and South." *Journal of Economic History* 16 (1956): 334–49.

Cohen, John S. "Fascism and Agriculture in Italy: Politics and Consequences." *Economic History Review* 32 (1979):70–87.

Cohen, Miriam. "Changing Educational Strategies among Immigrant Generations: New York Italians in Comparative Perspective." *Journal of Social History* 15 (1982): 443–66.

Colajanni, Napoleone. *Gli Avvenimenti di Sicilia e le loro Cause*. Palermo: Remo Sandron, 1896.

Coletti, Francesco. *Dell'Emigrazione Italiana*. Milan: Ulrico Hoepli, 1912.

Cortese, Nino. *Il Governo Napoletano e la Rivoluzione Siciliana del MDCCCXX–XXI*. Messina: Ufficine Grafiche Principato, 1934.

Covello, Leonard. *The Social Background of the Italo-American School Child*. Ed. Franceso Cordasco. Leiden: E. J. Brill, 1967.

Daniel, Pete. *The Shadow of Slavery: Peonage in the South, 1901–1969*. Urbana: University of Illinois Press, 1972.

De Ciampis, Mario. "Gli Italiani in America." *La Parola del Popolo* 26 (1976):63–91.

———. "Note sul Movimento Socialista tra gli Emigrati Italiani in U.S.A. (1890–1921)." *Cronache Meridionali* 6 (1959):255–73.

De Ciampis, Pasquale. "Storia del Movimento Socialista Rivoluzionario Italiano." *La Parola del Popolo* 9 (1958/1959):136–63.

DeGrand, Alexander. *Italian Fascism*. Lincoln and London: University of Nebraska Press, 1982.

Del Carria, Renzo. *Proletari senza Rivoluzione*. 2 vols. Milan: Ed. Oriente, 1966.

Della Miraglia, Emmanuele Navarro. *La Nana*. Bologna: Capelli, 1963.

———. *Storielle Siciliane*. Palermo: Sellerio, 1974.

DeMarco, William M. *Ethnics and Enclaves, Boston's Italian North End*. Ann Arbor, Mich.: UMI Research Press, 1981.

De Stefano, Francesco and Francesco Luigi Oddo. *Storia della Sicilia dal 1860 al 1910*. Bari: Laterza, 1963.

Diem, Aubrey. "Land Reform and Reclamation in Sicily." *Canadian Geographical Journal* 66 (1963):88–91.

Di Giovanna, Alfonso. *Inchiostro e Trazzere*. Sambuca di Sicilia: Ed. "La Voce," 1979.

Diggins, John P. "The Italo-American Anti-Fascist Opposition." *The Journal of American History* 54 (1967):579–98.

———. *Mussolini and Fascism: The View from America*. Princeton, N.J.: Princeton University Press, 1972.

Di Rudini, Antonio. "Terre Incolte e Latifondi." *Giornale degli Economisti*. 2nd Series, 10 (1895):40–131.

Di San Giuliano, Antonino. *Le Condizioni Presente della Sicilia: Studi e Proposte*. Milan: Fratelli Treves, 1894.

Dollo, Corrado et al. *I Fasci Siciliani*. 2 vols. Bari: DeDonato, 1975, 1976.

Dore, Grazia. "Socialismo Italiano negli Stati Uniti." *Rassegna di Politica e di Storia* 14 (1968):1–6, 33–40, 114–19.

Douglas, Norman. *Old Calabria*. London: Martin Secker, 1915.

Douglass, William A. *Emigration in a South Italian Town: An Anthropological History*. New Brunswick, N.J.: Rutgers University Press, 1984.

Eckaus, Richard S. "The North-South Differential in Italian Economic Development." *The Journal of Economic History* 20 (1961):285–317.

Falci, Raimondo. *Scienzati e Patriotti Siciliani negli Albori del Risorgimento*. Palermo: Arti Grafiche E. Priulla, 1926.

Falzone, Gaetano. *Storia della Mafia*. Milan: Pan Editore, 1975.

Faust, Levin. "The Rockford Swedes." *Swedish-American Historical Bulletin* 3 (1930): 61–72.

Fenton, Edwin. *Immigrants and Unions, a Case Study: Italians and American Labor, 1870–1920*. New York: Arno Press, 1975.

———. "Italian Immigrants in the Stoneworkers' Union." *Labor History* 3 (1962): 188–92.

———. "Italians in the Labor Movement." *Pennsylvania History* 26 (1959):33–143.

Ferrari, Robert. *Days Pleasant and Unpleasant in the Order of the Sons of Italy in America*. New York: Mandy Press, 1926.

Fiorentini, Vincenzo. "La Storia di un Nobile Cavaliere del Lavoro nei Campi Minerari dei Illinois." *La Parola del Popolo* 9 (1958/1959):120–26.

Foerster, Robert F. *The Italian Emigration of Our Times*. Cambridge: Harvard University Press, 1924.

Gabaccia, Donna. *From Sicily to Elizabeth Street: Housing and Social Change among Italian Immigrants, 1880–1930*. Albany: State University of New York Press, 1984.

———. "Migration and Peasant Militance, Western Sicily, 1880–1910." *Social Science History* 8 (1984):67–80.

Gambino, Richard. *Blood of My Blood*. Garden City: Doubleday, 1975.

———. *Vendetta*. Garden City: Doubleday, 1977.

Gestri, Lorenzo. "I Fasci Siciliani." *Movimento Operaio e Socialista* 23 (1977):506–21.

Gilkey, George R. "The United States and Italy: Migration and Repatriation." *Journal of Developing Areas* 2 (1967):23–35.

Ginsborg, Paul. "The Communist Party and the Agrarian Question in Southern Italy, 1943–48." *History Workshop* 17 (1984):81–101.

Giordano, Christian. *Handwerker- und Bauernverbände in der Sizilianischen Gesellschaft*. Tübingen: J. C. B. Mohr (Paul Siebeck), 1975.

Giordano, Paolo. "Italian Immigration in the State of Louisiana: Its Causes, Effects and Results." *Italian-Americana* 5 (1979):160–77.

Giusti, Ugo. *Le Correnti Politiche Italiane attraverso Due Riforme Elettorali dal 1909 al 1921*. Florence: Alfani e Venturi, 1922.

Gramsci, Antonio. *Selections from the Prison Notebooks*. New York: International Publishers, 1971.

Graziani, L. "Patron-Client Relations in Southern Italy." *European Journal of Political Research* 1 (1973):3–34.

Hall, W. Scott. *The Journeyman Barbers' International Union of America*. The Johns Hopkins University Studies in Historical and Political Science. Series 54. No. 3. Baltimore: The Johns Hopkins Press, 1936.

Harney, Robert F. "The Padrone and the Immigrant." *Canadian Review of American Studies* 5 (1974):101–18.

——— and J. Vincenza Scarpaci, ed. *Little Italies in North America*. Toronto: The Multicultural History Society of Toronto, 1981.

Hewitt, Nancy A. "Women in Ybor City: An Interview with a Woman Cigar Worker." *Tampa Bay History* 7 (1985):161–65.

Hilowitz, Jane. *Economic Development and Social Change in Sicily*. Cambridge, Mass.: Schenkman, 1976.

Hobsbawm, Eric J. *Primitive Rebels: Studies in Archaic Forms of Social Movement in the 19th and 20th Centuries*. New York: W. W. Norton, 1959.

Horowitz, Daniel L. *The Italian Labor Movement*. Cambridge, Mass.: Harvard University Press, 1963.

Iorizzo, Luciano John. *Italian Immigration and the Impact of the Padrone System*. New York: Arno Press, 1981.

Izzo, Luigi. "Free Trade and the Southern Question in Early Post-Unification Italy." *Mezzogiorno d'Europa* 3 (1983):473–80.

Juliani, Richard N. *The Social Organization of Immigration: The Italians in Philadelphia*. New York: Arno Press, 1980.

Kammerer, Peter. *Arbeit Gibt's Immer*. Frankfurt: Campus Verlag, 1987.

———. "Bauernkämpfe und Landreform, 1943–1953 in Süditalien." In Onno Poppinga, ed., *Produktion und Lebensverhältnisse auf dem Land*, pp. 236–52. Opladen: Westdeutscher Verlag, 1979.

Kertzer, David I. *Comrades and Christians. Religion and Political Struggle in Communist Italy.* Cambridge: Cambridge University Press, 1980.

Kessner, Thomas. *The Golden Door: Italian and Jewish Immigrant Mobility in New York City, 1880–1915.* New York: Oxford University Press, 1977.

——— and Betty Boyd Caroli. "New Immigrant Women at Work, Italians and Jews in New York City, 1880–1905." *Journal of Ethnic Studies* 5 (1978):19–32.

Klein, Herbert S. "The Integration of Italian Immigrants into the United States and Argentina: A Comparative Analysis." *American Historical Review* 88 (1983):306–29.

Labate, Valentino. *Un Decennio di Carboneria in Sicilia, 1821–1831.* Rome and Milan: Soc. Ed. Dante Aligheri di Abrighi, Segati, 1909.

Landi, Guido. "La Riforma Agraria in Sicilia." *Rivista di Diritto Agrario* 32 (1953): 315–53.

La Pena, Alberto, ed. *La Rivoluzione Siciliana del 1848, in Alcune Lettere Inedite di Michele Amari.* Naples: Alfredo Guida, 1937.

LaSorte, Michael. *La Merica: Images of Italian Greenhorn Experience.* Philadelphia: Temple University Press, 1985.

La Torre, Pio, *Comunisti e Movimento Contadino in Sicilia.* Rome: Ed. Riuniti, 1980.

Lawrence, William Francis. "European Immigration Trends of Northeast Louisiana, 1880–1900." *Louisiana History* 26 (1985):41–52.

Lepre, Aurelio. *Il Mezzogiorno dal Feudalismo al Capitalismo.* Naples: Soc. Ed. Napoletana, 1979.

Loncao, Enrico. *Considerazioni sulla Genesi ed Evoluzione della Borghesia in Sicilia.* Palermo: Tipografia Cooperativa fra gli Operai, 1899.

Long, Durward. "La Resistencia: Tampa's Immigrant Labor Union." *Labor History* 6 (1965):192–213.

Lopreato, Joseph. "Social Stratification and Mobility." *American Sociological Review* 26 (1961):285–96.

Lunberg, Anna. "The Italian Community in New Orleans." In John Cooke, ed., *New Orleans Ethnic Cultures.* New Orleans: The Committee on Ethnicity in New Orleans, 1978.

Lutz, Vera. *Italy: A Study in Economic Development.* London and New York: Oxford University Press, 1962.

Lyttelton, Adrian. "Revolution and Counter-Revolution in Italy, 1918–1922." In Charles Bertrand, ed., *Revolutionary Situations in Europe, 1917–1922.* Montreal: Centre Interuniversitaire d'Études Européennes, 1977.

Macaluso, Emanuele. *I Comunisti e la Sicilia.* Rome: Ed. Riuniti, 1970.

MacDonald, J. S. "Agricultural Organization, Migration and Labor Militancy in Rural Italy." *The Economic History Review.* 2nd Series, 16 (1963):61–75.

———. "Italy's Rural Social Structure and Emigration." *Occidente* 12 (1956):437–53.

———. "Some Socio-Economic Emigration Differentials in Rural Italy." *Economic Development and Cultural Change* 7 (1958):55–72.

——— and Leatrice D. MacDonald. "Chain Migration, Ethnic Neighborhood Formation, and Social Networks." *The Milbank Memorial Fund Quarterly* 42 (1964): 82–97.

———. "Institutional Economics and Rural Development: Two Italian Types." *Human Organization* 23 (1964):113–18.

————. "Italian Migration to Australia: Manifest Function of Bureaucracy versus Latent Functions of Informal Networks." *Journal of Social History* 3 (1970):249–75.

————. "A Simple Institutional Framework for the Analysis of Agricultural Development Potential." *Economic Development and Cultural Change* 12 (1964):368–76.

Mack Smith, Denis. *A History of Sicily*. 2 vols. New York: The Viking Press, 1968.

————. *Italy, a Modern History*. Ann Arbor, Mich.: University of Michigan Press, 1959.

————. "The Latifundia in Modern Sicilian History." *Proceedings of the British Academy* 6 (1965):85–124.

Magnaghi, Russell M. "Louisiana's Italian Immigrants Prior to 1870." *Louisiana History* 27 (1986):43–68.

Maione, Giuseppe. *Il Biennio Rosso*. Bologna: Il Mulino, 1975.

Mangano, Antonio. *Sons of Italy: A Social and Religious Study of the Italians in America*. New York: Missionary Education Movement, 1917.

Manzardo, Mario. "Struggles and Growth of Labor in Illinois: Some Italian Contributions." *La Parola del Popolo* 26 (1976):292–95.

Margavio, A. V. "The Reaction of the Press to the Italian-American in New Orleans 1880–1920." *Italian Americana* 4 (1978):72–83.

———— and J. Lambert Molyneaux. "Residential Segregation of Italians in New Orleans and Selected American Cities." *Louisiana Studies* 12 (1973):639–45.

———— and Jerome Salomone. "The Passage, Settlement, and Occupational Characteristics of Louisiana's Italian Immigrants." *Sociological Spectrum* 1 (1981):345–59.

Mariano, John. *The Italian Contribution to American Democracy*. New York: Arno Press, 1975.

Marino, Giuseppe Carlo. *Movimento Contadino e Blocco Agrario nella Sicilia Giolittiana*. Palermo: S. F. Flaccovio, 1979.

————. *Partiti e Lotta di Classe in Sicilia da Orlando a Mussolini*. Bari: DeDonato, 1976.

————. *Socialismo nel Latifondo: Sebastiano Cammareri-Scurti nel Movimento Contadino della Sicilia Occidentale (1896–1912)*. Palermo: Ed. Stampatori Associati, 1972.

Marino, Salvatore Salomone. *Costumi e Usanze dei Contadini di Sicilia*. Ed. Aurelio Rigoli. Palermo: Ando Ed., 1968.

Marsilio, Renato. *I Fasci Siciliani*. Milan and Rome: Ed. Avanti, 1954.

Martellone, Anna Maria. *I Siciliani fuori dalla Sicilia: l'Emigrazione Transoceanica fino al 1925*. Florence: Tipografia G. Capponi, 1979.

————. "Per una Storia della Sinistra Italiana negli Stati Uniti: Riformismo e Sindicalismo, 1890–1911." In Franca Assante, ed., *Il Movimento Migratorio Italiano dall'Unità Nazionale ai Nostri Giorni*, pp. 181–92. 2 vols. Geneva: Librairie Droz, 1978.

Merlino, S. "Italian Immigrants and their Enslavement." *Forum* 15 (1893):183–90.

Micciché, Giuseppe. *Dopoguerra e Fascismo in Sicilia, 1919–1927*. Rome: Ed. Riuniti, 1976.

Montalbo, Orazio. *Diciannove Anni di Vita e di Lotta*. Brooklyn: A. Guerriero Press, n.d.

Mormino, Gary R. *Immigrants on the Hill: Italian Americans in St. Louis, 1882–1982*. Champaign-Urbana: University of Illinois Press, 1986.

————. "Tampa and the New Urban South: The Weight Strike of 1899." *Florida Historical Quarterly* 60 (1982):337–56.

————. "We Worked Hard and Took Care of Our Own: Oral History and Italians in Tampa," *Labor History* 23 (1982):395–415.

———— and George E. Pozzetta. "The Cradle of Mutual Aid: Immigrant Cooperative Societies in Ybor City." *Tampa Bay History* 7 (1985):36–58.

————. *The Immigrant World of Ybor City, Italians and Their Latin Neighbors in Tampa, 1885–1985.* Champaign-Urbana: University of Illinois Press, 1987.

Moss, Leonard and Stephen C. Cappannari, "Patterns of Kinship, Comparaggio and Community in a South Italian Village." *Anthropological Quarterly* 33 (1960):24–32.

Movimento Operaio 6 (1954). Special Issue on I Fasci Siciliani.

Nelli, Humbert S. *From Immigrants to Ethnics: The Italian Americans.* Oxford and New York: Oxford University Press, 1983.

————. "The Hennessy Murder and the Mafia in New Orleans." *Italian Quarterly* 19 (1975–76):77–95.

————. *The Italians in Chicago, a Study in Ethnic Mobility.* New York: Oxford University Press, 1970.

————. "The Italian Padrone System in the United States." *Labor History* (1964): 153–67.

Neufeld, Maurice F. *Italy: School for Awakening Countries.* Ithaca, N.Y.: Cayuga Press, 1961.

Nicastro, S. *Dal Quarantotto al Sessanta.* Biblioteca Storica del Risorgimento Italiano. Milan and Rome: Soc. Ed. Dante Alighieri di Albrighi, Segati, 1913.

Nigrelli, Ignazio. "La Crisi della Industria Zolfifera Siciliana in Relazone al Movimento dei Fasci." *Movimento Operaio* 7 (1954):1050–66.

Papa, Antonio. "Guerra e Terra, 1915–1918." *Studi Storici* 10 (1969):3–45.

Peel, Roy V. *The Political Clubs of New York City.* New York and London: G. P. Putnam's Sons, 1935.

Piselli, Fortunata. *Parentela ed Emigrazione.* Turin: Giulio Einaudi, 1981.

Pitrè, Giuseppe. *La Famiglia, la Casa, la Vita del Popolo Siciliano.* Vol. 25. Biblioteca delle Tradizioni Popolari Siciliane. Palermo: Libreria Internazionale A. Reber, 1913.

————. *Proverbi Siciliani.* Vols. 8–11. Biblioteca delle Tradizioni Popolari Siciliane. Palermo: Luigi Pedone Lauriel, 1880.

————. *Usi e Costumi, Credenze e Pregiudizi del Popolo Siciliano.* Vols. 14–17. Biblioteca delle Tradizioni Popolari Siciliane. Palermo: Libreria L. Pedone Lauriel di Carlo Clausen, 1889.

Pozzetta, George E. "Immigrants and Radicals in Tampa, Florida." *Florida Historical Quarterly* 57 (1979):337–48.

————, ed. *Pane e Lavoro, the Italian-American Working Class.* Toronto: The Multicultural History Society, 1983.

————. "Italian Radicals in Tampa, Fla.: A Research Note." *International Labor and Working Class History* 22 (1982):77–81.

———— and Gary Mormino. "Immigrant Women in Tampa, the Italian Experience." *Florida Historical Quarterly* 61 (1983):296–312.

Preti, Domenico. "La Politica Agraria del Fascismo." *Studi Storici* 14 (1973):802–69.

Price, Charles A. *Southern Europeans in Australia.* Melbourne and New York: Oxford University Press, 1963.

Procacci, Giuliano. *La Lotta di Classe in Italia agli Inizi del Secolo XX.* Rome: Ed. Riuniti, 1970.

———. "Movimenti Sociali e Partiti Politici in Sicilia dal 1900 al 1904." *Annuario dell' Istituto Storico Italiano per l'Età Moderna e Contemporanea* 11 (1959):107–216.

Quaderni Storici 10 (1975). Special Issue on Fascism and Rural Life.

Quartaroli, Antenore. "La Tragedia Mineraria di Cherry, Ill." *La Parola del Popolo* 9 (1958–59):129–33.

Raia, Gianbattista. *Il Fenomeno Emigratorio Siciliano con Speciale Riguardo al Quinquennio, 1902–1906.* Palermo: Tipografia dell'Impresa Affari et Pubblicità, 1908.

Reece, J. E. "Fascism, the Mafia and the Emergence of Sicilian Separatism." *Journal of Modern History* 45 (1973):261–76.

Renda, Francesco. *l'Emigrazione in Sicilia.* Palermo: Ed. "Sicilia al Lavoro," la Cartografica, 1963.

———. *I Fasci Siciliani, 1892–94.* Turin: G. Einaudi, 1977.

———. *Il Movimento Contadino nella Società Siciliana.* Palermo: Ed. "Sicilia al Lavoro," 1956.

———. "Origine e Caratteristiche del Movimento Contadino della Sicilia Occidentale." *Movimento Operaio* 7 (1955):659–61.

———. *Risorgimento e Classi Popolari in Sicilia, 1920–1921.* Milan: Feltrinelli, 1968.

———. *La Sicilia nel 1812.* Caltanissetta: Sciascia, 1963.

———. *Socialisti e Cattolici in Sicilia, 1900–1904, le Lotte Agrarie.* Caltanissetta and Rome: Ed. Salvatore Sciascia, 1972.

Restifo, Giuseppe. *Sottosviluppo e Lotte Popolari in Sicilia, 1943–1974.* Cosenza: Pellegrini, 1976.

Reynieri, Emilio. "Emigration and Sending Areas as a Subsidized System in Italy." *Mediterranean Studies* 1 (1980):90–113.

Reynolds, George M. *Machine Politics in New Orleans, 1897–1926.* Studies in History, Economics and Public Law, No. 421. New York: Columbia University Press, 1936.

Riis, Jacob A. *How the Other Half Lives.* New York: Hill and Wang, 1957.

Romano, Salvatore Francesco. *La Sicilia nell' Ultimo Ventennio del Secolo XIX.* Palermo: Ind. Grafica Nazionale, 1958.

———. *Storia dei Fasci Siciliani.* Bari: Giuseppe Laterza e Figli, 1959.

Rosoli, Gianfausto, ed. *Un Secolo di Emigrazione Italiana, 1876–1976.* Rome: Centro Studi Emigrazione, 1978.

Rossi, Adolfo. *Die Bewegung in Sizilien.* Trans. Leopold Jacoby. Stuttgart: J. K. W. Dietz, 1894.

Rossi-Doria, Manlio. "Land Tenure System and Class in South Italy." *American Historical Review* 64 (1958):46–53.

———. *Riforma Agraria e Azione Meridionalista.* Bologna: Ed. Agricole, 1948.

Salvadori, Max. "Anti-Fascisti Italiani negli Stati Uniti." *La Parola del Popolo* 26 (1976):248–55.

Salvemini, Gaetano. *Italian Fascist Activities in the United States.* Ed. Phillip V. Cannistraro. New York: Center for Migration Studies, 1977.

———. *The Origins of Fascism in Italy*. New York: Harper Torchbooks, Harper & Row, 1973.

Saudino, Domenico. "Il Fascismo alla Conquista dell'Ordine Figli d'Italia." *La Parola del Popolo* 9 (1958–1959):247–56.

Scarpaci, Jean Ann. "Immigrants in the New South: Italians in Louisiana's Sugar Parishes, 1880–1910." *Labor History* 16 (1975):165–83.

———. *Italian Immigrants in Louisiana's Sugar Parishes: Recruitment, Labor Conditions, and Community Relations 1880–1910*. New York: Arno Press, 1980.

Scarpaci, J. Vincenza. "Labor for Louisiana's Sugar Fields: An Experiment in Immigrant Recruitment." *Italian Americana* 7 (1981):19–41.

Scaturro, Girolamo. "l'Esperienza Siciliana nella Lotta per la Terra." *Riforma Agraria* 4 (1956):436–40.

Scaturro, Ignazio. *Storia della Città di Sciacca e dei Comuni della Contrada Saccanese fra il Belice e il Platani*. 2 vols. Naples: Gennaro Majo, 1924, 1926.

Schepis, Giovanni. *Le Consultazioni Popolari in Italia dal 1848 al 1957, Profilo Storico-Statistico*. Empoli: Ed. Caparrini, n.d.

Schiavo, Giovanni Ermengildo. *The Italians in Chicago: A Study in Americanization*. New York: Arno Press, 1975.

Schifani, Carmelo. "Sulla Cooperazione Agricola in Sicilia nel Periodo fra le Due Guerre e Dopo la Seconda Guerra." *Rivista di Economia Agraria* 1 (1950):67–92.

Schmidt, Carl T. *The Plough and the Sword: Labor, Land, and Property in Fascist Italy*. New York: Columbia University Press, 1938.

Schneider, Jane. "Trousseau as Treasure: Some Contradictions of Late Nineteenth-Century Change in Sicily." In Eric B. Ross, ed., *Beyond the Myths of Culture: Essays in Cultural Materialism*, pp. 323–56. San Francisco: Academic Press, 1980.

———. "Of Vigilance and Virgins: Honor, Shame, and Access to Resources in Mediterranean Societies." *Ethnology* 10 (1971):1–24.

Schneider, Jane and Peter Schneider. *Culture and Political Economy in Western Sicily*. New York: Academic Press, 1976.

———. "Demographic Transitions in a Sicilian Rural Town." *Journal of Family History* 9 (1984):245–72.

———. "Economic Dependency and the Failure of Cooperatives in Western Sicily." In June Nash, Joyce Dandler, and Nicholas Hopkins, eds., *Popular Participation in Social Change*, pp. 289–303, The Hague: Mouton, 1973.

———. "The Reproduction of the Ruling Class in Latifundist Sicily, 1860–1920." In George E. Marcus, ed., *Elites: Ethnographic Issues*, pp. 141–69. Albuquerque: University of New Mexico Press, 1983.

Schneider, Peter. "Rural Artisans and Peasant Mobilization in Late Nineteenth Century Sicily." *Journal of Peasant Studies* 13 (1986):63–81.

Schneider, Peter, Jane Schneider, and Edward Hansen. "Modernization and Development: the Role of Regional Elites and Noncorporate Groups in the European Mediterranean." *Comparative Studies in Society and History* 14 (1972):328–50.

Schwieder, Dorothy. *Black Diamonds: Life and Work in Iowa's Coal Mining Communities 1895–1925*. Ames: Iowa State University Press, 1983.

Scoppola, Pietro. "Cattolici e Moti Sociali in Italia intorno al 1900." *Quaderni di Cultura e di Storia Sociale* 1 (1952):171–76, 220–26, 262–68.

Sereni, Emilio. *Il Capitalismo nelle Campagne 1860–1900*. Turin: Einaudi, 1968.

————. *Storia del Paesaggio Agrario Italiano*. Bari: Laterza, 1961.

Serio, Ettore. "Il PCI in Sicilia." *Nord e Sud* 13 (1966):78–87.

Siegenthaler, Jürg K. "Sicilian Economic Change since 1860." *The Journal of European Economic History* 2 (1973):363–415.

Silverman, Sydel. "Agricultural Organization, Social Structure, and Values in Italy: Amoral Familism Reconsidered." *American Anthropologist* 70 (1968):1–20.

Sitta, Pietro. *Le Migrazioni Interne: Saggio di Statistica Applicata*. Genoa: Tipografia del R. Istituto Sordomuti, 1893.

Sladen, Douglas. *In Sicily*. 2 vols. London: Sands and Co., 1907.

————. *Sicily, the New Winter Resort*. New York: E. P. Dutton, 1907.

———— and Norma Lorimer. *Queer Things about Sicily*. London: Kegan Paul, Trench, Trübner, 1913.

Smith, Judith E. *Family Connections: A History of Italian and Jewish Immigrant Lives in Providence, Rhode Island, 1900–1940*. Albany: State University of New York Press, 1985.

Somogyi, Stefano. *Bilanci Demografici dei Comuni Siciliani dal 1861 al 1961: Contribuito alla Storia Demografica della Sicilia*. Palermo: Università di Palermo, Istituto di Scienze Demografiche, 1971.

Sonnino, Sidney. *I Contadini in Sicilia*. Florence: Vallecchi Ed., 1925.

Sorbi, Ugo. *Le Cooperative Agricole per la Conduzione dei Terreni in Italia*. Rome: Tipografia Pol. dello Stato, 1955.

Speranza, Gino C. "Many Societies of Italian Colony: Their Uses and Abuses Discussed by an American Citizen." *New York Times*, March 8, 1903.

Squarzina, F. *Produzione e Commercio dello Zolfo in Sicilia nel Secolo XIX*. Turin: Industria Tipografica, 1963.

Sylvers, Malcolm. "Sicilian Socialists in Houston, Texas, 1896–1898." In *Gli Italiani negli Stati Uniti*, pp. 389–98. Florence: Istituto di Studi Americani, University of Florence, 1972.

Talamo, Clara Manlio-DeMarco. *Lotte Agrarie nel Mezzogiorno, 1943–44*. Milan: Mazzotta, 1972.

Tarrow, Sidney G. *Peasant Communism in Southern Italy*. New Haven and London: Yale University Press, 1967.

Tasca, Angelo. *The Rise of Italian Fascism, 1918–1922*. Naples: Istituto Italiano per gli Studi Storici in Napoli, 1967.

Titone, Virgilio. *Origini della Questione Meridionale*. Vol. 1. *Riveli e Platee del Regno di Sicilia*. Milan: G. Feltrinelli, 1961.

Tomasi, Lydio. *The Italian American Family: The Southern Italian Family's Process of Adjustment to an Urban America*. Staten Island: Center for Migration Studies, 1972.

————, ed. *Italian Americans: New Perspectives in Italian Immigration and Ethnicity*. Staten Island: Center for Migration Studies of New York, 1985.

Tomasi, Silvano. *Piety and Power: The Role of Italian Parishes in the New York Metropolitan Area*. Staten Island: Center for Migration Studies, 1975.

————, ed. *Perspectives in Italian Immigration and Ethnicity*. New York: Center for Migration Studies, 1977.

——— and Madeline H. Engel, eds. *The Italian Experience in the United States*. New York: Center for Migration Studies, 1970.

Trèves, Anna. *Le Migrazioni Interne nell'Italia Fascista; Politica e Realtà Demografica*. Turin: Einaudi, 1976.

Vaina, Michele. *Popolarismo e Nasismo in Sicilia*. Florence: Ed. Italiana di A. Quatinni, 1911.

Vecoli, Rudolph J. "Contadini in Chicago: A Critique of 'The Uprooted.'" *Journal of American History* 51 (1964):404–17.

———. "The Formation of Chicago's Little Italies." *Journal of American Ethnic History* 2 (1983):5–20.

———, ed. *Italian American Radicalism: Old World Origins and New World Developments*. New York: American Italian Historical Association, 1973.

———. "Pane e Giustizia: A Brief History of the Italian American Labor Movement." *La Parola del Popolo* 26 (1976):55–61.

———. "Prelates and Peasants: Italian Immigrants and the Catholic Church." *Journal of Social History* 2 (1969):217–68.

Velona, Fort. "Genesi del Movimento Socialista Democratico e della Parola del Popolo." *Parola del Popolo* 9 (1958–59):19–31.

Vetri, Giuseppe. "Le Origini del Fascismo in Sicilia." *Nuovi Quaderni del Meridione* 14 (1976):33–81 and 295–315.

Villari, Luigi. *Italian Life in Town and Country*. New York: G. P. Putnam's Sons, 1902.

Villari, Pasquale. *La Sicilia e il Socialismo*. Milan: Fratelli Treves, 1896.

Villari, Rosario, ed. *Il Sud nella Storia d'Italia*. Bari: Laterza, 1961.

Vivarelli, Roberto. *Il Dopoguerra in Italia e l'Avvento del Fascismo, 1918–1922*. Vol. 1. Naples: Istituto Italiano per Studi Storici in Napoli, 1967.

———. "Italy, 1919–21: The Current State of Research." *Journal of Contemporary History* 3 (1968):103–12.

———. "Revolution and Reaction in Italy, 1918–1922." *Journal of Italian History* 1 (1978):235–63.

Yans-McLaughlin, Virginia. *Family and Community: Italian Immigrants in Buffalo, 1880–1930*. Ithaca: Cornell University Press, 1977.

Zaninelli, Sergio. *Storie del Movimento Sindicale Italiano*. Vol. 1. Milan: Celne, 1971.

Zariski, Raphael. *Italy: The Politics of Uneven Development*. Hinsdale, Ill.: The Dryden Press, 1972.

Index